Phenomenological Approaches
to Popular Culture

Phenomenological Approaches to Popular Culture

edited by

Michael T. Carroll

and

Eddie Tafoya

Bowling Green State University Popular Press
Bowling Green, OH 43403

Library of Congress Cataloging-in-Publication Data
Phenomenological approaches to popular culture / edited by Michael T.
Carroll and Eddie Tafoya.
        p.   cm.
    Includes bibliographical references.
    ISBN 0-87972-809-4 (cloth) -- ISBN 0-87972-810-8 (pbk.)
    1. Civilization, Modern--1950- 2. Popular culture--History--20th
century. 3. Phenomenology. I. Carroll, Michael Thomas, 1954-
II. Tafoya, Eddie.
CB430.P46 1999
909.82'5--dc21

                                                        99-045937

Cover design by Dumm Art

CONTENTS

ACKNOWLEDGMENTS

We would like to express our appreciation to Prof. William W. Woods of Schreiner University and Prof. Diana Royer of Miami University for their constructive criticism. Thanks also to Joan Snider, Cesaera Pirrone-Alers, Imelda Rodriguez, and Patricia Hewitt for their assistance with editing and research.

"The Practice of Perception: Multi-Functionality and Time in the Musical Experiences of a Heavy Metal Drummer" by Harris M. Berger originally appeared in *Ethnomusicology* 41.3 (copyright 1997 by Board of Trustees of the University of Illinois) and is used here with permission of the University of Illinois Press.

"The Spell of the Sensuous: Casino Atmosphere and the Gambler" by Felicia Campbell was published in a shorter version in *The Business of Gaming: Economic Management Issues*, edited by William R. Eadington and Judy A. Cornelius (Reno: Institute for the Study of Gambling and Commercial Gaming, University of Nevada, 1999). This expanded version appears in this volume with permission.

"The Bloody Spectacle: Mishima, The Sacred Heart, Hogarth, Cronenberg, and the Entrails of Culture" by Michael T. Carroll originally appeared in *Studies in Popular Culture* 15.2 and is reprinted here with permission.

"On American Time: Mythopoesis and the Marketplace" by Steven Carter was originally published in the *Journal of American Culture* 17.2 (1994) and is reprinted here with permission.

"Viewing Television: The Metapsychology of Endless Consumption" by Beverle Houston originally appeared in *Quarterly Review of Film Studies* 9.3 (1984) (copyright Gordon and Breech Publishers) and is reprinted here with permission.

"This Is Not a Text, or, Do We Read Images?" by Don Ihde originally appeared in *Philosophy Today* 40.1 (1996) and is reprinted here with permission.

"Phenomenology, Linguistics, and Popular Literature" by Janice Radway originally appeared in the *Journal of Popular Culture* 12 (1978) and is reprinted here with permission.

—Michael T. Carroll and Eddie Tafoya

INTRODUCTION

BEING AND BEING ENTERTAINED:
PHENOMENOLOGY AND THE STUDY OF POPULAR CULTURE

Michael T. Carroll, Eddie Tafoya, and Chris Nagel

In the available accounts of the theories and methods of popular culture studies, phenomenology is conspicuously absent: in otherwise admirable works, such as Strinati's *An Introduction to the Theories of Popular Culture* and Bigsby's *Approaches to Popular Culture,* we find discussions of quantitative sociology, Marxism and the Frankfurt school, psychoanalysis, myth criticism, feminism, structuralism and semiotics, but hardly a word on the usefulness of the thought of Husserl, Schutz, Heidegger, and Merleau-Ponty. There are reasons for this omission that can be understood through an overview of both the development of popular culture studies (we speak here primarily of developments in Great Britain and the United States, although we need to be aware of important developments in Australia, Germany, and other nations) and the phenomenological movement (we speak here primarily of the original German movement and to some extent, developments in France and their latter assimilation into Anglo-American critical discourse).

The rather late emergence of identifiable works, academic departments, organizations, and journals devoted to the study of popular culture is the result of two fundamental assumptions that have, until very recently, guided traditional academic inquiry. The first, which is historical, asserts that in order to insure a meaningful analysis of a given cultural development, it is better that the development in question be held, temporally speaking, at a distance, and while, as Peter Burke shows us, there is much historical work to be done on the popular culture of the past, popular culture is often construed as being synonymous with the contemporary or the near contemporary, and therefore much of popular culture, according to this maxim, falls outside the range of legitimate study. The second assumption is cultural in nature and holds that the mission of the university is to present what Matthew Arnold called "the best and the brightest," an idea that, although well-intended, nevertheless employs a set of exclusionary aesthetic codes which render large areas of

1

cultural production—and popular production in particular—"unworthy" of study and analysis (cf. Eagleton 60-63), which of course raises questions concerning the practice of exclusion based on social class as detailed by Lawrence Levine. These two assumptions dovetail: vaguely-defined Arnoldian notions of "excellence" and "the best and the brightest" served to reinforce the academy's historical conservatism by defaulting to Dr. Johnson's "test of time" as the only way to certify the worthiness of a cultural production, and thus the student of culture and literature, by definition, was reckoned to be in no position to judge contemporary productions. That had to be left to non-academic reviewers, independent intellectuals, and as far as academe was concerned, to future scholarship.

We can see the effects of these operating assumptions in the way specific areas of humanistic study have evolved. For example, well into the 18th century, the study of English literature was largely nonexistent owing to the priority given to classical languages and literature over the vulgar tongues. It was not at an English university, but a Scottish one, the University of Edinburgh, particularly with the appointment of Hugh Blair as Regius Professor in 1780, that the study of literature and rhetoric in English first became part of the curriculum. Likewise, the study of American literature was not a collegiate enterprise in the age of Poe, Hawthorne, and Whitman. Again, change came from outside: an Englishman, D. H. Lawrence, in his *Studies in Classic American Literature* (1918), provided the United States' cultural establishment with a model of how to approach American literature, and only then was it included in the curriculum. And the work of Poe, which was once generally regarded as questionable diversionary reading at best, eventually became the object of psychoanalytic and formal criticism. This development was furthered in the early 1970s when feminist critics began to demonstrate the value of studying the most popular literary productions of the 19th century—the work of women writers like Susan Warner and Lydia M. Child—which had been largely overshadowed by the study of Poe, Hawthorne, Emerson, Melville, and Whitman. But this process is also true in a more general way. That is, during the era of Balzac and Dickens, novelists were seen as entertainers and chroniclers; in the 1940s, literary critics like Mark Shorer applied the poetic analysis of the "new critics" to works like *Wuthering Heights,* thus opening the novel, the most popular of literary forms, to academic inquiry.

Popular culture as a general field of study went through a process similar to that of the more specific designation of vernacular literature, subject to the same resistance of the academy to the vernacular in general. The mid-nineteenth-century folklore movement—what Burke calls the "discovery of the people"—was in part directed by the awareness (on the part of a like-minded group of scholars) that the social changes brought on by industrialism would largely eradicate older forms of cultural expression that had been generally regarded as being too humble to warrant academic study. Folklore studies were to become an important, perhaps the most important factor, in the emergence of popular culture studies, for "folk" and "popular" are cognate, often inseparable forms that traditionally had been excluded by the academy's emphasis on "elite" culture, which is, in spite of any efforts to keep these categories separate, entangled with the "folk" and the "popular" (as in the case of Homer, who has been, at one time or another, all three). As folklore studies developed, however, its primary interest, as with ethnology in general, was with indigenous practices that were established long before the arrival of industrial capitalism, whose cultural manifestations remained largely unexamined and untheorized.

Of course, changes did not go totally unobserved; often, the novelists, whose form of expression was itself part of this new culture, became its primary chroniclers, as in Flaubert's incisive description of the consumer who is herself consumed in *Madame Bovary*. Marx and Engels, as analysts of the conditions of industrialism, were in an ideal position to describe these developments; however, for the most part, the Marxist cultural studies that eventually developed (we speak particularly of Adorno, Horkheimer, and the work of the Frankfurt School in the 1940s), much like the conservative criticism that the Marxists otherwise opposed, were more directed toward condemning popular culture rather than analyzing it (cf. Hoppenstand 59).

In the mid to late nineteenth century the social sciences, which then were emergent disciplines, came as a response to two new sources of human "data": industrial society itself and the greater access to non-Western primary cultures that had been afforded by imperialism and improved methods in transportation and communication. Comteian sociology and the British school of anthropology both attempted to analyze these two newly available areas of research. In the course of the development of these disciplines, it became increasingly obvious that the methods of the humanist scholar and those of the natural scientist were both inadequate, and thus, eventually, new methodologies came into being—the structure-function approach of Bronislaw Malinowski would inform the development of formal anthropology, while sociology, particularly in the United States, would take its cue from Durkheim's methods of quantification. But an "anthropology of the present" hadn't yet been conceived, and Durkheimian quantification does not provide a satisfactory method of cultural description: culture, as George Lewis notes, is a concept that "has always been difficult to operationalize for research purposes" (71) (although the early example of Q. R. Leavis, in her *Fiction and the Reading Public* [1932] shows the fruitfulness of sociological approaches to popular literature). While the emergence of American literature studies and later, American Studies, foreshadowed the ultimate reception of popular culture in the academy, during the first half of the twentieth century, the humanities in general remained conservative, following Arnoldian dictates.

In the late 1960s, as an echo of the civil rights movement, new "area studies," often defined by gender and ethnicity (women's studies, Black Studies, Native American Studies), and a body of critical work concerned primarily with popular culture began to emerge. Like other area studies, the new field took shape as a methodological orphan, borrowing tools on an as-need basis from various established disciplines, according to the needs and the orientation of the researchers. In England in the late 1950s, Richard Hoggart and Raymond Williams developed "cultural studies," which became fully institutionalized in 1964 with the establishment of the Centre for Contemporary Cultural Studies at Birmingham University. The British cultural studies movement begins as a response to the influential work of F. R. Leavis (esp. his magnum opus, *The Great Tradition* [1948]). While Leavis argued for a broader educational dissemination of culture, he viewed culture, as did Arnold, as part of a limited cannon of the "great tradition." Hoggart and Williams were also interested in a broader distribution of what Bourdieu calls "cultural capital" but, as During notes, this new generation of critics

experience[d] Leavisism ambivalently. On the one hand, they accepted that its canonical texts were richer than contemporary so-called "mass culture" and that culture ought to be measured in terms of its capacity to deepen and widen experiences; on the other, they recognized that Leavisism at worst erased, and at the very least did not fully come into contact with the communal forms of life into which they had been born. (3)

The British cultural studies movement also needs to be understood as a significant change in the direction of Marxist and Marxist-influenced approaches to popular culture. This post-Frankfurt Marxism has developed more subtle, less condemnatory views of popular culture, as in the work of Raymond Williams, Stuart Hall, and Pierre Bourdieu (cf. Real 146). Another important development occurs with the dissemination of French structuralism, which is itself part of the developments outlined above, for it demonstrated a movement in linguistics from a purely historical philology towards a greater concern with everyday speech practices and the way various cultural practices are structured like a language (in the late 1950s, Roland Barthes' *Mythologies* provided a fine example of structuralist views of popular culture; his essay on professional wrestling being particularly effective in showing "junk" culture in a more positive light). The Birmingham School would add structuralism to its already established ethical and methodological bases in Marxism and humanism. In the United States in the late 1960s and early 1970s, offshoots from folklore studies and the American Studies movement would lead to the creation of the Department of Popular Culture at Bowling Green State University in Ohio. While this circle was broadly constituted in its methodological perspective and, as with its British counterpart, committed to a program of curricular reform, it took particular inspiration from the myth and genre studies that emerged from folklore and literature departments. Here we need to credit the influence of Carl Jung who, in his final (and collaborative) effort, *Man and His Symbols* (1964) employed many examples from popular culture, including references to *Dr. Jekyll and Mr. Hyde,* rock and roll, James Thurber's cartoons, and modern advertising, thus helping critics and public alike to appreciate the archetypal depths of popular culture. We should also credit the work of the Canadian critic and genre theorist, Northrop Frye, whose *Anatomy of Criticism* (1957) proved to be influential in the 1960s and beyond, and in terms of popular culture studies, John Cawelti's *Six Gun Mystique* (1971), served to establish a rigorous genre approach. Cawelti's book might be regarded as the defining work of this loosely defined school, although again, having said that, a cursory review of article titles in the *Journal of Popular Culture, Journal of American Culture,* and *Studies in Popular Culture* reveal a variety of approaches, from myth criticism to empirical historical narrative. (We should note that currently there are two competing terms, "cultural studies" and "popular culture studies," the former having an English and Continental orientation, the latter, American.)

American area studies were then theoretically enriched by the application of new European approaches: the structuralism of Roland Barthes (who was introduced to American thinkers in the mid-1960s by Susan Sontag), the deconstructive method of Jacques Derrida (who made his American debut in 1966 and whose work was, by the early 1970s, assimilated into American literary studies by the Yale school of deconstruction), the reader-response criticism of German scholars like Wolfgang Iser and Hans Robert Jauss, and American versions of the reader-oriented method (Stanley Fish, Jane Tompkins), and the theoretical feminism and semiotics (developed from Lacanian psychoanalysis) of Julia Kristeva and Helené Cixous. Whatever their background, the researchers who established the area studies movement had stumbled onto important domains of human existence that had not adequately been addressed by the established disciplines, and as has often been the case in the history of knowledge, they approached their task through interdisciplinarity and methodological pluralism.

While the phenomenological movement proper begins in Germany with the work of Edmund Husserl in the opening decade of the twentieth century, we need to acknowledge the roots of the movement in philosophy's "epistemological crisis." Hume's radical scepticism posed a philosophical problem that resolved itself in a "bifurcation" (to use A. N. Whitehead's famous phrase) into Kantian idealism and British Empiricism, two mutually exclusive ways of interpreting the problem of reality. For Husserl, another crisis—that crisis of scientific thought which achieved notoriety in the 1920s—provided an opportunity to merge these two traditions, with phenomenology providing a grounding of empirical science in the pre-scientific realm of primary experience.

Although phenomenologists disagree concerning the appropriate degree of formality and rigor in phenomenological inquiry, there is enough agreement to permit a general statement of the phenomenological method, its aims and results. The fundamental component of all phenomenological investigation could be described in reference to Husserl's concept of the "natural attitude." The natural attitude is our ordinary way of approaching experience, which assumes an established realm of objectivity, intersubjectivity, and selfhood. Within the natural attitude, the things we experience have what Alfred Schutz terms a "taken-for-granted" character: ordinarily, objects, other persons, and ourselves count for us in reference to an implicit positing of their actuality. In taking things for granted, we approach them as holders of certain values for us. In ordinary experience of popular culture, we are confronted with light entertainments, cheap thrills perhaps, and we simply take them up as such. The artifacts hold these meanings in themselves—they are or have become their values for us, and in our ordinary encounter with them we have no need of interpretation. The CBS Evening News is just that in everyday experience—a segment of cultural life with a certain meaning and use constantly attached to it and carried along with it.

What is obscured in the natural attitude is just how the things we experience come to count as actual objects with certain meanings. In the most general sense, phenomenology is an attempt to lay bare how the natural attitude and the taken-for-granted character of experience is constructed. In other words, phenomenology seeks the essences of things that appear in experience. Under the phenomenological attitude, our approach to popular culture aims at the manner in which these artifacts hold certain cultural meanings—just how they come to appear to be essentially light entertainments and cheap thrills. The CBS Evening News maintains and can be identified with its cultural meaning, but it remains possible to discover the way this meaning accrues to it.

The first step in phenomenological investigation is to set aside ("bracket" or "parenthesize") the assumption of the natural attitude. This move, Husserl's phenomenological "epoché," results in a field of appearances stripped of their presumed actuality. Husserl compares bracketing to Descartes' methodological doubt. Similarly to methodological doubt, phenomenological bracketing prohibits the philosophical investigator from making any assumptions about actuality. But as Husserl notes, Descartes' doubt has a negative character: doubt is not an unassuming attitude toward our common belief in actuality, but a challenge to that belief. Instead, phenomenological bracketing leaves all beliefs in actuality intact, but merely set aside. Another comparison could be made to the notion of theatrical "suspension of disbelief." By suspending disbelief, a member of a theater audience permits the emotions evoked by the drama to count as genuine emotions, and the events to count as actual events. The phenomenological attitude could be considered the reverse of this process, a kind of suspension of *belief,* in which what ordinarily counts as actual is taken up without regard for its actuality.

From the phenomenologically reconstructed point of view, all phenomena are left open to an investigation into what makes them phenomena, what makes them phenomena of a particular sort, and what makes them count as real, meaningful objects for ordinary experience. The investigation takes the form of description which is both creative and rigorous. Phenomenology is not usually concerned with providing logical definitions of terms, arguments to demonstrate the metaphysical place of things, nor even to prove the validity of the descriptions themselves. Instead, phenomenological description creatively evokes an experience of something in order to guide other investigators towards the same something. A rigorous phenomenological description evokes this experience of something and guides others to it. The validity of the description is to be found in experience, in "the things themselves." In a sense, phenomenological method could be considered a way of training perception to attend to the phenomena that present themselves.

In *The Phenomenological Movement,* Herbert Spiegelberg outlines seven steps of the method, cautioning that there is no universal agreement among phenomenologists about the method or its ultimate and achievable aims. Generally, a phenomenological study of culture could dispense with the most transcendental steps of the method, which pertain to the conditions of the possibility of knowledge and objectivity. In fact, most phenomenologists do not extend themselves into this sphere, remaining within the vast realm of what Schutz called the "mundane." Mundane phenomenology takes up only the first three of Spiegelberg's seven steps: Investigating Particular Phenomena, Investigating General Essences, and Apprehending Essential Relationships (659ff.).

In investigating particular phenomena, the researcher picks out a relatively independent phenomenon (a presumptive object), distinguishes its elements and structure, and attempts to guide the perceptions of others to the same phenomenon with description. The description cannot pretend to be exhaustive or definitive, and in fact such a description would work at cross purposes to phenomenology. The description is a set of clues about the experience of the particular phenomenon.

The description is also the means of finding the general essence of the phenomenon. The clues to the experience direct perception to the heart of the matter, we might say, or what makes it just this phenomenon. The abstract essence can be studied in its own right by making it the object of further description.

The importance of this abstracted essence becomes clear in apprehending essential relationships. There are, Spiegelberg says, two polarities of essential relationships, internal and external, which determine the way the essence of something is encountered: through a technique Husserl called "free imaginative variation" we find essential relationships by seeing how an essence is "exploded" by adding unnecessary elements or subtracting necessary elements (680-81). The internal relationships of the essence determine what is absolutely required for the phenomenon to be a phenomenon of one type and not another. Similarly, the external relationships of this essence to other essences show in what connections a phenomenon of a particular type can be found. To give a simple example, a triangle's three angles and three sides form a set of internally essential relationships. They can be varied with respect to one another, but any figure lacking three angles, or having more than three angles, is no longer a triangle, just because the internal relationships of a triangle require these elements be held together. In the case of external relationships (relationships between essences), it is clear that any shape must have some color, just because the external relationships between shape and color must always be held together (everything with shape must have color; everything with color must have shape).

The upshot of this for popular culture studies is twofold. First, phenomenology provides a way to investigate the social construction of the meaning of cultural artifacts, discovering rather than presuming their significance. The values of cultural artifacts can be revealed where they lie, in the constituted artifacts themselves. Setting aside our everyday belief in their meanings, we can bring to light the structure of things that underlies and supports these meanings. Through describing and investigating the essences of these artifacts, phenomenological study sets out just what they are, just what is necessary to their being what they are, but without presumptively positing any of this. A phenomenological account of the cultural meaning of film, of zoos, of television, of casinos, or of anything else, reaches essences and essential relationships through the clues of description, opening cultural analysis for anyone who follows the path back to the phenomenon.

Second, phenomenology is radically anti-ideological in the sense that no phenomenological description relies on the presumption of a fixed hermeneutic principle. Phenomenologists do not primarily seek to find how cultural artifacts are encoded or engendered, how they exploit the masses or coarsen civilization. Working beneath these ideological interpretations, phenomenological description can show how meaning in general is created—that is, how things come to be what they are for us. Essential descriptions of phenomena could, in fact, be seen as the grounding for interpretations that rely on ideological principles. It is all too easy for gender or race critics to be ignored on the basis that their views are outlandish or irrelevant political opinions, as long as the manner in which cultural artifacts become accepted as meaningful objects is left obscure. Finding the essence of the phenomena and its relationships to other essences through description instead of by stipulation allows other researchers to see how an analysis arises. For this reason, we believe, phenomenology is an important or even a necessary step in cultural analysis.

These two aspects of phenomenology also determine a relationship to other schools of cultural studies (and we'll have more to say about this in a moment). Putting a researcher's interpretive schema under suspension (as another kind of belief in the actuality of things) gives us an opportunity to investigate the essential connections between interpretation and its objects. For example, the interpretive schema of feminist critique can be seen in relation to objects of feminist critique, and that relation can be shown to obtain essentially, in the very structure of the objects. The result of such an inquiry could have aspects of phenomenology and feminism, indeed gaining explanatory power in the bargain.

For the phenomenologist, everything depends on perceiving the essential structures of things, and the strength of the analysis is carried by the force of the description. This is the meaning of the call to arms originally sounded by Husserl himself: "to the things themselves."

If we return to our initial supposition that the term "phenomenology" is oddly absent in the discourse regarding the theory and methodology of popular culture studies, sooner or later we need to ask why this is the case. One possible answer has to do with the "linguistic turn" and the question of language in cultural studies, the humanities, and the social sciences. Concurrent with the development of interdisciplinary area studies and phenomenology, as outlined above, was another methodology—that of semiotics and structuralism, which finds its source in the work of Ferdinand de Saussure and Roman Jacobson. While Saussure's theory of structuralism was developed around 1913 in his lectures at the University of Geneva (published posthumously as *A Course in General Linguistics*), his impact, and that of Jacobson, was not widely felt until Levi-Strauss and Roland Barthes achieved their academic notoriety. While one will find a certain methodological parallel between the phenomenological activity and the stucturalist activity, Detweiler accurately notes the fundamental difference: while the Husserlian phenomenologist aims to "discover how consciousness forms a system of being and meaning," the structuralist aims to reveal how "system forms the being and meaning of consciousness" (17). Therefore, while consciousness is the main concern of the phenomenologist, for the structuralist, it is at best secondary. System and language preoccupy the structuralist; consciousness and experience preoccupy the phenomenologist.

If the epistemological crisis in Enlightenment philosophy comes from a probing of the subject-object problem resulting in a "bifurcation" of knowledge, the interaction between structuralism and phenomenology would expose a similar bifurcation of consciousness and language. It was the primary work of Derrida to critique the linguistic problem in Husserl. In his first major contributions (*An Introduction to Husserl's Origins of Geometry* [1962] and *Speech and Phenomena* [1967]), Derrida deconstructs Husserl's transcendentalism by showing the problematic nature of Husserl's opposition of two terms: *Ausdruck* and *Anzeigen* ("expression" versus "indication") in a way that favors the former, which is related to the immediacy of the voice and perception, while the latter is related to writing, which lacks the immediacy of speech. But as Derrida shows, Husserl himself was suspicious of his own construction, acknowledging that the two are not so easily separable. Ultimately, Derrida uses this problem to formulate his theory of *différance,* the always absent quality of the transcendental signified and the notion that signs only refer to other signs in the ceaseless play of unstable significations that frustrate any final resting point in some meaning that is exterior to the sign system. It is at this moment, Derrida claims in his signature essay, "Structure, Sign, and Play," that "language invaded the universal problematic; that in which, in the absence of a centre or origin, everything became discourse . . . that is to say, when everything became a system in which the central signified, the original or transcendental signified, is never absolutely present outside a system of differences" (84-85).

Powerful though it was, and continues to be, the Derridian critique is itself not beyond critique. First, as Hazard Adams observes, in the post-structuralist paradigm, questions of the self are "dissolved into the world of language" (19), thus indicating that an eclipsing of phenomenology may simply deliver us into the hands of a new formalism, and ironically, formalism, particularly in literary studies, was decisively rejected by the deconstructionists. Second, particularly as it concerns phenomenology as a methodology in the humanities and social sciences, deconstruction ultimately failed to dispose of the problem of subjectivity. Even the structuralist/post-structuralist slogan, "language speaks man," compelling though it may be, fails to reduce the problem of experiencing the world to one of signification and the ceaseless play of language. Third and finally, we need to remember, as should be obvious from our overview, that phenomenology is by no means bound by its transcendentalist origins; that is, while the most ambitious aims of Husserlian phenomenology are that of providing a pre-scientific basis for the system of the sciences and providing a method (the epoché) of revealing the essence of experiences and, beyond that, the unmediated, transcendental ego, even Husserl himself, in an Appendix to the *Crisis,* confronts the problems of the system of analysis that was his life's work, giving up on his more grandiose aims, acknowledging that the "transcendental subject . . . is grounded in the historicity of a cultural life-world rather than grounding it" (Kearney 115). The work of both Alfred Schutz and Maurice Merleau-Ponty were of fundamental importance in pushing phenomenology beyond its original transcendentalist framework, and more recently, we have Don Ihde's postulation of a "postphenomenology" that, in consultation with developments in neopragmatism, new historicism, and post-structuralism, is "nonfoundational and nontranscendental" and that "makes variational theory its most important methodological strategy" (7). While this suggests that a new "postphenomenology" is particularly suited for popular culture studies, we need to remember that there has been a close, though unrecognized, relationship between the aims of phenomenology and the aims of popular culture and other area studies, for just as these studies have proposed to expand the academy in order to include the study of things that had traditionally been excluded, the revolutionary impulse of phenomenology sought to liberate philosophy from the academy and return it to the realm of everyday lived experience. Witness the response of Jean-Paul Sartre when he came under the influence of Husserl:

I was carried away: nothing appeared to me more important than the promotion of street lamps to the dignity of a philosophical object. I had the obscure recollection of a thought that perhaps I have never had: that truth drags through the streets, in the factories and, apart from ancient Greece, philosophers are eunuchs who never open their doors to it. One year later, I read Husserl in Berlin; everything was changed forever. (qtd. in Kearney 3)

The essays that follow do not propose to conform to the more rule-governed aspects of phenomenology, and the aim of the collection as a whole is suggestive rather than orthodox and definitive. In gathering these contributions, a useful schema emerged corresponding to the thematic concerns of the individual essays. In keeping with this, the text is organized according to four clusters: textuality, performativity, spectatorship, and the social construction of reality.

Our textuality cluster contains two essays that deal with specific literary works, in the tradition of phenomenological literary criticism established by Ingarden, and later, Poulet, Iser, and any number of critiques that draw on phenomenology (most notably that of Heidegger), and two that deal with the broader questions of textuality.

We begin with an essay by Janice Radway first published in the *Journal of Popular Culture* in 1978. In this essay, Radway, who went on to become a leading figure in phenomenological approaches to popular literature, rejects the "traditional aesthetic modes" that have been used to evaluate popular literature and, drawing on both Merleau-Pontian phenomenology and Saussurian structuralism, finds a more tenable approach, one that is defined by the way texts function within the overall cultural system. Radway does an excellent job of placing before us a more workable set of criteria for analyzing and evaluating all the genres of popular literature, though her choice of examples here is restricted to the Gothic mode.

Following Radway's essay, James Brusseau gives consideration to a notorious work of popular literature, Bret Easton Ellis' third novel, *American Psycho*. The reception of *American Psycho* stands as one of the great scandals in recent literature—a violent and repetitive work that stopped the career of this "spokesman of Generation X" in its tracks. Rather than dwelling on the reception of *American Psycho* or its shortcomings in terms of normative aesthetics, Brusseau demonstrates how the reading experience this unusual novel engenders can be productively grasped through reference to Jean Baudrillard's theory of the simulacra.

Following Brusseau's essay, Tafoya examines the fool archetype as he appears transculturally, from the New Testament to the Marx Brothers, and most significantly, in Robert Pirsig's *Zen and the Art of Motorcycle Maintenance.* In so doing, Tafoya draws on the work of Heidegger and Ihde to probe the phenomenology of this popular archetype.

The contributions of Don Ihde to phenomenology, and in particular, the relations between phenomenology and technology as well as phenomenology's relationship to contemporary methodological movements, are well-known. In the essay included here, "This Is Not a Text, or, Do We Read Images?" Ihde begins with a questioning of postmodern theory's "literalization" of the world before opening a phenomenological description of various image technologies—from their uses in scientific research to entertainment, including both the political uses of images in network news and the image-sequences of MTV. Ihde probes these technologies in terms of their hermeneutic function, their role in what he calls embodiment relations, to truth claims and fictionality. In so doing, he exposes the limitations of approaches that acknowledge textuality to the exclusion of life-world relations.

The second cluster of essays center on the phenomenology of performance in the popular culture environment. In his contribution, Sam McBride calls our attention to achievements of performance artist Laurie Anderson, who, in the early 1980s, made the crossover from avant-garde artist to pop culture icon/performer, and her complex approach to performativity ultimately influenced rock concert performances, most notably that of the Irish band, U2. McBride demonstrates that in her major works, most notably *United States,* Anderson consistently probes, conceptually and socially, the problem of objectivity/subjectivity in a way that parallels the work of Merleau-Ponty. As McBride notes, Anderson has made a "questioning of the boundary between subject and object . . . a consistent theme in her performances for the past twenty-five years."

Continuing with the theme of performativity, Daniel Mackay turns his analytic gaze on role-playing games like Dungeons & Dragons, a form of entertainment that moved from marginal cult status to the mainstream in the 1970s. Through productive use of a variety of thinkers (Richard Schechner, Gary Fine [in his adaption of Irving Goffman], Roland Barthes, and Wolfgang Iser), Mackay compellingly reveals that the intersubjective experience of the role-playing game is both complex in terms of the role-players' use of various perceptual frames. Mackay also argues that while these games have caught the unwanted attention of the self-appointed cultural guardians who quite often see these games as a time-wasting at best and satanic ritual at worst, fantasy role-playing games do indeed provide a socially fulfilling activity and a model for effectiveness in the "real lives" of the participants.

We continue with Felicia Campbell's look at casino gaming. Drawing on David Abram's anthropological work on shamanism (which employs Merleau-Ponty's theory), Edward Allen's comic novel, *Mustang Sally,* and her own observations of the gambling environment as well as the testimony of others, Campbell draws our attention to the altered state of consciousness into which the gambler enters while in the surreal world of Las Vegas casinos.

Our performance cluster is rounded out with Harris M. Berger's work on popular music. In this essay, Berger applies both Husserl's theory of time-consciousness and recent ethnomusicological research to the study of rhythm in heavy metal music, with particular attention to the experiences of the musicians themselves. Berger's admirable work goes a long way toward dispelling the notion that popular music is "simple."

The third and largest cluster of readings revolves around the central "activity" of the subject in the popular culture *lebenswelt:* spectatorship. With a title that puns on Bentham's then-optimistic, now-ominous plan for a world of constant surveillance, the "Panopticon," Ralph Acampora calls us to seriously consider a place that has been for over a century a staple of urban popular culture—the zoological garden, or as it came to be known, following a Victorian slang made famous in a music hall song, the zoo. By examining the objectification of the animal body and the "somaesthetics of visiting" as well as broader political and ecological questions, Acampora indeed demonstrates that zoos tell us as much about human beings as they do about animals.

We then take leave of the zoo and head for Disneyland with Peter Steeves, the "phenomenologist in the magic kingdom." Disneyland, Disney movies, and the whole Disney corporate enterprise have certainly received their share of attention from the critical community, and just when you thought that all that can be said about Disney has been said, Steeves shows us (and this is the intended value of this anthology) that the phenomenological perspective can always lever up new and valuable observations. Steeves notes the odd parallel between the activity of the tourist and that of the phenomenologist as a prelude to an investigation of meaning, being, and identity in the theme park environment.

Next, we stop at yet another pilgrimage site in the world of popular culture. The heritage centre, as Karl Simms explains, is an enterprise that combines the entertainment aspects of the theme park environment with the purported cultural preservation mission of the traditional museum. This development is particularly evident in postindustrial Britain, where heritage centres have taken the place of what once were workplaces.

Using Husserl's "Crisis" and the second edition of Malraux' *Museum Without Walls* as point of departure, Simms looks at the act of gazing upon the culture of the Other before turning the analysis to the knowledge-as-entertainment represented by the modern heritage centre.

We then return to the question of image technologies and the work of the late Beverle Houston, a major figure in the theory of television spectatorship. While the methodological grounding of Houston's work is that of Lacanian psychoanalysis, Kristevian semiotics, and ideological critique, the goal is in keeping with phenomenology's intention of offering a demystification of mundane experience, and this essay illustrates a particularly powerful phenomenological application. Houston, with reference to programming from the early 1980s, such as *Fantasy Island,* shows how television coordinates with the structures of the subject's desiring, feeding off of a "dream of wholeness and the lack that motors it" to in turn feed the audience with its nonstop "total flow."

Our inquiries into spectatorship come to a close with Carroll's study of the spectacle of bodily violation as it appears transculturally, from Yukio Mishima's obsession with the *seppuku* ritual to the image of the Sacred Heart of Jesus, from Hogarth's rendering of a medical autopsy in *The Reward of Cruelty* to the films of David Cronenberg. Carroll shows how, as different as these images are, they derive their spectacular power through an appeal to a transcendental gesture.

Our final two essays ask broad questions regarding what Alfred Schutz calls the "social construction of reality." In his contribution, Chris Nagel performs a classic phenomenological epoché by putting aside our received notions about truth and advertising. As with Steeves' essay, Nagel shows that asking about the truth-value of the object can never substitute for an examination of how it appears to us. Nagel then refers to Merleau-Ponty and Schutz to develop a description of the intersubjective relationships engendered by the television ad. What is implied by Nagel's work is that while advertising may be viewed as merely a tool to stimulate consumption, given its ubiquitousness, it is better to view it as a fundamental element of contemporary culture and a shaper of contemporary intersubjectivity.

Finally, we come to a work that makes broad and compelling claims about the cultural phenomenology of time in America. Moving from literary references from classic American literature (Irving and Twain) to Fitzgerald's *The Great Gatsby* and finally, to an examination of contemporary media culture, Steven Carter draws on Heidegger and Fraser to interrogate the American's peculiar denial and disassociation from time.

These essays, then, provide a fairly broad display of the ways in which phenomenological approaches can illuminate popular culture studies. We must point out, however, that this set does not cover all of the phenomenological approaches to popular culture; to do that, we suggest that one consult the work of Vivian Sobchack and Jenny Nelson, among others. Furthermore, it is not our purpose here, as stated earlier, to advocate any methodological orthodoxy or to advance a program. In the pragmatic spirt of methodological pluralism, we wish only to put a few more wrenches and spanners in your hermeneutic toolbox. We hope they come in handy.

We believe this work is timely: while for some time, structuralism, with its foregrounding of the rule-governed structures of the culture system, and Frankfurt style Marxism, with its emphasis on the dominant hegemonic force of the "culture industry," have dominated cultural studies, more recently, critics and scholars have begun to argue with the assumptions of these methodologies. As Strinati argues, a new school of "cultural populism" has come into being, producing work that goes beyond the "culture industry" critique à la Frankfurt School in order to investigate the responses of the audience and the pleasure it derives from popular entertainments (255-60; cf. McGuigan). Here we find a reawakening of the phenomenologist's imperative of describing the ground of experience, and thus perhaps it is time to turn to phenomenology in order to reinvigorate the study of popular culture. Perhaps the best way to "take popular culture seriously" is to take it nonreductively, as it is, as it appears to us, as it affects us—that is, to take it in the phenomenological attitude. And in our roles as teachers, we hope this collection will prove helpful in our collective attempts to provide students with ways of understanding the popular spectacle that they confront, for better or worse, every day of their lives.

Works Cited and Consulted

Adams, Hazard, and Leroy Searle. *Critical Theory Since 1965*. Tallahassee: Florida State UP, 1986.

Adams, Hazard. "Introduction." Adams and Searle, 1-22.

Adorno, Theodor, and Max Horkheimer. "The Culture Industry: Enlightenment as Mass Deception." During, 29-43.

Barthes, Roland. *Mythologies*. 1957. Trans. Annette Lavers. New York: Hill and Wang, 1972.

Bigsby, C. W. E., ed. *Approaches to Popular Culture*. London: Edward Arnold, 1976.

Browne, Ray B. *Against Academia.* Bowling Green, OH: Bowling Green SU Popular P, 1989.

Burke, Peter. *Popular Culture in Early Modern Europe.* Rev. reprint. Aldershot: Scholar P, 1994.

Cantor, Norman F. *Twentieth Century Culture: from Modernism to Deconstruction.* New York: Lang, 1988.

Cullen, Jim. *The Art of Democracy: A Concise History of Popular Culture in the United States.* New York: Monthly Review, 1966.

Derrida, Jacques. "Structure, Sign, and Play in the Discourse of the Human Sciences." Adams and Searle, 83-94.

Detweiler, Robert. *Story, Sign, and Self: Phenomenology and Structuralism and Literary-Critical Methods.* Philadelphia, PA: Fortress P, 1978.

During, Simon, ed. *The Cultural Studies Reader.* London and New York: Routledge, 1993.

——. "Introduction." During, 1-28.

Eagleton, Terry. *The Function of Criticism: From the Spectator to Post-Structuralism.* London: Verso, 1984.

Hoppenstand, Gary. "Ray and Pat Browne: Scholars of Everyday Culture." *Pioneers in Popular Culture Studies.* Ed. Ray B. Browne and Michael T. Marsden. Bowling Green, OH: Bowling Green SU Popular P, 1999. 33-65.

Ihde, Don. *Postphenomenology: Essays in the Postmodern Context.* Northwestern UP, 1993.

Jung, Carl, and M. L. von Franz, Joseph L. Henderson, Jolande Jacobi, and Aniela Jaffé. *Man and His Symbols.* Garden City, NY: Doubleday, 1964.

Kearney, Richard. *Modern Movements in European Philosophy.* Manchester and New York: Manchester UP, 1994.

Leavis, F. R. *The Great Tradition.* 1948. London: Chatto and Windus, 1962.

Leavis, Q. D. *Fiction and the Reading Public.* 1932. Norwood, PA: Norwood Editions, 1977.

Levine, Lawrence. *Highbrow/Lowbrow: The Emergence of Cultural Hierarchy in America.* Cambridge, MA: Harvard UP, 1990.

Lewis, George H. "Dramatic Conversations: the Relationship between Sociology and Popular Culture." *Symbiosis: Popular Culture and Other Fields.* Ed. Ray B. Browne and Marshall Fishwick. Bowling Green, OH: Bowling Green SU Popular P, 1988. 70-84.

McGuigan. J. *Cultural Populism.* London: Routledge, 1992.

Nelson, Jenny L. "The Dislocation of Time: A Phenomenology of Television Reruns." *Quarterly Review of Film and Video* 12.3 (1990): 79-92.

Real, Michael. "Marxism and Popular Culture: The Cutting Edge of Cultural Criticism." *Symbiosis: Popular Culture and Other Fields.* Ed. Ray Browne and Marshall Fishwick. Bowling Green, OH: Bowling Green SU Popular P, 1988. 146-59.

Sobchack, Vivian. "'Surge and Splendor': A Phenomenology of the Cinematic Historical Epic." *Representations* 29 (Winter 1990): 24-49.

Spiegelberg, Herbert (with the collaboration of Karl Schuhmann). *The Phenomenological Movement: A Historical Introduction.* 3rd ed. The Hague: Martinus Nijhoff, 1982.

Strinati, Dominic. *An Introduction to the Theories of Popular Culture.* London and New York: Routledge, 1995.

I.

TEXTUALITY

1

PHENOMENOLOGY, LINGUISTICS, AND POPULAR LITERATURE

Janice A. Radway

In formally linking popular literature and phenomenology I do not imply that what follows is a strict phenomenological analysis of the popular literary text. Unlike Roman Ingarden and Mikel Dufrenne, who use the phenomenological method first formulated by Edmund Husserl to isolate and describe the characteristic structure and mode of existence of the literary work of art, I am primarily interested in exploring the process by which meaning is made manifest, whether in a literary text, a film, or a television melodrama. Consequently, my method might be more accurately viewed as a variant of structuralism, since I employ the characteristic linguistic analogy to explain how radically different kinds of significance can be revealed through the manipulation of a previously acquired sign system.

However, I wish to distinguish my work from that of purely structuralist critics such as Roland Barthes, Tzvetan Todorov, Will Wright, and Hayden White. I am convinced that the late French phenomenologist, Maurice Merleau-Ponty, provided an important corrective to the structuralist conception of language by placing linguistic behavior within a complex and comprehensive epistemology. Thus I have used his phenomenology of language to explain both how and why two creators can employ similar generic conventions and yet produce two enormously different products, one of which is lauded as a "work of art" while the other is dismissed as "popular culture."[1] In keeping with this interest in phenomenological linguistics, this essay acknowledges the differences between Merleau-Ponty's conception of language and that of the orthodox structuralists. Furthermore, the essay argues that it is indeed possible to make positive assertions about the differences between elite artistic expression and popular culture if we understand that man always uses language to "mean" and that he can and must use that language in two entirely different ways. Therefore, while my theory of popular literature is not itself a phenomenology, it is directly derived from the phenomenological analysis of language conducted by Maurice Merleau-Ponty in *The Prose of the World* and *The Visible and the Invisible*.[2]

My interest in phenomenological linguistics and its applicability to popular culture studies derives both from a prior interest in the aesthetic criticism of popular art, and from my belief that traditional modes of aesthetic analysis have been supremely unsuccessful in dealing with the special characteristics of popular forms of expression. I originally began this study with the hope of suggesting alternative methods for the evaluation of popular literature, but as I became more and more involved in questions of judgement and evaluation I realized that I could not formulate proper norms until I had some idea how popular literature functions for the reader, and how it differs from those works we traditionally call elite literature or art.

Aware of the growing influence of structuralism on literary criticism, I initially turned to the phenomenology of Merleau-Ponty rather than to purely structuralist analysis.[3] Phenomenology is a philosophical method for the investigation of reality, first articulated by Edmund Husserl and later modified by Martin Heidegger, Jean-Paul Sartre, Paul Ricoeur and Merleau-Ponty himself. It is essentially a science of the various objects and events of the world as they are given in human consciousness. Merleau-Ponty has called it a "transcendental philosophy . . . for which the world is always 'already there' before reflection begins— as an inalienable presence" (*PP* vii). It is a rigorous attempt to offer an account or description of space, time and the world *as we live them.* Consciousness is always consciousness of something for a phenomenologist. According to Merleau-Ponty, an object or phenomenon cannot be said to exist except as the intended goal of an act of consciousness.

Although Maurice Merleau-Ponty died in 1961 while immersed in a major writing project designed to study language in depth, he had already included substantial material on the subject in several previous volumes. His conception of language is loosely based on the theories of Ferdinand de Saussure, whose work provided the linguistic foundation so essential to structuralism. Merleau-Ponty's theory of language is formulated as part of his larger investigations into perception and it is therefore derived from a complex conception of the relationship between the human subject and his environment.

In his major work, *Phenomenology of Perception,* Merleau-Ponty argues that the human body is not a separate physical entity which merely comes into contact with an already fully constituted world, but rather a structure that is open to the world and correlative with it (*PP* xii-xix). He maintains that the world is inseparable from the perceiving subject, who is in the world by virtue of his incarnation as a body. This "being-in-the-world" precedes any reflective consciousness a person may have of that world; as a result, he lives in direct contact with beings, things, and his own body. He lives, in short, in a universe of experience, and his perception is really a form of communication between his body and the universe. Perception is a dialectical process, in which an organism shifts its attention from one position to another, focuses on some intended goal, and thereby organizes the surrounding field. As a result of such an act, that goal is understood as a *perceived* object.

Merleau-Ponty continues to argue that the primary means available to man for bringing this pre-conscious contact with the world to conscious awareness is his ability to use language and to give definite form to his inchoate experience by expressing the constituent parts of that experience in words. Language, then, for Merleau-Ponty, is not a discrete system cut off from all other non-linguistic knowledge of the world, but rather a medium in which experiential knowledge or pre-conscious experience is given conscious, objective existence by a speaking subject. As he says in the early essay "Indirect Language and the Voices of Silence," "signs do not simply evoke other signs for us and so on without end, and language is not like a prison we are locked into or a guide we must blindly follow; for what those linguistic gestures mean and gain us such complete access to that we seem to have no further need of them to refer to it finally appears at the intersection of all of them" (81).

My theory of the differences between elite and popular literary texts is directly derived from Merleau-Ponty's distinction between the Creative and Empirical use of language, a distinction which is itself an extrapolation of Saussure's notion that language exhibits a peculiar dual nature. Merleau-Ponty points out in another early essay, "On the Phenomenology of Language," that language can be thought of as a stable institution or system composed of signs, their roughly equivalent meanings, and syntactic rules governing their communication. Although he does not use Saussure's designation, *la langue,* to refer to language considered as a system, it is to it that he refers when he admits that men could not communicate their experiences to others if they did not know how to operate within a shared system of signs and meanings. Merleau-Ponty refers elsewhere to language considered as a system as *le langage parlé,* or spoken language (*PW* 10), which is essentially the residue of past acts of signification and the record of already acquired meaning ("Phenomenology of Language" 85). Language can therefore be thought of as a completely adequate system of words and meanings which must be learned and acquired by every speaker and then used in the process of expression and communication.

Language-in-use, (Saussure's *la parole*) is the reverse side of *la langue,* and Merleau-Ponty argues that such speech cannot properly be conceived without the notion of language ("Phenomenology of Language" 86). In discussing speech, Merleau-Ponty limits it in a way Saussure does not. Saussure argues that *la parole* is the executive side of language, involving both the combinations by which the speaker uses the code of the linguistic system in order to express his own thoughts and the psychophysical mechanism which permit him to externalize these combinations (14). Merleau-Ponty narrows the focus, however, and defines Speech or *le langage-parlant,* literally, speaking language—as a contingent, temporal, individual act which *necessarily* goes beyond the limits of the language institution itself and which constantly adds to the possibilities of expression contained within it (*PW* 10). Real Speech events are capable of and responsible for the modification of language as a system because, when an individual uses language in a certain way, he makes words signify that which they have never meant before, thus adding to or altering their sedimented meanings.

In the essay, "On the Phenomenology of Language," Merleau-Ponty is careful to stress the fact that language can never be reduced to either one of its two aspects, i.e., *le langage parlé* or *le langage parlant.* In other words, one cannot argue that speech events are the chronological antecedents of language considered as a system, since there can never be a speech event which does not use the elements of that system. Merleau-Ponty continually stresses the fact that language as *system* is inextricably bound up or intertwined with language as event and he deliberately attempts to avoid the structuralists's preoccupation with *la langue.*[4] He always thinks of language phenomenologically—as a system-in-use—and his designation of it as Speech refers not to the simple act of speaking, or to the system of sedimented meanings, but rather to the convergence or intertwining of the two aspects effected by an actual speaker.

When a person has acquired the use of his language as a system and has learned to speak to others, he can be said to possess *linguistic competence.* Competence (a term adapted from Noam Chomsky) refers to the body of knowledge any fluent speaker possesses which allows him to formulate "grammatical" utterances and to judge the intelligibility of utterances directed to him by others. To describe a speaker's competence would involve "the explicit representation, by a system of rules or norms, of the implicit knowledge possessed by those who successfully operate within that system" (Culler 9). However, even though competence is not generally subjected to explicit reflection and thus remains merely tacit, it nevertheless controls and directs the speaker's attempts to make sense and to discern the sense in what others say.

For example, while I may not know all the rules of English grammar as they are currently represented and articulated in my culture, as a native speaker of the language I have an internal awareness of what makes sense and what does not. Although I may be aware that "erasers smile curdled" is nonsense, at least according to traditional norms, I may not be able to explain what rules have been broken or to explain why those particular words can't be combined in that way. Nevertheless, I do know they should not be, if they are to make sense. Competence, then is knowledge of that collection of words, their meanings, and the syntactic rules and laws governing the use of those words in proper context which makes up language. Merleau-Ponty's argument is that any speaker who defies such rules in order to make new meaning speaks "Creatively," while a speaker who adheres to rules and remains within the linguistic system uses language "Empirically."

In the Creative use of language—that is, in true Speech—Merleau-Ponty maintains that the speaker seeks to give objective, verbal presence to some portion of his *pre*-verbal, *pre*-conscious existence. However, because this part of his experience has never previously been brought to consciousness, there is no name for it within the existent language system, and hence no way to express it. The speaker must "deform" the familiar words of the language he speaks in order to force them to secrete a meaning they have never had before. Merleau-Ponty calls this process "the coherent deformation." He defines it as that operation which arranges available words and their meanings in a new sense, thereby taking "not only the hearers *but the speaking subject as well* through a decisive step ("Phenomenology of Language" 91). The point is that the new meaning is not objectively present, even for the speaker, until the very moment he embodies it in words. Consequently, this meaning cannot be said to exist prior to the utterance itself; as a result, it is actually the temporal manifestation or result of the process whereby familiar words are combined and uttered in a new way. As Merleau-Ponty says, "Speech . . . does not translate ready-made thought, but accomplishes it" (*PP* 178).

In combining words in a new way, the speaker must inevitably defy some syntactic rule or contextual norm. This set of new combinations creates the new meaning precisely because it enables the words to interact in strange and unfamiliar ways. The "deformation" upsets the listener's expectations and his ability to make normal sense of the words used. But deformation or not, the speech act is nonetheless coherent because the words themselves are known to the listener, and, by discerning the new "rules" governing their combination, he can begin to understand what they mean in this new context.

What Merleau-Ponty describes here is that magical process which occurs when one suddenly sees through the previously opaque language of a difficult speaker or writer and instantly understands all that has been obscure up to that moment. Such *eclaris sement* or enlightenment can occur at all levels, whether one is confronted by modest changes in a few words introduced by a minor metaphor or by the reorientation of a whole language system created by the statement of a new philosophical theory. In either case, familiar words are combined in such a way that they are momentarily thrown out of focus for reader or listener, who then must await the breakthrough of meaning which will give the discourse internal coherence and form.

Diametrically opposed to the Creative use of language is Empirical use, in which a speaker puts signs together as if each word actually "contains" its meaning absolutely, once and for all. When language is used Empirically, both speaker and listener rely wholly on the meanings of the signs as they are traditionally employed. In Empirical speech, therefore, the subject depends on sedimented meaning, that collection of relationships between sign and signification which he learned as a child while seeking to master use of the system as a whole.

Empirical use of language, then, is nothing more than the "opportune recollection of a pre-established sign" which itself seems to possess a definitive sense (Merleau-Ponty, "Indirect Language" 144). A speaker employs the sign and its traditional sense conservatively, neither changing nor augmenting its use value in any way. He stays within the limits of the language system and adheres to all or virtually all of those rules, norms, and expectations which form his linguistic competence (Merleau-Ponty, "Indirect Language" 44; 46).

At this point, one may justifiably ask what all this has to do with popular literature. If we can accept the structuralist premise that literature can be thought of analogically as a language system, capable of individual speech acts in the form of texts, then the connection becomes clear. When I propose to use linguistics as a model for the study of literature I do not mean that we should simply conduct linguistic analysis of the language used in texts. Rather, I propose to consider literature as a *system* of varying levels of organization, each with its own fundamental units and traditional rules or norms governing the combination of those units. Although it is not possible or even necessary to elaborate here on those organizational levels, I would point out that aside from its linguistic organization, a text may also exhibit a general narrative or plot organization, a particular generic structure and a peculiar character presentation among others. In any case, I do not believe a reader can come to a text without previous expectations—as Jonathan Culler explains:

a text can be a poem only because certain possibilities exist within the tradition; it is written in relation to other poems. A sentence of English can have meaning only by virtue of its relations to other sentences within the conventions of the language. The communicative intention presupposes listeners who know the language. And similarly, a poem presupposes conventions of reading which the author may work against, which he can transform, but which are the conditions of possibility of his discourse. (30)

As might be anticipated, Culler calls this body of conventions our "literary competence." It governs our ability to compose and to understand entirely *new* texts, as surely as our linguistic competence governs our ability to comprehend the speech acts of others. To read a text as a literary text, therefore, is to come to it with certain preconceived ideas about the way sentences are put together in literature and how such sentences refer or do not refer to a world. Similarly, to read a text we must rely on our previous knowledge about the ways in which specific textual units are combined in the production of certain generic forms, just as we come to the genre itself with certain ideas about that genre's relation to the world and its consequent significance. In sum, one might say that we always approach an unfamiliar text with specific expectations and norms in mind, and that our ability to understand that text is necessarily affected—and often limited by—the flexibility of those expectations.

I want to make it absolutely clear that in discussing literary competence and its effect on the composition and comprehension of unfamiliar texts, I am not saying that the meanings of those texts are wholly determined by the system itself, or that they are freely manufactured by a reader and the competence he brings to them. While any text must undoubtedly be read and construed with respect to a previous knowledge of how other texts function, a text nonetheless possesses in itself that structure or form which serves as the latticework, foundation, or vehicle for the meaning as it is actualized in the act of reading. The text is that structure or form, in the same way the environment is a style or structure even before its various elements are marked off as objects in the mind of the perceiver.

The meaning of the text, therefore, can be thought of as the tacit component of the words, sentences, paragraphs, and larger units which make up the entity that is the text as a whole. One can argue that this meaning is "created" by the author because he is the manipulator of the words. However, once the words are written, the text is apparently free of its author. The meanings contained therein are not directly dependent on him or on the original significative intention that brought them into existence. Those meanings simply await a reader who, in the act of reading, confronts the visible form of which they are the invisible depth.

It is impossible to say, then, whether the meaning of a text, as it is construed by the reader, is the result of the author's creative intentions or simply an effect produced by the power of language itself. Certainly, the author cannot compose without the benefit of an already fully constituted language, and what he wishes to say must in some way be determined by the language he speaks. However, like any speaker, he can use language "creatively" or "authentically" (as Merleau-Ponty calls it) and when he does, he stamps the language with his own personal imprint. If he is successful in this, the reader, who may be momentarily disoriented, can eventually detect, beneath the familiar words, the new context, form or structure which causes those words to mean in a different way.

By continuing to extend the comparison between literature and language, it is possible to develop the useful notion of a literary continuum, along which specific texts may be located with respect to the number of rules, norms, and expectations of the literary system which they either observe or violate. Texts can be arranged functionally, according to the ways in which they work for readers with respect to literary competence. Given, for example, some absolute, ideal notion of literary competence, certain texts will break a large number of rules, some only a few; and others none. On the revolutionary side of this proposed continuum, we might place all those literary texts which upset conventions, pioneer in the formation of unusual structures and create new meaning. These works we traditionally, although not necessarily, label "elite" literature. Some are so far outside the literary institution as it exists at the moment of creation that they are extremely difficult to read and comprehend. In such instances, the "deformation" effected in the reader's competence is so great that what he reads is no longer coherent for him. Often a certain amount of time must elapse during which readers are pushed by the style of the work to the point where they can intuitively grasp the peculiar semantic richness of the words and forms used and begin to articulate that understanding by "translating" it into other roughly equivalent words. Works such as these which readily come to mind are Pound's "Cantos," Eliot's "The Wasteland," and Faulkner's *The Sound and the Fury.*

There are literary cases, however, in which only a few conventions and expectations are overturned and the consequent "deformation" in the reader's competence is less severe. In such instances the text may often adhere to traditional norms governing generic form and plot construction but ignore others governing character development or mimetic reference to a world. I should place some of the novels of Henry James at this point on the continuum. In any event, when such words, by combining textual units in unfamiliar ways, operate outside the literary system, they not only create new meanings, but also, by creating new structures, establish new rules and norms. This kind of "creative" text parallels Merleau-Ponty's conception of the Creative use of language.

However, if we argue that our ability to comprehend a literary work is governed by expectations and norms which are part of an accepted literary system, and that any number of these norms can be ignored or violated in the creation of texts, it is necessary also to argue that it is equally possible for a text to remain within the system and to conform to all or nearly all of these same conventions. It is my belief that the texts we traditionally label "popular literature" or tend to dismiss as "mass entertainment" are those which choose not to violate conventions, upset expectations or create new forms.[5] Such "popular" writers respect and manipulate familiar forms and structures, thus relying on the standard or sedimented significance generally associated with them. These texts are fundamentally *referential,* in that their conservative use of literary and linguistic forms enables the reader to discern automatically the traditionally accepted significance or meaning associated with those forms. As a result, the reader literally penetrates, or sees through those forms, to the worlds they delineate. Such texts are also primarily *formulaic* in that they rarely function outside a reader's competence, and thus assiduously avoid disappointing the reader's expectations. It is at this end of the continuum that I would locate Edgar Rice Burroughs' *Tarzan of the Apes,* Jack Schaefer's *Shane,* and Arthur Hailey's *Hotel.*

As might be expected, I see a direct parallel between the empirical use of language described by Merleau-Ponty and the formulaic manipulation of narrative patterns, plot structures and character types in popular literature. When a writer or speaker uses language empirically, he combines the words of the language system according to standard rules of syntax and thus reveals only the generally accepted sedimented meanings of those words. It is therefore possible to think in similar fashion of the "popular" author as one who arranges the common elements of the literary text into familiar sequences which depend upon generally accepted, well-known meanings providing the reader with the experiences he anticipates. Texts such as these are literally "conservative," in that they do conserve and preserve the literary system as it exists at the time. They are truly "popular" and "of the people," in the sense that they operate almost entirely within the linguistic and literary competencies and expectations of the mass of readers. As a result, these readers find such works truly pleasant to read because they reaffirm the validity of the strategies and conventions that they, as readers, have for making meaning of the world. Popular texts can therefore be accurately described as entertainment—precisely because they enable their readers to deny, even if only for a short while, the problem of an unavoidably disordered and alien world.

To read an *empirical* text, then, is to reaffirm what we already know as members of a culture; it is to underscore the accuracy and efficacy of our everyday strategies for comprehending the world. Because popular texts remain within the linguistic and literary systems from which they are composed, their function is to stabilize or strengthen both those systems. Such texts function, therefore, as linguistic and literary anchors, because they insure the continued survival of both systems as shared cultural resources. At the same time, they give verbal existence to the containing culture's basic, universal concerns. Continued use of the two institutions, then, as they are familiarly known, and understood, tends to perpetuate the life and vitality of both.

Although it is impractical here to demonstrate that the distinctions I have drawn are, in fact, real distinctions appearing among actual literary texts, it is possible to describe briefly the procedures followed in arriving at my conclusions.[6] I selected a single genre—the Gothic novel—and attempted to describe the fundamental narrative units and rules of combination basic to the genre. After establishing the pattern of structure peculiar to the Gothic novel throughout its long history, I then analyzed several contemporary American texts casually identified as "Gothic," in order to discern whether they used the structure I had isolated and how they changed it if they had. The texts chosen were *The Golden Unicorn* and *Spindrift* by Phyllis Whitney; *Sanctuary* by William Faulkner, and *The Member of the Wedding* by Carson McCullers.

Of course I was not surprised to discover that both Whitney novels used narrative units and structural combinations which were nearly identical to the underlying patterns of such traditional gothics as *The Castle of Otranto* and *The Mysteries of Udolpho*. However, I was surprised to find that both *Sanctuary* and *The Member of the Wedding* are, indeed, Gothic novels—not because they simply incorporate Gothic properties into otherwise non-Gothic plots, but because they actually are founded on the standard Gothic meaning-structure. Although both novels significantly alter that structure and consequently reveal radically different "meanings," those meanings are, nevertheless, products of a conscious, visible deviation from the original Gothic pattern. It became clear that while Phyllis Whitney uses the Gothic system empirically and thus reiterates the genre's standard significance, both Faulkner and McCullers "deform" the "system" and thus extend its capacity to "mean" by drawing it into previously uncharted areas.

We must avoid the temptation, of course, to place greater value on one side of the literary continuum than on the other. If we are indeed serious about the analogy between literature and language, then we cannot ignore the fact that language has a dual nature; that it is a stable, sedimented system, but one capable of radically creative speech acts. Furthermore, we must recall that the creative character of these speech acts is not discernible except against the background of other more conservative acts which reinforce the traditional structures and meanings contained within the system. I believe we must recognize that literature is a similar system—complete with basic units, rules of combination, and strategies for reading. We must acknowledge, therefore, that it too is capable of being used to formulate revolutionary, creative texts whose function is to extend the whole system's capacity to "mean." However, those texts are also creative only with respect to the traditional norms and familiar conventions of more conservative works whose primary function is to preserve the system and to emphasize its basic effectiveness in delineating the world. Because creative expression is always initially dependent on empirical expression, which is itself the result of some previously completed creative act, it seems clear to me that equal status must be accorded both.

While I have only applied the notions of creative and empirical expression to the realm of literature, I feel certain it is equally possible to treat music, cinema, and architecture as language systems. The first task in such an enterprise will be the analytical decomposition of particular symbols in terms of those elements in the generation of individual works within the system. Once this arduous task has been accomplished, it will be possible to focus on individual works as Creative or Empirical uses of the system in question. This procedure, then, should move us much closer to an understanding of the relationship between American society and the elite and popular culture it produces.

Notes

1. The theory referred to here and discussed throughout this essay is developed at length in my doctoral dissertation, *A Phenomenological Theory of Popular and Elite Literature*. This study includes a summary of Merleau-Ponty's phenomenological philosophy, a detailed statement of my theories about popular and elite literature, and a case study of the Gothic novel.

2. Maurice Merleau-Ponty, *The Prose of the World* and *The Visible and the Invisible*. While these two volumes are not formal phenomenologies of language, they do analyze man's use of language from a phenomenological perspective and consequently situate linguistic behavior within a complex conception of man's perspective and consequently situate linguistic behavior

within a complex conception of man's ability to "know" the world as a result of his insertion in it. For the exposition of a formal phenomenology of language, see James M. Edie's *Speaking and Meaning: The Phenomenology of Language.*

3. For a comprehensive critique of structuralism, see Frederic Jameson's *The Prison House of Language: A Critical Account of Structuralism and Russian Formalism.*

4. I think it worthwhile to note here that Frederick Jameson's principle objection to structuralism is its inadvertent negation of the temporal or diachronic aspect of language use which results from the insistence on the relational or synchronic nature of the linguistic system itself. It seems to me that because Merleau-Ponty refuses to *divide* language into two distinct aspects in the first place, he avoids collapsing an essentially and fundamentally historical event into a timeless, synchronic present. For an extended discussion of this, see Jameson, 342.

5. I do want to point out, however, that absolute correlation between these two categories is not necessary nor has it always occurred. Indeed, certain texts which I would classify as creative because they deformed familiar structures to establish new meanings, have achieved a measure of popularity. Examples which immediately suggest themselves are F. Scott Fitzgerald's *The Great Gatsby,* Sinclair Lewis's *Babbitt,* and Kurt Vonnegut's *Slaughterhouse Five.* The point I wish to make here is that most of the texts we traditionally identify as "popular" are also those which are functionally empirical in nature. To explain, however, why certain creative texts can and do become popular would entail a very long digression at this point. Suffice it to say, therefore, that even though such texts are *actually* creative, they possess certain peculiar characteristics which enable readers to approach them as if they are empirical.

6. See note 1, above.

Works Cited

Culler, Jonathan. *Structuralist Poetics: Structuralism, Linguistics, and the Study of Literature.* Ithaca: Cornell UP, 1975.

de Saussure, Ferdinand. *Course in General Linguistics.* Ed. Charles Bally and Albert Sechehaye with Albert Riedlinger. Trans. Wade Baskin. New York: McGraw-Hill, 1954.

Edie, James M. *Speaking and Meaning: The Phenomenology of Language.* Bloomington: Indiana UP, 1976.

Jameson, Frederic. *The Prison House of Language: A Critical Account of Structuralism and Russian Formalism.* Princeton UP, 1972.

Merleau-Ponty, Maurice. "Indirect Language and the Voices of Silence." *Signs.* Trans. and with an introduction by Richard C. McCleary Evanston: Northwestern UP, 1964.

——. "On the Phenomenology of Language." *Signs.*

——. *Phenomenology of Perception.* Trans. Colin Smith. London: Routeledge and Kegan Paul, 1962.

——. *The Prose of the World.* Trans. John O'Neill. Evanston: Northwestern UP, 1964.

——. *The Visible and the Invisible.* Trans. Alphonso Lingis. Evanston: Northwestern UP, 1969.

Radway, Janice A. *A Phenomenological Theory of Popular and Elite Literature.* Diss. Michigan SU, 1977.

2

VIOLENCE AND BAUDRILLARDIAN REPETITION
IN BRET EASTON ELLIS'S *AMERICAN PSYCHO*

James Brusseau

Bret Easton Ellis's *Less Than Zero* (1985) was a critical and sales success (75,000 hardcover copies in the first year and a first paperback run of 100,000 copies). By the late 1980s he was being hailed as the voice of Generation X and so, in spite of the commercial and critical flop of his second book, *The Rules of Attraction* (1987), Simon and Shuster anticipated strong sales for his third novel, *American Psycho* (1991). Thousands of copies were printed and stored on warehouse pallets. But, by October 1990, word got out that many Simon and Shuster employees were disturbed by the novel's excesses. Copies of the manuscript were leaked to New York publishing and reviewing circles and months before the official publication date in January 1991, the public received advance warning, particularly through a review in *Time* by R. Z. Sheppard: *American Psycho,* we were told, is unrelentingly violent; the reader sees fingers nailed individually to wood planks, hears the hiss of brains escaping their skull cavity through cracks the size of ax blades, watches victims be skinned alive. If Ellis' intent was, as he claimed, to provoke, to let people find out about "their own limits as readers," he succeeded (qtd. in Hoban 36).

Before anyone in the Simon and Schuster publicity department could intervene, the literary rumor mill was grinding so fast, so wildly, that Richard Snyder, chair of Simon and Shuster, actually read the book. His conscience would not permit him to publish it (Hitchens 7). In mid-November 1990, he canceled *American Psycho* (Kennedy 426), sent the already printed copies to the shredders, sent the manuscript back to Ellis, and wrote the $500,000 author's advance into the accounting ledgers as a straight loss. The book was too violent and misogynistic.

Opportunistically, or perhaps for the cause of free literary expression,[1] Sonny Mehta of Alfred A. Knopf agreed to publish it as part of the Vintage Contemporaries paperback series (Penguin had already declined the reprint rights). The novel didn't sell well, and its aesthetic shortcomings—its redundancy in particular—did not escape the critics. A few tentatively defended the book on its merits (Hitchens, Rawlinson) with the strongest support from Joe McGinniss, author of *Fatal Vision* and Ellis's creative writing professor and mentor at Bennington College. He wrote that *American Psycho* surged "from the deepest, purest motives . . . It's a quantum leap beyond his earlier books" (qtd. in Hoban 36). Norman Mailer also expressed some sympathy for Ellis, although ultimately he felt that the novel's execution did not live up to the promise of its concept.

In spite of these defenses, most reviewers agreed with Terry Teachout of the *National Review,* who proclaimed that "everything bad you've read about [*American Psycho*] is an understatement . . . it is, in the truest sense of the word, obscene" (45). Many reviewers focused on the novel's repetitiveness: as Naomi Wolf (writing for *The New Statesman*) remarked, Ellis "grinds through about thirty cycles of clothes, restaurant menus, cunnilingus, and then, watch out! It's the old nailgun through the palms again!" (34). Ellis describes the suits his characters wear over and over, even though they're always the same. He renders the stereotypical yuppie dialogue over and over; it never changes. The novel's misogyny also raised concern: the Los Angeles chapter of the National Organization of Women (NOW) quickly established a hot line to encourage the public to boycott Random House, Knopf's parent organization (Hoban 34). As for the murders: it's just pound, pound, pound, the same thing, over and over again. And when you've reached the final page, you haven't gotten anywhere or learned anything—even about murder.

Yet, *American Psycho* can be seductive; in spite of its too obvious aesthetic shortcomings, this is a book many readers work all the way through even if they won't admit it. For this reason, it is, paradoxically, a popular book (it's by a popular author, it's infamous, notorious, and for some, compelling, which is ultimately perhaps the sole aesthetic criteria for popular literature) while not being very popular (in terms of overall sales). This presents an interesting problem in terms of popularity, aesthetics, violence, and the phenomenology of reading.

We can begin to interrogate the problem by reconsidering a central concept in the Western philosophic and literary tradition: for something to exist at the most crucial level, it must not be said, it can't be said, it is unsayable. Consequently, Plato's dialogues, relentless as they are in their adherence to this central idea, always end (as they start, as they proceed) in ambiguity. This veneration of silence has enjoyed an uncanny philosophical persistence. Jacques Derrida expounding upon the problem of signification, which he claims is one of unnamablility, states that ". . .

there is no name for it [*différance*] at all . . . not even that of "*différance*" which is not a name . . ." (26). From Plato to Derrida, metaphysics conspires to gag us: we think of truth (or its stubborn absence) as immutable, but once it assumes textual form, it can be erased or changed or misinterpreted. So, to protect it and ourselves from clumsy interpretation, we only hint, allude, evoke.

In *The Republic,* right at the start, when Socrates is walking home, he is intercepted by Glaucon who asks for the pleasure of his company. Socrates tries to refuse, but Glaucon aggressively asks whether Socrates and the friends accompanying him outnumber Glaucon and his friends. After a quick count, Socrates concedes to go to Glaucon's house. Violence never reaches the explicit degree of happening—it's not said, but it is there. At least Socrates believes it is.

On the other end of history and at the other end of the textual spectrum, Toni Morrison employs a similar rhetorical strategy regarding violence. The narrative chain of her short story "Recitatif," approaches and approaches and approaches a particular violent scene. On each succeeding page a smudged memory, a detail, an effect is added. At first it is just a day that "Maggie fell down;" later there are others there who have something to do with it, who might even have forced her down, or worse. But the account ends with the question: "What the hell happened to Maggie?" (453). We don't know what happened. This gives the story power. Far from being a shortfall or qualification, this technique of silence makes the violence real. Exactly how it does that is a separate question about literary language. Here, only the implications are important. Authors manipulating the literary gadget of reticence equally inscribe themselves on the long, distinguished list of writers headed by Plato. They all valorize by saying nothing, and by saying it judiciously.

There is also, as Jean Baudrillard suggests, a second reason for the injunction to silence: sentimentality.[2] We don't say it because we don't want to. Would you want to hear it, if you could? Would you want to see Beauty or touch *différance*? No, the promise of these intellectual black holes tugs strongest in their absence, without the anticlimax of revelation. This situation breeds a modern necessity. It no longer suffices to surrender before the metaphysician's impossible task. As emotional beings trapped in denial, we have to insist—to ourselves even—that we can't say the words of philosophic dreamers from Plato to Derrida. Therefore, according to Baudrillard, we have the modern necessity of a "deterrence machine," something to stop us from saying it (*SS* 61-62). Therefore we have Disney World. The Magic Kingdom is how we say we can't say it here. For the traditional categories of the inexpressible—

such as Beauty and Justice—this is obvious. Fairies and princes with their magic phrases summon up unblemished heroes and kingdoms who exploit no one. That they are sensible and articulable at Disney grants us the desirable assurance that out there, beyond the parking lot, they can't be conjured up. The play on our desires turns metaphysics into masochism—we enjoy the denial. That's why we pay to go in. And though it's supposed to be for children, eventually we all get hooked by the disingenuous moral that there are things none of us can pronounce though we wish we could, and there are spells none of us know though undoubtedly they are locked away in some ancient book somewhere. This moral runs industriously through the history of philosophy, keeping lips stitched from ancient Athens to contemporary Paris.

But, Baudrillard argues, Disney has now reached epistemological overdrive. Going well beyond its ostensible function of eliciting a zone of fantastic words and keeping them out of quotidian existence, Disney has actually begun confusing the real and unreal, the sayable and unsayable. For Baudrillard, Walt Disney World is not only the way the world isn't, the set of words that can't be said out here beyond the walls. Disney also holds the power to present the world as it at least sometimes is, as a surface of confusion between the real and imaginary, the unsayable and sayable; it is "the perfect model of all the entangled orders of simulation" (*Simulations* 23). So much so, and so confused, that it no longer makes sense to try straightening the two orders out. Far more prudent to suspend the distinction altogether. The world does not cut neatly into words and the inarticulable. In fact, it doesn't cut at all but rather mingles and then gels into a planet without the West's great and long-lived silences of disciplined reality.

For example: imagine yourself wreaking havoc in Walt Disney World. Bring a .45 caliber automatic pistol and pockets full of ammunition. Start shooting. First, you'll notice that the actors you've seen on TV take bullets with much greater conviction than actual people who look stupid for a moment and then drop obtusely onto the pavement. Actors convulse, shriek, and drag themselves toward some illusory safety. Far more real. And the prop-blood flows better and grislier than the translucent bodily stuff which coagulates too quickly or else is too thin, and doesn't even look like real blood. While you're firing away, families will gather to watch the show. Caring fathers and chivalrous husbands shove their wives and daughters up front for better views. You point the trembling barrel between a six-year-old's eyes and the child shrieks appropriately, but the older brother and both parents chuckle and smile, already relishing years of family dinner table recollections about the day little Tommy was so scared by the Disney show, and then the crack. This is really good. People push as close as they can, some on tiptoes, children on their father's shoulders. At the same time, the sheriff from Western Town, who has never seen your face in the dressing room, becomes ambiguously suspicious. Suspicious of you, but also suspicious of himself for being suspicious. While the crowd applauds, he overcomes his own hesitations and tries, vainly, to apprehend you. The dazed father, blue oxford shirt and corduroy pants blotched, joins in the attack. At this, some of the families start moving back, but others push into the abandoned spots in front. Some burly guys appear and start pulling things apart. Most of them sport uniforms labeled Disney Enterprises Security, but one of them is dressed as a duck. Later, the Orlando Police are getting confused about who are regular police, who are Disney police, and who are performers dressed as police. The sheriff is mixed up in all this somewhere, too. Meanwhile, you march for the employee exit. On the way, someone intercepts you and asks rudely, even forcefully, for your autograph.

This is the way the world is, Baudrillard claims. Not necessarily violent, but hopelessly confused. In the above, the confusion most evidently swirls between the awkwardly broad categories of real and unreal. But this could easily be extended to a more specific mix-up of Justice and Injustice (when the real officers of the law arrive, more justice isn't done, the confusion just increases). Or, even further, to an enigmatic confusion between the unsayable and sayable. Imagine someone shouting "Put down that gun in the name of God!" in the midst of your performance. But who? And in what terms? If he is an actor confusing you for an actor, then "Put down that gun in the name of God!" is a perfectly sayable Disney kind of sentence, the reference to God is not really to a transcendent entity but to a dramatic device designed to heighten excitement. On the other hand, if it is a real police officer terrified by the situation, the same sentence would likely have as its referent just that God that we humans can't say. So, the confusion: real and unreal, just and unjust, unsayable and sayable. This blemishes the long-venerated horizon of intellectual and religious silence.

It's much the same with *American Psycho*. Consider the confusion surrounding the status of the book's characters. Most of Ellis' personages are straight fictions, but some aren't. Steve Rubell and Ivana Trump are both mentioned (121). So, the question: are these fictitious characters or are they real ones stuck into a fictitious background? More confusing still are characters like Stash, who may or may not be the same Stash who appears in Tama Janowitz's novel *Slaves of New York*. And what about the psycho himself, twenty-six-year-old Patrick Bateman, a pathological yuppie Wall Street investment banker with a taste for designer clothes, upscale restaurants, drugs, and torture—wasn't he in an earlier Ellis novel? We could follow these questions through, step by step, and end up back in Baudrillard's simulacra, with reality split and rearranged by the same epistemological and ontological uncertainty that curves through Disney World.

What would constitute Disney violence? The answer lies in a peculiar understanding of repetition. For Baudrillard, repetition bounces on without a primary source, without a component of central identity. Repetition is the ongoing act of copying for which there is no original. The moment a psycho infiltrates Disney, there is no ultimate differentiator, no original, no way to separate what is really going on from what is just an appearance (a copy) of what is going on. Sheriffs, security officers, town police, actors, and laborers all roll out of the machine one after the other without any clear designation of their status. Thus, in the Magic Kingdom gone wrong, the only judicial official who has any idea what is really happening isn't even a policeman but a fake Western sheriff, a copy sheriff—a copy that is not genuine and not not genuine (this is different than the binary pairing of genuine:not-genuine). It wasn't as though this sheriff had attended the police academy and flunked out near the course's end and thus wound up as the next best and closest thing, almost the real thing, a police impersonator. He never attended a police academy: he's an actor—his knowledge of police work comes from Clint Eastwood. Dirty Harry, then, serves as the original, the model for his action and his understanding. But the Hollywood screen which modeled the sheriff's honorable and dangerous mission was itself copied not from the San Francisco police, but from a formula for box office success with all its rhetorical flourish, with its "Go ahead—make my day." In turn, these things were copied from statistical data sheets and an almost forgotten stand-up routine in some dingy comedy club. We could keep following this back, but the further we go, the less plausible each consecutive origin will seem. Instead of climbing out of Plato's cave, we are tunneling deeper into it.

Baudrillard recommends a halt to sifting through less and less likely candidates for originality. He insists that the magnitude of this confusion cuts off every escape route but one: simply giving up the endeavor of making order. Thus, beneath all the make-up and costumes and fantasy and happy endings, the Disney Empire also communicates a more ecstatic message: there is no longer anything to be confused about since nothing should hold any pretension to being "reality" or its opposite, or even mixed together in a recognizable way. Under normal circumstances Disney preserves well-ordered, planned confusion, but only until the moment some psychopath reveals the whole thing as a fraud.

In the language of repetition, simply accept that there is no original. Accept it, even though, admittedly, this default is absurd. On the theoretical front, it leaves innumerable questions unanswered about the organization of subjective experiences and cognition. Undoubtedly, this intellectual condition is as ludicrous as ridiculously digging up increasingly unlikely candidates for originality. But in the vertiginous situation where Walt Disney serves as the oracle of truth, absurdity might as well be the preference.

Baudrillard's striking ersatz-metaphysical stance has a powerful implication: we are ungagged on both the metaphysical and sentimental fronts. There is no secret, thus no reason to whisper. There is no original to protect from the dirty words coming from our mouths and pens. And there is no reason to engage in a sentimental protection of the cherished unknown because now we know it's not there. Or, better yet, we don't know it's there and don't know it's not there. We suspend the debate. As a result, there is no more unconquerable territory for speech. This, however, comes at a cost: we can talk, but we can't really talk about anything because words no longer have any penetrating meaning. Words possess no force because they lose the hidden element of their referent.

Literary language has always been predicated on its duality, something both explicit and implied—something ineffable, something out there, unsaid, mysteriously hovering over the text, giving it force. Or to put it another way, what powers literary language is the part of its reference that escapes understanding and that we know escapes understanding—just like what powers love is the part we can't possess, the dashes of time we can't recapture. Ask Gatsby. Whether it's the violence in Plato or Toni Morrison, it's the same: they speak, or so we think, because their crucial parts remain incompletely spoken. When nothing is hidden, there is nothing to want, nothing to drive for, nothing to arouse us. Anyone who has ever been to a nude beach already knows this. Like totally exposed bodies, totally exposed words deprived of secret places shed impact.

One need not, however, go to a nude beach—a trip to Walt Disney World supplies the verification. But this time, before you start shooting, start telling people you're going to shoot. They will chuckle and point you out to their friends. They will watch instead of running. Some will even pretend to be afraid. Firing a few shots in the air won't clear up this confusion but instead draws more gawkers. Baudrillard's repetition undergirds the rhetoric of this exposure and this futility. Each recurrence—a warning, a shot, another shot—has the peculiar quality of adding nothing to what is repeating. It adds nothing because, paradoxically but not contradictorily, nothing is repeating—there is no original to repeat. You repeat your violent threat by saying it, by shouting it, by shooting in the air. No one gets any more scared. This is repetition without point, without center, without unsaid, without original.

And this is also the repetition of *American Psycho*. Take this typical scene: Patrick and Evelyn are talking about how their wedding would be, were they to get married:

"I'd want a zydeco band, Patrick. That's what I'd want. A zydeco band," she gushes breathlessly. "Or mariachi. Or reggae. Something ethnic to shock Daddy. Oh I can't decide."

"I'd want to bring a Harrison AK-47 assault rifle to the ceremony . . . so after thoroughly blowing your fat mother's head off with it I could use it. . . ."

"Oh, and lots of chocolate truffles . . . ," she says excitedly. "And we'll hire someone to videotape it!"

"Or an AR-15. You'd like it Evelyn: it's the most expensive of guns, but worth every penny." I wink at her. But she's still talking. . . . (124)

Or this scene:

"Well, it's easy to find a good fur now," Daisy says slowly. "Since more ready-to-wear designers have now entered the fur field, the range increases because each designer selects different pelts to give his collection an individual character."

"It's all so scary," Caron says, shivering.

"Don't be intimidated," Daisy says. "Fur is only an accessory. Don't be intimidated by it."

"But a luxurious accessory," Libby points out.

I ask the table, "Has anyone ever played around with a TEC nine-millimeter Uzi? Its a gun. No? They're particularly useful because this model has a threaded barrel for attaching silencers and barrel extensions." I say this nodding.

"Furs shouldn't be intimidating." Taylor looks over at me and blackly says, "I'm gradually uncovering some startling information here."

"But a luxurious accessory," Libby points out again. (204)

These are simple examples about words in the text passing between characters. True, it takes place in New York City, but Disney's infection is complete. The words evaporate, just like threats in Disney World.

Next, shift the dynamic; string it between the novel's speaking words and the listening ears of the reader. Concentrate on the violent words that constantly repeat. Pound, pound, pound, that's what American Psycho does. The carnage is graphically, boisterously displayed: ". . . bring the knife up and push the tip of it into the socket, first breaking the protective film so the socket fills with blood. . . ." (128). One after the other, more scenes will follow, each indifferentiable from the previous except in page number (*cf.* 164; 176). In the pages up to here, all well before two hundred in a book of four hundred, at least three other deaths are casually mentioned or eluded to. The brute repetition makes no pretension to artistic subtlety, no page makes a claim to push past the one before. The scenes are not increasingly graphic or increasingly violent or increasingly careless or increasingly sadistic or increasingly anything. Consequently, part of one sentence about one bloody episode suffices to document them all. This is what is curious: not the absence of development, but the unambiguity of the absence. There is no attempt to extend or advance past the last episode and the pages don't want there to be any advancement. They don't try to add anything (a similar critique, for example, was leveled at the notorious agricultural inventories performed by the narrator of Robbe-Grillet's *Dans Le Labyrinth*). As mentioned at the outset, *American Psycho*'s detractors concentrate on this. Thus, they usually fault the work for its failure to conform to an established aesthetic criteria: each successive murder should be conveyed as a symbolic parallel to a growing insanity by the murderer. For these critics, Freccero notes, there needs to be "an inner truth . . . located in the psyche of the serial killer" (52). True, this absence of an "inner truth" revealed through symbolism is a fault according to the aesthetic criteria, but it's a requirement that doesn't seem to concern this particular novel. Ellis claims that his aesthetic strategy for the novel is rooted in juxtaposition: the ongoing juxtaposition of "absurd triviality and extreme violence" (Ellis qtd. in Hoban 36). But there's more to it than juxtaposition: the stakes it works for are Baudrillardian.

Consider one of the novel's more fantastic lines: "I think I'm losing it" (214). The pronouncement is set up both by the immediately preceding paragraphs and by the whole first half of the book which has been nothing if not a testament to a mind already irretrievably gone. Immediately before uttering his reflection, the murdering protagonist eyes a prostitute. Violent memories run through his head. He stares at her as she dresses and says it, with complete sincerity, "I think I'm losing it." So—now he's losing it. After more than five separate and perfectly unjustifiable, cold-blooded murders and various pointless assaults, the last of which he has just acknowledged aloud, now it occurs to the anti-hero that things might be getting out of control? True, he is losing it, but what he's losing is not his touch with common legal norms and prosaic sanity—that was gone before the first page. What he's losing is his defense against the intrusion of Baudrillardian reality, his defense that each one of these murders is drawing him closer to something still unfound, something stubbornly ineffable, that one thing out there that every book reaches for, not just *Moby Dick* and *The Great Gatsby,* but also *Tristam Shandy* and *The Crying of Lot 49.* Each of these, no matter how traditional or uncanny, can easily be shown to fit into the ancient legacy of want, of trying to reach something, of trying to say something that isn't quite communicable in direct referential language. So they repeat it from different, incomplete angles. What Patrick Bateman, the American Psycho, realizes is not that the murders are wrong or might be the symptoms of insanity, but that all of them so far have been exactly like their portrayal in the book: born from nowhere, aimed nowhere, without a stable referent. Each one is complete, complete because there is no hidden origin for these actions. And because there is no hidden origin, the words shed impact and so the writing isn't about anything. On this point, it's worth noting that Ellis took his inspiration from the summer of the 1987 stock market crash when he was "hanging out with a lot of Wall Street Guys." According to Ellis, "they didn't talk about their jobs at all—only about how much money they made, the clubs and restaurants they went to, how beautiful their girlfriends were. It was all about status, about surface" (qtd. in Hoban 36).

Of course, it's easy to write a bad book, one that isn't about anything. Everyday publishers like Vintage Contemporaries receive unsolicited manuscripts that could add nothing of value to the corpus of literature. *American Psycho* is like them, yet different because it circles around nothing so unabashedly and wholly without apology; it contributes on a different level by seducing its readers into Baudrillard's vacant metaphysical space. Pound pound pound. Murder after murder after murder. And slowly but surely the orthodox expectation of original meaning wears away. This is the work of the book and this is why it takes just short of four hundred pages to do it. Every page is necessary.

The critical realization: there is no violence in *American Psycho.* For all the ax blades and chain saws, power drills, and blood splotches, nothing violent occurs. To be fair, nothing not violent occurs either. What does occur is the effacement of the central idea from which all the particular acts are copied. The very idea of violence—the seeming core of Ellis' interminable writing—disappears as the book segues into Baudrillardian repetition. Obtrusively, repetition no longer makes a point or gestures to an original. And it does that in the only way possible. Not by saying there is no point—that would leave the mysterious, unsayable locus intact, as a stubborn question that relentlessly seeks to know what it is that is not being pointed to. *American Psycho* succeeds by saying in certain and complete terms exactly what the no point is. It repeats it over and over again. It is nothing, presented as violence, presented as wholly explicit violence.

More directly, it is the increasing ease with which readers digest each subsequent bloody scene until at some point they start passing right through. Erased by our weariness and boredom with the same thing again and again, the words diffuse from the paper. First you stop caring about the descriptions and then you stop noticing them. Eyes skim along the lines. Finally, only the blank page lingers. On the next level, the disappearing words begin suggesting, then pushing, and finally shoving that white paper forward. Baudrillard comes with them, with the idea of experience circling round and round a point no one sees anymore—not even a trace of it.

We need to change our strategy for evaluating Ellis's book. The parameters should not be literary but philosophic. The book accomplishes nearly the hardest task in thought: it shows that something isn't; it manifests what doesn't exist as exactly that. Thus, the book's back cover misleads the potential purchaser and misrepresents the text when it tries to spark reader interest by noting that "Bret Easton Ellis has . . . captured the insanity of violence in our time or any other." Wrong. Nothing could be further off; the book illustrates precisely nothing of violence. What it illustrates is that violence doesn't exist because it can be said so easily. If reviewers force *American Psycho* to talk about prosaic issues of late 20th century America, the book fails miserably; it strangles in its own monotonous circles. If these continue to be the parameters for discussion, then the book should be panned. But these shouldn't be the parameters.

The entrance into Baudrillardian space answers a difficult question: why, once you start reading this book, do you keep reading even though you sensed right from the start that you weren't getting anywhere or going anywhere? It's because this book's uselessness carries a specific sense. Reverse into the sense by inverting the question: Why would you stop reading? Phenomenologically, reading normally stops when the book isn't going anywhere, when it can't get any traction. But you only sense you are stuck if there is a tangible place you aren't going. No place you're not going means you can't feel stuck. *American Psycho* is strange like that. It isn't going anywhere, but because the sense of a goal and place you would want to go or not want to go has worn away, the excuse or reason for stopping has disappeared. The reader can't find any reason to stop. That's the experience of reading *American Psycho*. You don't want to go on, nobody wants to go on, but everybody I've talked to has. They get caught in the trap of reading in a place without an original, in a place where you can't stop even though doing more reading makes no difference.

So you read on in *American Psycho,* pushed along by your own inertia, unable to say why or why not. That is the unfamiliar attraction of the book, achieved by its repetition, over and over, of these murders which don't get any more or any less anything. They just repeat, like things without an original will do. Readers of *American Psycho* need to be careful because the book is contagious. Not contagious of violence; not like it will encourage anyone to go on a wild spree. The overriding threat rises from infection by what Baudrillard calls "hyperreality," the state of absolute resignation before the collapse of real and unreal. Resignation to the point where you forget you're resigned and you'll read or write anything.

Notes

1. An important issue that's not treated in this paper is that of literary censorship. This aspect of the *American Psycho* scandal censorship surfaced in a number of the reviews, and the more notorious scrapes with censorship encountered by Robert Mapplethorpe, Two-Live Crew, and Madonna were obvious points of comparison. See Freccero for a full treatment of this topic. (Ed.)

2. While Baudrillard does not actually use the term "sentimentality," it is clearly implied in the way he organizes his ideas about Disneyland.

Works Cited

Baudrillard, Jean. *Simulacra and Simulation.* 1981. Trans. Sheila Faria. Ann Arbor: U Michigan P, 1994.

——. *Simulations.* Trans. Paul Foss, Paul Patton, Philip Bleitchman. New York: Semiotext(e), 1983.

Derrida, Jacques. *Margins of Philosophy.* Chicago: U Chicago P, 1982.

Ellis, Brett Easton. *American Psycho.* New York: Vintage Contemporaries, 1991.

——. *Less Than Zero.* New York: Vintage, 1985.

——. *The Rules of Attraction.* New York: Vintage, 1987.

Freccero, Carla. "Historical Violence, Censorship, and the Serial Killer: The Case of *American Psycho.*" *Diacritics* 22.7 (1997): 44-58.

Hitchens, Christopher. "Minority Report." *The Nation* 7 Jan. 1991: 7.

Hoban, Phoebe. "'Psycho's Drama." *New York* 17 Dec. 1990: 232-37.

Janowitz, Tama. *Slaves of New York.* London: Picador, 1986.

Kennedy, Pagan. "Generation Gaffe." *The Nation* 1 Apr. 1991: 426-28.

Mailer, Norman. "The Children of the Pied Piper." *Vanity Fair* Mar. 1991: 154+.

Morrison, Toni. "Recitatif." *Calling the Wind: 20th Century African-American Short Stories*. Ed. Clarence Major. New York: Perennial, 1993.

Rawlinson, Nora. Review of *American Psycho*. *Library Journal* 116.1 (1991): 147.

Sheppard, R. Z. "A Revolting Development." *Time* 29 Oct. 1990: 100.

Teachout, Terry. "Applied Deconstruction—*American Psycho* by Bret Easton Ellis." *National Review* 24 June 1991: 45-46.

Wolf, Naomi. "The Animals Speak." *New Statesman* 12 Apr. 1991: 33-34.

3

EMPTY-HEADED MUSINGS:

THE HOLY FOOL IN ROBERT PIRSIG'S

ZEN AND THE ART OF MOTORCYCLE MAINTENANCE

Eddie Tafoya

In a scene from the 1931 film *Horsefeathers,* a bum approaches Pinky the dogcatcher, played by Harpo Marx, and says, "say buddy, can you help me out? I'd like to get a cup of coffee." The silent Pinky responds by reaching into his pocket and lifting out a cup of coffee, replete with saucer and rising steam, which he then places in the solicitor's hands (*Horsefeathers*). While this could easily be dismissed as a corny filler gag, it nevertheless asks a vital question about the archetype of the Fool and his audience. Why would a bum beg from the disheveled Pinky who, with his crushed top hat, oversized trench coat, blank stare, and ill-fitting shirt, appears even more destitute than he does? If the tramp is seen as a stand-in for the audience (especially the 1931 audience still reeling from the stock market crash) much comes into focus: we approach the Fool because we identify with him and thus seek a psychological handout; we ask that he assure us that he is the Fool and that we, by implication, are the nonfools; that if we can identify him as the outsider, we must sit comfortably within the inner rings. The Fool, then, is Otto's *mysterium terribile et fascinans* manifest in the human condition—we identify with him as we separate ourselves from him; we are repulsed but cannot turn away; we ask his favors but can never be sure what he will deliver.

Perhaps it is exactly this kind of comic mysteriousness that accounts in some measure for the Fool's omnipresence. From the Norse, Ethiopian, Chinese, and Native American trickster myths to Cosmo Kramer of the hit 1990s television show *Seinfeld,* from the Fool of *King Lear* to Forrest Gump, from Don Quixote to the 1997 movie *Slingblade,* the Fool maintains a constant presence in the worlds of myth, literature, and popular culture. Like the Fool of various tarot decks who appears to be wandering nonchalantly over a cliff's edge, the Fool stands at the border of one reality and is ready to drop off into the next; he remains ready to deliver the unexpected in a way that makes us question the bedrock of our experience. Whether he is introducing the magical into the mundane, planting a germ of chaos into rigid order, or inverting power paradigms, the Fool's function by and large is to shock us out of our egoism and make us consider, at least for a moment, that the universe might not be as ordered as we have manipulated ourselves into believing.

Perhaps then it is not simply the monomythic and bloody heroics that account for Western Man's devotion to Jesus as a fundamental religious and political icon, but His foolishness as well. Not only does Jesus function as a Fool with His constant challenge to standard paradigms and enigmatic pronouncements such as "Blessed are the poor," and "love your enemy," but quite often the demands of the Gospel are too wild for any rational person to take seriously. What rational person would, for example, consider a lifestyle such as that called for in Luke 9 (and also echoed in the Gospels of Matthew, Mark, and Thomas) in which He asks His followers to go out preaching the Good News and "take nothing for your journey, no staff, nor bag, nor bread, nor money; and do not have two tunics"? (Luke Ch. 9:3). It is quite likely that anyone following the command would be declared insane and irrational by virtue of his adherence to Jesus' words (a sentiment that is echoed in Saint Paul's announcement that he and Timothy are "fools for Christ's sake" [1 Cor. 4:10]). I suggest then that Paul may not be too far off the mark as Jesus's show can easily be equated with the fool's show, especially when one considers the relationship between tragedy and comedy in light of Socrates' closing remarks that come at the end of *The Symposium,* about how "the genius of comedy was the same with that of tragedy, and that the true artist in tragedy was an artist in comedy also" (Beavers). Despite their savage brutality, the Gospels tell of a pariah who, like Elwood P. Dowd of Mary Chase's play *Harvey* or Chief Broom of Ken Kesey's novel *One Flew Over the Cuckoo's Nest,* sees, feels, and hears what others cannot; they depict a zealot who, like Don Quixote, lives and dies for his cause (and there is ample material to argue that Jesus, like Quixote, was ultimately wrong). Finally, Jesus' show culminates in one of world literature's most perfectly structured but least humorous political and social satires: He is convicted in a mock trial, given a fake crown and title, and paraded through the streets in a travesty of a royal procession. If we were to look past seventeen centuries of socioreligious codes we would see that the plot structure of the Passion is strikingly similar to that of the courtroom scene of the Marx Brothers' classic movie *Duck Soup* which, ironically enough, appeared exactly 1900 years after the traditional date of the Crucifixion. In Jesus' trial Pontius Pilate, governor of

Judea, serves as prosecutor, judge, jury, and even defense attorney when he proclaims to those demanding crucifixion that "I can find no crime in this man" (Matthew 27:23; Luke 23:3). Then, when Pilate asks Jesus if he is, indeed "King of the Jews," Jesus, rather than attempting to save his own skin says, "You have said so"—a retort which would not only be considered a wisecrack but unequivocally foolish if uttered by virtually anyone else under similar circumstances (imagine O. J. Simpson saying something similar to Lance Ito). Jesus' statement, however, is nothing less than the Fool's brilliance as it, in the spirit of the comedy of manners, *carnival,* Feast of Fools, or Marx Brothers routine, inverts the incident power paradigm as it turns the judge and prosecutor into the accused in a manner recalling the way *Harvey* questions the common understanding of "sanity." The drama eventually boils over into mass hysteria that culminates with the Crucifixion.

In *Duck Soup,* Groucho Marx plays Rufus T. Firefly, president of the mythical country of Freedonia, and when Chicolini (played by Chico Marx) is tried for espionage, Firefly becomes his Pilate, also serving as judge, prosecutor, jury, and—upon his pronouncement that "[t]his man's story moves me deeply," likewise becomes a voice for the accused. As the trial begins, Firefly calls across the courtroom saying, "Chicolini, I'll give you eight to one we find you guilty." Instead of rising to his own defense, Chicolini responds: "'ats'a no good. I can get ten to one at the barber shop" (*Duck Soup*). This scene culminates in an extravagant song and dance, the famous "Freedonia's going to war" production number, which is also mass hysteria (in this case, war hysteria) presented with all the lavishness of a Hollywood musical.

Jesus and the Marx Brothers share the same function: each introduces an element of chaos into a highly structured environment so as to reveal it as artificial and transitory, or in other words, by virtue of their unabashed foolishness, they allow the nonfools to make fools of themselves. Just as Chicolini not only escapes his hot seat but becomes one of the victors and in all probability seals his place in Freedonian history and myth, Jesus, through the Crucifixion, not only takes the most powerful icon of anti-insurrectionary Roman power, the crucifix, and turns it into the symbol of Christian power and salvation, but soon the situation is reversed beyond the wildest imaginings of even the most gifted soothsayers of first century Galilee: rather than bowing down to emperors such as Caesar or Domitian, within four centuries Rome finds itself collectively bowing down to the poor bastard transient insurgent called Jesus.

Other parallels persist as well. In his 1969 book *The Fool and His Scepter: A Study in Clowns and Jesters and Their Audience,* literary critic and Jungian psychotherapist William Willeford relays the story of a simpleton who, upon being discovered standing before a mirror with his eyes closed, explains that he hopes to see "what he looks like when he is asleep." The anecdote illustrates, explains Willeford, how the Fool not only "stands at the boundary of consciousness" but is also master of Kierkegaardian irony in that he is the owner of a

strange two-fold consciousness which makes each one of us realize only too well that [we are] . . . mere bubble[s] of temporary existence threatened at every moment with extinction, and yet . . . unable to shake off the sensation of being a stable entity existing eternal and invulnerable at the very centre of the flux of history. (Willeford 234)

As with Jesus or Chicolini, this split in the Fool's consciousness consequently renders him not only the protagonist in his comedy, but also his own audience. He becomes a "detached commentator" who is ready to observe himself sleeping, wait for more lucrative odds while betting on his own demise, or stand outside of himself in order to see the minuscule but vital role he plays in the cosmic drama as he declares to the universe at large, "not my will but yours be done."

A less obvious example of precisely this dynamic comes by way of Robert Pirsig's 1974 cult classic tome, *Zen and the Art of Motorcycle Maintenance,* a story in which the detached commentator and foolish ventures are not only the central source of anxiety, but are indispensable to understanding the story's plot, protagonists, theme, and philosophy.

Zen and the Art of Motorcycle Maintenance involves two entwined story lines, the first of which moves chronologically and concerns a nameless narrator, his son Chris, and two companions, John and Sylvia Sutherland, traveling from Minnesota to the Dakotas on motorcycles; the second, meanwhile, concerns the narrator's re-assembly of a fragmented past in order to make peace with an entity he calls Phaedrus, who is soon revealed as both his alter-ego and the person he was before his nervous breakdown.

While on the surface it appears that the narrator is a learned man capable of long soliloquies on both Eastern and Western intellectual history and mysticism, his foolishness soon emerges out of the parallel narratives. Just as Jesus centers his life around an invisible "Kingdom of God" or Elwood P. Dowd centers his around a friendship with an invisible six-foot-three-inch rabbit, Phaedrus perceives the world in a singular way that renders him the laughingstock among his university faculty colleagues. The narrator sacrifices his job, marriage, family, and sanity in his pursuit of something he calls "Quality," that which he has deduced as the Ground of Being. Not only is the narrator ready to recognize the singularity of his perception and the toll it is taking on him, but he is also quite willing to become the detached commentator and undergo painstaking analyses of his own madness. His description of his insanity, for instance, does not only apply to Jesus, Elwood Dowd, Chief Bromden, and a host of other fools, but it also recalls the vantage point of the Fool of the Rider-Waite Tarot deck (among others) and the innocent venture that takes him a step beyond the platform of common experience. Pirsig writes:

. . . each child is born as ignorant as any caveman. What keeps the world from reverting to the Neanderthal with each generation is the continuing, ongoing mythos . . . the huge body of common knowledge that unites our minds as cells are united in the body of man. To feel that one is not so united, that one can accept or discard this mythos as one pleases, is not to understand what the mythos is.

There is only one kind of person, *Phaedrus said,* who accepts or rejects the mythos in which he lives. And the definition of that person, when he has rejected the mythos, *Phaedrus said,* is "insane." To go outside the mythos is to become insane. (316; my emphases)

The narrative stance, underscored by the otherwise redundant repetition of the tag line "Phaedrus said," shows how the narrator places himself in a position to see both the mythos and the non-mythos, the *tierra firma* and the *tierra incognita* of common experience; he appears to be observing himself from afar as if looking back on his own ego and persona, where he can actually draw a distinction between what he is, what he is not, and what he may become.

This split consciousness and the resulting narrative stance from a step beyond the accepted norm accounts for the existential anxiety that mortifies the protagonist throughout the course of the book, a motif that is underscored by the narrator's finding himself at various spatial and psychological edges. In the penultimate chapter, for instance, the narrator arrives at a cliff's edge that "juts out into the ocean but now is . . . surrounded by banks of fog" (366). Similarly, while lounging at a barbecue one afternoon, the narrator compares himself directly to Christopher Columbus, and quite easily adopts the attitudes of both the explorer and those contemporaries who thought of him as a fool about to drop off the edge of the Earth. The narrator tells his friends:

"Columbus has become such a schoolbook stereotype it's almost impossible to imagine him as a living human being anymore. But if you . . . project yourself into his situation, then sometimes you can begin to see that our present moon exploration must be like a tea party compared to what he went through. Moon exploration . . . [is] really just a branch extension of what Columbus did. A really new exploration, one that would look to us today the way the world looked to Columbus, would have to be in an entirely new direction . . . present-day reason is an analogue of the flat earth of the medieval period. If you go too far beyond it you're presumed to fall off, into insanity. And people are very much afraid of that. I think this fear of insanity is comparable to the fear people once had of falling off the edge of the world. Or the fear of heretics. There's a very close analogue there.

"But what's happening is that each year our old flat earth of conventional reason becomes less and less adequate to handle the experiences we have and this is creating widespread feelings of topsy-turviness. As a result we're getting more and more people in irrational areas of thought . . . occultism, mysticism, drug changes and the like . . . because they feel the inadequacy of classical reason to handle what they know are real experiences." (151-52)

In other instances the psychological borders and the borders of his own ego-consciousness are challenged. Consider, for example, the scene in which the narrator and Chris are racing across the Great Plains, and he finds himself (to use a Buddhist cliché) becoming "one with his environment":

The engine responds beautifully—seventy . . . eighty . . . eighty-five . . . we are really feeling the wind now and I drop my head to cut down the resistance . . . ninety. The speedometer needle swings back and forth but the tach reads a steady nine thousand . . . about ninety-five miles an hour...and we hold this speed . . . moving. Too fast to focus on the shoulder of the road now . . . We whizz through the flat open land, not a car anywhere, hardly a tree, but the road is smooth and clean and the engine now has a "packed," high rpm sound that says it's right on. It gets darker and darker.

A flash and *Ka-wham*! of thunder, one right on top of the other. That shook me, and Chris has got his head against my back now. A few warning drops of rain . . . at this speed they are like needles. A second flash-WHAM and everything brilliant . . . and then in the brilliance of the next flash [I see] that farmhouse . . . that windmill . . . oh, my God, he's been here! . . . throttle off . . . this is his road . . . a fence and trees . . . and the speed drops to seventy, then sixty, then fifty-five, and I hold it there. (26)

The thunderclap, the reaction to it, and the frightened tone of the passage hint at a mystery that is complicated further on the next page as the other characters question his decision to slow down. Eventually, Sylvia tells him, "You look like you'd seen a ghost" (27). At dinner that evening ghosts return as the subject of conversation and while at first the narrator claims not to believe in ghosts, soon (in true fool fashion) he inverts the paradigm of Western thought, reverses his own opinion, and claims that mathematics and the Law of Gravity are modern-day ghosts. He then proceeds to disassemble systematically a significant border between modern and primitive man, ultimately revealing the hubris of Western rationalists. Because the monologue begins with the narrator's acknowledging his reversal, we can assume that this is nothing he has ever considered before and that the ensuing speech is, like the motorcycle trip, a journey into the *tierra incognita* and the "badlands" that is being thought out as it is being spoken. The narrator continues a lengthy discourse, saying:

"Laws of nature are human *inventions* [Pirsig's emphasis], like ghosts. Laws of logic, of mathematics are also human inventions, like ghosts. The whole blessed thing is a human invention, including the idea that it isn't a human invention. The world has no existence whatever outside the human imagination . . . Your common sense is nothing more than the voices of thousands and thousands of these ghosts from the past. Ghosts and more ghosts. Ghosts trying to find their place among the living."

John looks too much in thought to speak. But Sylvia is excited. "Where do you get all these ideas?" she asks.

I am about to answer them but then do not. I have a feeling of having already *pushed it to the limit* [my emphasis], maybe beyond, and it is time to drop it. (31-32)

The parallelism of these two scenes is revealing. In the first instance the narrator is traversing the open plains of the American West (what we can call, oxymoronically, "the Old Frontier") and shifts the motorcycle engine into high gear, pushes it to the limit, and slows down to a "normal speed" after he hears the bark of a demiurge symbolized by the thunderclap, an automatic allusion to Thor or Zeus. In the second example he traverses the plains of Western Thought, shifts his intellectual engine into overdrive, propels himself into unknown regions of the psychic landscape, feels that internal cycle being pushed to the limit, hears an internal and silent peal, and slows his mind down to a more "normal" speed. The penetration into the geographical badlands eventually leads to the narrator's describing himself as "a pioneer . . . looking onto a promised land" (79).

The second instance, meanwhile, hints of an advancement into the fog of madness, into the abyss of the unknown and of limitless possibilities, that which Westerners might best term as "the future" or what a

Tarot card reader might interpret as the "chaos before reason." It also points to Leslie Fielder's book *The Return of the Vanishing American* and its conclusion that the Natty Bumpos and Huckleberry Finns of the future will move into a frontier of madness (185). Just as Jesus sweat blood in the moments preceding the supplication of His own will to that of the Father so as to construct a more perfect future, or just as the Tarot Fool steps from his precipice, the narrator repeatedly deposits himself at the edge of one reality and ends up gazing into the abyss of another; he remains consistently aware that sooner or later he too must leap into the unknown and into the pit of chaos in order to construct a better future—a future personified in Chris.

The symbol of the motorcycle when taken in light of this anxiety takes on prime importance. While on one level the narrator is the frontiersman and the cycle his steed, on another the motorcycle symbolizes the potential abandonment of the ego. Just as the capsule of the automobile separates a person from his environment and, in Pirsig's words, reduces everything around the traveler to "just more TV" (4), thereby equating the windshield with the Heideggerian *gestell* as it frames and crops the visual experience of the environment, the capsule of the ego separates the "I" and the "not-I," the observer from the observed and the subject from the object. In a passage that aligns philosophically with Heidegger's notion of "being-in-the-world" Pirsig says that a motorcyclist, unlike the person in the car, is "completely *in* the scene [Pirsig's emphasis] and is not just watching it anymore, and the sense of presence is overwhelming" (4).

Perhaps this sense of presence is too overwhelming. While a psychologically healthy person might experience negligible tension while shooting across the open plains of the West and allowing the experience to consume him, the psychologically frail might very well feel himself to be "falling apart" when he discovers himself in this position. In his 1990 book *Technology and the Lifeworld: From Garden to Earth* Don Ihde discusses "embodiment relations" between man and his tools that, like the narrator's motorcycle, "entail larger, more complex artifacts and . . . a somewhat longer, more complex learning process," but can nevertheless become extensions of the operator's body. Ihde explains how

[i]n a finely engineered sports car, for example, one has a more precise feeling of the road and of the traction upon it than in the older, softer-riding, large cars of the fifties. One embodies the car, too, in such activities as parallel parking: when well embodied, one feels rather than sees the distance between car and curb—one's bodily sense is extended to the parameters of the driver-car "body." . . . The experience of one's "body image" is not fixed but malleably extendable

and/or reducible in terms of the materials or technological mediations that may be embodied. (Ihde 74)

Precisely this kind of "bodily extension" exacerbates the existential terror for Pirsig's narrator, who seems to view himself as some kind of cosmic balloon about to burst or float away. Consequently, we see throughout the text how the narrator's angst drives him to compulsively reassure himself of his corporeal presence via immediate contact with the here-and-now— items such as long lists, multi-tiered charts, and tedious descriptions of motorcycle maintenance that on first reading are jolting interruptions of an otherwise gripping narrative flow.

Chapter Four, for instance, begins with a list of items taken along on his trip, items arranged into categories such as "Clothing," "Personal Stuff," and "Books," and very little—neither combs, pens, nor wallet— is too trivial to mention. In subsequent chapters the reader must trudge through: 1) A conceptual breakdown of the "motorcycle" into two groups, "components" and "functions" (86-87); 2) two inventories of the differences between "classical understanding" and "romantic under- standing" (60-61; 69-70); and 3) a list of "logical statements" concerning the running of his motorcycle, also broken down into several categories, including "statement of the problem," "hypotheses as to the cause of the problem," and "experiments designed to test each hypothesis" (93).

Furthermore, in a passage illustrating how the Cartesian mind is always conscious of itself, that to be aware of an object is to be aware of being aware, the narrator goes through painstaking analyses of subject- object relations and continually finds that the meeting point between the realms is increasingly ambiguous, so much so that not even his Church of Reason can rescue him:

That's all the motorcycle is, a system of concepts worked out in steel. There's no part in it, no shape in it, that is not out of someone's mind. . . . I've noticed that people who have never worked with steel have trouble seeing this—that the motorcycle is primarily a mental phenomenon. They associate metal with given shapes—pipes, rods, girders, tools, parts—all of them fixed and inviolable, and think of it primarily as physical. But . . . steel can be any shape you want if you are skilled enough, and any shape but the one you want if you are not. . . . These shapes are all out of someone's mind. . . . Hell, even the steel is out of some- one's mind. There's no steel in nature. Anyone from the Bronze Age could have told you that. All nature has is a potential for steel. There's nothing else there. But what's "potential"? That's also in someone's mind! . . . Ghosts (88)

Upon careful inspection, it appears that what is significant about these passages is not so much what is being said but rather what is not being said—not the careful planning being revealed but the anxiety that is being hidden. Just as Rodney Dangerfield must readjust his tie after each joke or Johnny Carson must brush his cheek or stick his hand in his pocket after each joke (and the movements become even more vigorous after the particularly funny ones), the narrator, who has already suffered one nervous breakdown, finds himself groping for tangible realities after his excursions into what he calls "the high country of the mind" (111). Thus, the meticulous lists and charts reinforce the "hereness and now-ness" of the world as they keep him connected to it. So important is this need for psychological grounding that what was once "routine maintenance" soon becomes obsessive and sacramental, and neither the narrator nor Pirsig make any bones about it. Just as religious sacraments are, as Freud and others observed, obsessive compulsive acts set within a religious context and which serve to help the practitioner maintain the illusion that he has some control over his self and environment, through his compulsive adjusting, tuning, and monkeying with his machine, the narrator assuages his own angst by continually reassuring himself of his corporeal presence as it manifests through the motorcycle. The motorcycle is not merely what Ihde describes an extension of his body but actually is his body. Not only does Pirsig makes this point directly when he declares

The real cycle you're working on is a cycle called yourself. The machine that appears to be "out there" and the person that appears to be "in here" are not two separate things. They grow toward Quality or fall away from Quality together. (293)

He then goes on to extend the Freudian comparison between religious and neurotic ritual almost ad nauseam. The description of the tune-up that begins Chapter 8, for example, sounds hauntingly like a description of a rote memorization of "The Our Father": "I've done the tuning so many times it's become a ritual. I don't have to think much about how to do it anymore" (83). Just as a prayer is a ritual one uses to keep himself free from harm, the ritual of cycle maintenance is to ward off any evils that might accompany an unreliable, dangerous, or maladjusted machine. Again, though, Pirsig pushes the limit, and soon interweaves a discourse on Reason with a detailed description of mechanical work until the distinction between the two almost fades completely:

The first tappet is right on, no adjustment required, so I move onto the next. Still plenty of time before the sun gets past those trees . . . *I always feel like I'm in church when I do this.* (my emphasis; 85)

The comparison is soon taken to absurd proportions when it is buoyed up with a quote from a 1918 speech by Albert Einstein:

In the temple of science are many mansions . . . and various indeed are they that dwell therein and the motives that have led them there.

Many take science out of a joyful sense of superior intellectual power; science is their own special sport to which they look for vivid experience and the satisfaction of ambition; many others are to be found in the temple who have offered the products of their brains on this altar for purely utilitarian purposes. Were an angel of the Lord to come and drive all the people belonging to these two categories out of the temple, it would be noticeably emptier but there would still be some men of both present and past times left inside . . . those who have found favor with the angel are somewhat odd, uncommunicative, solitary fellows, really less like each other than the hosts of the rejected. (98)

Then, after two paragraphs of Pirsig's narrative followed by an ambiguously presented passage that is a continuation of Einstein's speech but could be easily read as Phaedrus's addendum, the comparison is taken still further:

The state of mind which enables a man to do work of this kind is akin to that of the religious worshiper or lover. The daily effort comes from no deliberate intention or program, but straight from the heart. (98)

While prayers may palliate, they cannot completely soothe existential fears because they address the essence but do nothing for the existence— and despite the lack of the names of any existentialist philosophers in his broad-stroke sketch of Western philosophy, the narrator and Phaedrus are undeniably sympathetic to the existentialists, as is evinced through statements such as "The only Zen you find on the tops of mountains is the Zen you bring up there" (220) and the Nietzschean overtones of his diatribe against being a "good slave" (209). The narrator's angst, then, can only be dispelled through action or, as Pirsig and the Buddha might say, through "right action." And it is this intuitive understanding of what constitutes "right action" that accounts for both the narrator's anxiety and his fascination with Jules Henri Poincaré and the way in which the French Renaissance man "illustrated how a fact is discovered" (239). The connection to the Book of Genesis is undeniable: God summons the universe into the light of being with the divine pronouncement "Let there be light"; similarly, Adam and his progeny call the objects of the world into the light of consciousness via naming; Poincaré seeks to understand precisely this process.

Despite any conclusions it might draw, Phaedrus's philosophy (as revealed through his castigation of the university system, the lengthy passage on Poincaré, and his constant concern that "the cart of civilization" might have to "creak along a little slower" because of uninspired students [175]) is founded firmly upon his belief that man, willy-nilly, is a central participant in the creation process. Phaedrus implicitly rejects the more common reading of the Edenic myth and standard lesson that the expulsion from Eden was the result of Man's hubris or disobedience. Rather, he seems to agree with a more radical element—Christian commentators such as Harvey Cox (see Cox xi) and Karen Armstrong (see Armstrong 270)—who argue that the mythological first humans were created to tend the garden and were subsequently expelled when they refused to stand up for the lesser inhabitants by letting a serpent (a symbol of limited Free Will because he has no arms, legs, or thumbs and cannot walk erect) steer the coarse of creation. In other words, like the bureaucrats of Nazi Germany who were seduced by their feelings of impotence and allowed the holocaust to happen, Adam and Eve were banished from the garden for relinquishing their Free Will unto the serpent—their choice was not to choose and this indecision ultimately stalled the creation process of which they were both stewards and participants.

If Phaedrus accepted the popular demiurge of Augustine or Jonathan Edwards, the cosmic father figure who demands blind obedience and punishes us whenever we get too big for our britches, the thunderclaps mentioned above and the looming violations of various borders would have been comforting reminders that he must *not* push the limit—and this is clearly not the case. Although the narrator is occasionally self-absorbed at the expense of his son, wife, friends, and students, he never appears the least bit concerned with *theyness* or anyone else's judgements. Rather, his anxiety stems from his *refusal,* rather than his *desire,* to be like God; from his turning away from acts of *imitatio dei,* the imitation of God manifest through service to others (see Armstrong 78) or, in this case, service to Chris and Chris' future. This is expressed directly in this passage in which the narrator rationalizes his fear of going further up the mountain he and Chris are climbing:

You go up the mountain and all you're gonna get is a great big heavy stone tablet handed to you with a bunch of rules on it.

That's about what happened to [Phaedrus].

Thought he was a goddamned Messiah.

Not *me* [Pirsig's emphasis], boy. The hours are way too long, and the pay is way too short. Let's go. (220-21)

The narrator's concern is quite reasonable, when taken in light of Cox's or Armstrong's take on Genesis 3. Just as heightened Free Will or the heightened ability to make decisions is what makes a being human, it is also his greatest burden and that which kills him. According to psychologist Julian Jaynes, the stress that weakens the body and leaves it open to the ravages of age and disease is an inevitable by-product of decision-making and nothing else; or more specifically, stress is a direct result of the pause of doubt intrinsic to the decision-making process (93-94). Pirsig's narrator seems to understand this intrinsically—to him man, indeed, is condemned to be free.

Consequently, the image of the Tarot Fool becomes the central metaphor of *Zen and the Art of Motorcycle Maintenance* because of its multivalence: it is simultaneously an image of a departure from the mythos, of Columbus sailing off the edge of the earth, and the Jesus who had succumbed to Satan's temptation to fling himself off of Herod's tower; it is also an image of Kierkegaard's leap of faith and the Heideggerian hero abandoning all interpretive frameworks and accepting both Being and beings on their own terms—the philosophical equivalent of cutting oneself loose in space; it is also Sartre's hero who is different from the animals and plants by virtue of his ability (and duty) to hurl himself into the future.

And finally, it is Phaedrus himself who, in the climax of the book, finds himself dropping off the edge of reality and into a pit of madness. After a lengthy section about how Zen teaching is built upon expanding one's consciousness through koans designed to confuse the student so as to deposit him at the "zero point of consciousness," Phaedrus himself becomes empty-headed. As has been proven by Chinese thought-control prisons, a thought must be expressed in order to be kept. Thus Phaedrus, like the brilliant seminarian who plows through years of philosophical and theological study and ends up taking a vow of silence, falls into the Fool's trap and succumbs to yet another inverted paradigm: rather than the empty-headed fool seeking to become the wise man, the wise man seeks, via his abandonment of words and therefore all thought, to become silenced and as empty-headed as any fool who has taken a vow of silence—be it Buddha beneath the bodhi tree, a Benedictine Monk isolated in a monastery, a yogi atop a mountain, Chief Bromden, or Harpo Marx. In this passage Pirsig describes the moment that is simultaneously the collapse of Phaedrus's ego, his individuation, and his mental breakdown:

He stares at the wall in a cross-legged position upon a quilted blanket on the floor of a bedless bedroom, his thoughts moving neither forward nor backward, staying only at the instant. His wife asks if he is sick, and he does not answer. His wife becomes angry, but Phaedrus listens without responding. He is aware of what she says but is no longer able to feel any urgency about it. Not only are his thoughts slowing down, but his desires, too. And they slow and slow, as if gaining an imponderable mass. So heavy, so tired, but no sleep comes. He feels like a giant, a million miles tall. He feels himself extending into the universe with no limit. (358)

Phaedrus here is not merely becoming one with his environment but one with the universe. As with Jesus' succumbing to the will of the universe or the Fool's traipsing off a cliff, this scene serves to remind us that within each of us thrives the potential to arrive at a place each of these characters has already visited, where a pariah is likely to pull a cup of coffee out of his pocket or rise from the dead and thus serve as a living reminder of the pronouncement of Luke 1:37 that "with God all things are possible." The Fool reminds us that the dissolution of the boundaries of the ego that results from an exalted metaphysical experience is exactly the same as the abandonment of the ego that results from corporeal death; that within any person hides the potential that he may soon be looking back through himself and into the core of human anxiety and seeing within it the potential for that moment when he and "the Father are one," where the Alpha meets the Omega and one must love his neighbor because his neighbor is himself; it is the potential moment when the individual, like Jesus at Gethsemane, or Forrest Gump, who runs across the country "for no particular reason," is called upon to surrender his will to that of the universe of which he is an integral part; when he must allow the cosmic forces to do with him whatever they deem necessary.

Works Cited and Consulted

Armstrong, Karen. *A History of God: The 4000-Year Quest of Judaism, Christianity and Islam.* New York: Knopf, 1994.

Beavers, Anthony F., gen. ed. "Symposium: Ch. 14: Conclusion." *Exploring Plato's Dialogues: A Virtual Learning Environment on the World-Wide Web.* U of Evansville, Evansville, ID. URL: http://plato.evansville.edu/texts/jowett/symposium14.htm (19 July 1998).

Cox, Harvey G. *On Not Leaving It to the Snake.* New York: Macmillian, 1967.

Duck Soup. Dir. Leo McCarey. Perf. Groucho Marx, Harpo Marx, Chico Marx. Paramount, 1933.

Fiedler, Leslie. *The Return of the Vanishing American*. New York: Stein and Day, 1968.

Horsefeathers. Dir. Norman McLeod. Perf. Groucho Marx, Harpo Marx, Chico Marx. Paramount, 1931.

Jaynes, Julian. *The Origin of Consciousness and the Breakdown of the Bicameral Mind*. Boston: Houghton Mifflin. 1976.

Pirsig, Robert. *Zen and the Art of Motorcycle Maintenance*. New York: Bantam, 1975.

Willeford, William. *The Fool and His Scepter: A Study in Clowns and Jesters and Their Audience*. Chicago: Northwestern UP, 1986.

4

THIS IS NOT A TEXT, OR, DO WE READ IMAGES?

Don Ihde

Magritte's enigmatic title, "Ceci n'est pas un pipe," placed upon his "image" of a pipe poses a problem not unlike the problem of the "Text" in the family of post-, a-, or non-Modern theories currently fashionable in Euro-American philosophical contexts. Clearly the "image" pipe is *not* a real pipe, yet the confusion which the title, juxtaposed with a realistic painting of a pipe, produces raises a wide set of questions worthy of surrealistic inquiry.

One might invert the same problematic as applied to this essay: in some sense it *is a text* and thus to claim it is not would be to perform or claim a kind of trickery that belies its mode of being-as-taken. But in Magritte's case it is the "image" that is not the (real) pipe. Thus one might begin somewhat analytically and note that there are a number of matters that need to be sorted out: (a) the presumed referent, an actual pipe—but which "refers," the title disclaiming reference, or the image with implicit reference?—(b) if the latter, it is a representation, or an image which somehow representationally refers; and (c) then there is the ironic disclaimer found in the sentence itself, "This is not a pipe."

But this will not do precisely because the very field in which referents, representations, and various kinds of metaphorical structures obtain is also that which is under contestation in post-, a-, and non-Modern contexts. This family of contesters of modernism has both a positive and a negative side. Its positive side might be called its "textualism" or "discoursism" and it finds itself proponent of a kind of metaphorical totalization in which the phenomena of (a) reading, (b) writing, and (c) texts are spread out over the entire social and cultural "worlds" to be analyzed. Everything becomes a "text" or "text-like" with the characteristics of indeterminacy, arbitrariness, and finitude. It could be called in a significant sense, a "literarization" of the World. The "reverence texts" that themselves help establish this mode of analysis are primarily those stimulated and arising out of Foucault, Derrida, and Lyotard in the fashionable Euro-American discourse, but adumbrated both in very widespread "social constructionism" approaches as well as a "bodies" approach particularly developed by late twentieth century feminism. The negative side is the critique that addresses what are sometimes identified as Modern stances regarding a number of related phenomena. Let us look briefly at what is being contested:

1) Any "realistic" theory of reference is contested. From structuralism on, and particularly among the poststructuralists, reference or reality-referencing disappears in the notions that language refers only to itself or is a play of signifiers/signified within an arbitrary or—as I shall put it—literary fictive mode of construction. Positively, what emerges is some finite, indeterminate mode of "discourse," "episteme," or other largely socially or fictively constructed "text-like" phenomenon.

2) Similarly, "perception" while frequently used in postmodern contexts also is contested with respect to what I shall call "Body One," a located, sensory body. In its most radical form, one finds the Derrida position as one that claims "there never was perception" (103), in that the discovery of "presence" always takes place within some form of non-presence that, in turn, relates back to inscription or trace or writing; or in less radical form, "perception" is seen to be a Modern invention—along with Man—in Foucault's sense that perception is socially constructed and as such can be both invented and dis-invented in some present or future episteme. In short, the perception that remains is solely the cultural perception that is socially constructed.

3) Bodies, in my sense of "Body One" as a being-here, located, sensory being with specific styles of movement, are also contested, either in a conservative sense as being malleable down to a highly reduced biological dimension, or replaced as a social body, whether in the form of the body of the condemned (as in Foucault), or as a breasted being whose breasts are clearly socially constructed (as in Young [ch. 11]). In my language, "Body Two," a social body, substitutes entirely or almost entirely for one's "own" or "lived" body in the Merleau-Pontyean sense.

Moreover, one must also recognize that the combatants have clearly gained territory, so much so that to try to return the contest to one in which "reference," "perceptions," and "bodies" simply regain previously lost ground would be seen as a retrogressive and thus defensive move. Thus I shall not take that tack. Quite contrarily, I want to take an example-set which may be located precisely *between* the combatants, but one in which the issues of reference, perception, and body re-emerge with a new and different kind of urgency for examination. That example set will revolve around what I shall call image technologies.

Image Technologies

One highly proliferating technological development in the late twentieth century has been the class of image technologies that span the entire social and cultural worlds from the most popular forms of imaging—as for example in MTV—to the most exciting science research frontiers in which radical advances in medical imaging technologies are matched by equally new image technology advances in earth and space sciences; in short, from the most micro- to the most macro-phenomena of scientific interest.

This development has spawned, in my university, an interdisciplinary "Image Group" that contains members from the Radiology Department of the Health Sciences Center, to film theorists, to philosophers. And we are learning some interesting things from one another—in part precisely because we bring such very different interests and concerns. I shall begin with a few report-like remarks on some of our results.

Let us begin with an image technology far at the popular and non-scientific end of the spectrum covered: MTV. This style of imaging is largely a bricolage format in which some song is accompanied by a series of discontinuous, interfaded, highly suggestive image chains. Analysts are quick to point out that the layers of meaning are multiple, that there are subliminal "messages" being conveyed, and that the operations have a depth psychology—i.e., Freud-Lacan-etc.—structure with both hidden and manifest, unconscious and conscious significations.

Note that here there is no question of any kind of "truth-functioning" or reality referencing, at least in any scientific sense. That is, the images do not transparently "refer" to some external event or reality as would be the case with a television monitor showing who is entering the door. Rather, if these images are in any way "text-like," they are like fictive texts. Fiction, after all, is not even constrained by any known set of physical, biological, or even social constraints. In fictive modes one can imagine speeds faster than that of light, cyborgs which do not exist, and one can stretch the limits of one's body beyond even a quasi-biological embodiment. This development is particularly extrapolated in virtual reality developments and displayed in such movies as *The Lawnmower Man*.

This is not to say that the imaging itself is not constrained—it is constrained by the state-of-the-art of the technology itself. And initially I want to take note that these constraints will pervade the entire spectrum of imaging technologies. For example, in what may seem too obvious and trivial an example, whether one is referring to MTV or to an MRI scan of the brain, the image-space is *framed space*. This implies that what is presented is presented as already distinct from ordinary or lived-bodily space precisely by the limited and selected-out "framing" of the image presentation. Additionally (apart from techno-fantasies that also appear in fictive form), this presentation is an on/off presentation. It is not the "involuntary" constancy of the on-so-long-as-conscious presence of ordinary experience. Thus, doubly, the framed and the on/off (which is a temporal frame) nature of the imaging distinguishes it from the fullness of an embodied lifeworld. Here, already, there is an implicit metaphorical connection to *reading*. To watch MTV is to set aside time from ordinary actional life, as in picking up a book to read, and to, moreover, suspend actional "belief" and enter into—not the book, but the imaging progression. This carry-over even overlaps the bodily insofar as the sitting-there is a partially disengaged mode of position.

Second, to date all mass image technologies also *lack depth*. (Holograms are, of course, exceptions.) Optical technologies yield, in television and cinema, a greatly foreshortened field for vision, and in such medical technologies as MRI, CAT, sonographic and other image scans, a mere slice or cross section of the imaged object (a brain, for example). And while contrivances are added to help overcome this limitation— such as the use of high speed illusions using old fashioned Renaissance perspective effects in science fiction cinema, or the additive technique of reconstructing more three-dimensional effects from multiple cross sections in medical imaging—the real time imitations are clearly notable.

These effects are thus "reductive" when compared to plenary, constant, and active or full sensory experience. They are effects that keep imaging technologies as at most "virtual" rather than actually substitutable realities. But, were I to leave the analysis there I would thereby miss what is *additive* or *magnified* technologically in imaging. To locate this phenomenon, I shall turn briefly to the more scientific use of imaging, which, while using similar state-of-the-art technologies, does so within a very different set of trajectories and constraints from the popular end of the spectrum.

Needless to say, the "intent" of a scientific use of imaging does have a truth-function. It is essential that the image "truly represent" that which is imaged. Medically, the CAT or MRI scan must show the abnormal growth to be there, and not that it be some artifact of the machine itself. (This is always a technical problem in the development of and in the reading from new image technologies.) But, interestingly, the way to attain that truth effect is not by means of anything like a "literal isomorphism" that a simple corresponding "representation" would give. (In older empiricist epistemology, representations could be considered to be correspondent if and only if they isomorphically replicated the thing being replicated. They were thought of as copies of the thing itself.

Technologies *transform* all possible representations and are never purely correspondent. In this respect they are "hermeneutic.")

Within the multiple uses of scientific imaging, there is a spectrum which does run from partial isomorphism to variations upon isomorphism that vary away from the "literal" or copy form, towards a certain kind of "fictive" or technologically enhanced form of variation. A sonogram, for example, shows in real time the shape, movement, and configuration of a fetus (albeit in somewhat blurred and black and white display). One can recognize the body parts, thumb sucking, and identify sex very early on. Moving to an MRI brain scan, one retains in a more clear fashion certain shape characteristics and thus spatial isomorphisms, but from a more sharply defined and now computer enhanced set of contrasts. These can even be further enhanced by the use of "false color," which is also used in earth satellite photography to highlight organic phenomena in contrast to inorganic ones. Note even here, although the "intent" is to highlight in such a way as to reveal some "real" phenomenon, the complex techniques are very close to the fixing that can be done through digitally enhanced photography, which today in journalism contexts has become an ethical issue. What had been the implicit, although always naive, photographic claim for "realism" now gets deeply called into question. Hyperrealism in digitally manipulated photography is one variant away from isomorphism, but a strange one in that it is a variation that makes the thing look "more real" than it is.

Returning to scientific contexts, non-isomorphic variants today include such processes as light- or heat-enhancement techniques which clearly exceed normal bodily sensory capacities, but that nevertheless reveal "real" features of things. Militarily developed light-enhancement technologies allow seeing in the dark in ways that approximate feline capacities; and heat-enhancement photography can show the heat shadow of a fighter plane that just took off from a runway, thus revealing a close past in a dimension again approximating rattlesnake sensory capacity. Note that in this case, while none of the imaging described mimics old fashioned copy-epistemology notions, it does, through variational means, "refer" to "real" effects.

Let us now move to a third use context for imaging technologies, one that lies between fictive and scientific constitutions: politics. In a series of documentaries undertaken by Bill Moyers, one program analyzes what is taken as "truth" in news programs. Moyers cleverly juxtaposes a smug Michael Deaver's claim concerning media manipulation with the news clips that were manipulated and with the reporter's responses to what had happened. In one such sequence, the news clip carries the verbal news that President Reagan was about to veto a piece of legislation favorable to labor, while the visual showed him happily drinking beer in a South Boston bar with workers. Deaver triumphantly proclaims that the pictures of "Reagan with the working stiffs" clearly overcome and even contradict the critical verbal report and that he knows that what is seen, not heard, is what will be "believed." The reporter, after the fact, concurs that even when in contradiction, the positive, visual image is virtually always taken as "true" in contrast to the action that is merely verbally described. When this video was shown to our medical members of the Image Group, there was what amounted to a gasp of recognition, but virtual disbelief that such overt manipulation of a news program could and did occur.

I will now complete my suggestive example-set with two more illustrations. First, the movie *Capricorn One* (1978) humorously called into question one of the great techno-scientific feats of the twentieth century—the first voyage of a human to the moon. (Some may recall that some of the first television shots of the moon landing were not, in fact, transmissions, but "simulations.") The movie—which actually echoed some cultures' beliefs rather than created them—shows in effect how the whole voyage could simply have been a media hoax. All of the shots of landing, the first steps on the moon, the corny statement concerning "one small step for man, one giant step for Mankind," were portrayed as staged, thus undercutting again the implicit "truth" of imaging through television.

And finally, there was the Gulf War, which in typical exaggerated fashion Jean Baudrillard claims "never existed." Here, again on the news, was displayed a new style of techno-war that featured "smart bombs" repeatedly going down ventilator shafts, anti-missiles which were "shown" intercepting incoming Scuds, and other feats of precision warfare (repeated in the same clips over and over again to audiences who strangely both simultaneously believed and doubted the veracity of the presumed "realism"). Later analyses claim than instead of the claimed 95% Patriot accuracy of interception, at most 24% were successful, and then often with disastrous results from falling debris from both missiles; that far smaller Iraqi forces were actually engaged; and that the far greater "collateral" damage that occurred was due to dumber-than-planned bombs. And when, in the development of anti-missiles, we learn that warheads were artificially heated to enhance the possibilities of a hit for demonstration purposes, the "cooking" of a techno-scientific test causes doubt to border over from the political to the institutionally "scientific" itself.

My example-set now has a spectrum, all of which utilize image technologies, but set in contexts varying from sheerly fictive, where no truth claim is made, to the political where truth claims are embedded in deep ambiguities of contestive and yet intermixed power plays, and in which truth is very hard to recover to the scientific uses that, under controlled constraints, nevertheless wish to make a strong truth claim, but that utilize modes of variation and enhancement that overlap exactly the previous two domains.

Applied to this example-set could be the similar spectrum of philosophical contests that are now occurring in the post-, a-, and non-Modern disputes. Overgeneralizing, the anti-Modernists tend to move the debate strongly to the left hand side of the fictive-politics-science spectrum. All phenomena are taken to portray the socially and fictively constructed features of this domain. In part, this echoes the cognate sensibilities and a shift of Euro-American fashionability themes away from the sciences (which had been the favored territory of the analytic philosophies) and towards the literary (with comp-lit now a virtual twin to Continental philosophy). When science is looked at as phenomenon, it is looked at as cultural institution, filled with both the imaginations of the fictive and the power-plays of discourse-power, gender, race, and social construction that remains comfortably in the mid- to left-side of the spectrum. Much of the "strong program," feminist criticism, and other social constructionist analysis—and often with great insight—portrays science in this way. Yet, while a critic like Evelyn Fox-Keller, characterizing deep gender differences both in science and in personality conflicts (quoting Mary Ellman) quips: "Faced with the charge that 'women always get personal,' Ellman counters, 'I'd say men always get impersonal. If you hurt their feelings, they make Boyle's law [sic] out of it.'" And, later extrapolating into noting that science results, in spite of gender and personalities, in generalizations like Boyle's Law, Fox-Keller adds, "The fact that Boyle's law [sic] is not wrong must, however, not be forgotten" (10-11).

At this point, it might be possible to see the image spectrum I have outlined as populated by association with three distinct social and theoretical communities: at its fictive extreme (MTV), there is no pretension towards truth or reference claims, and perceptions are simply imaginative variations without even sought for structures. In the middle, the political or Foucault-like area, it is realized that whatever is portrayed, simply by virtue of the naive but powerful perceptual-bodily "belief" that "seeing is to believe," is therefore manipulable within some power domain or discourse or episteme, and thus social constitution is a kind of power-knowledge. This, then, leaves the far right of the spectrum to the scientific community, which necessarily comes off as, if objective in any sense, clearly also somewhat naive with respect to what image transparency with respect to truth claims might be. Yet, interestingly, it is this community that is often the least naive with respect to the technical processes that actually yield the results, however isomorphic or enhanced, and that is the most sophisticated in guarding against and recognizing "instrumental artifacts." Therefore, instead of reverting to the easy result of taking technology—in this case the class of image technologies—as simply neutral and open to multiple uses depending upon the telos of the communities involved, I want to focus in more closely upon the human or community-technology relations more critically.

Critical Instrumental Realism

In much of my earlier work on technology (cf. *Technology and the Lifeworld; Instrumental Realism*), I differentiated between different types of human technology relations, sometimes intimating that what I call *embodiment relations* are often preferred to others.[1] These relations are ones in which the technology not only becomes maximally transparent, but which quasi-symbiotically becomes a kind of extended embodiment (in my Body One sense here). Contact lenses, the well-crafted hand tool, but also larger and more complex technologies that allow us to get at the environment mediatedly, but through a perceptual-bodily ease, are all examples. In all these cases the technology is incorporated into perceptual-bodily actions as per the formalism:

$$(I\text{-technology}) \rightarrow world$$

Image technologies, however, are interesting cases. In terms of my earlier distinctions, image technologies would ordinarily be thought of as *hermeneutic relating* technologies, although in particular cases retaining certain embodiment features. A hermeneutic relation is one that varies far enough from bodily isomorphism (including both space and time factors) to be more "text" or "language"-like than body-like. Thus, for example, while a real time television monitor directed at a bank teller's position can be thought of as a kind of technologically mediated and extended vision, its out-of-body position, its distance, and its obvious highly reduced field removes it in part from the immediacy of embodiment. Yet, like all image technologies, it retains and portrays—unless one is critical—its pretension toward "seeing is believing," and we are all dramatically aware of this in the recent Rodney King and Los Angeles truck driver video cases. These uses retain a "body-like" seeing. But, in terms of my earlier work, most image technology fits better into hermeneutic rather than embodiment relational schemes. That is to say, the perceptual focus is upon the display screen, through which there is a presumed reference, as in the formalism:

$$I \rightarrow \text{(technology-world)}$$

And for this very reason the question of "reading" images carries both positive and negative weight.

Image technologies, however construed, insofar as they retain perceptually isomorphic features, also presumptively carry with them the aura of seeing-believability. The bank robber, either viewed in real time by the guard upstairs, or later in a more video-like repeat time display, or Rodney King shown on national news via the doubly transformed video/ television display, carry this "eyewitness" quality. Here the continuum from the oldest photography to the latest complex manipulations of hyperreal imaging carry the same implicit seeing-believing claim. And this is the case *in spite of the fact that we know better.*

At bottom, this seeing-believability is tied to our basic and "primitive" bodily engagement with the World, our actional commitment that is echoed and mimicked through imaging technology displays. But, if this bodily-perceptual engagement is a constant, so also is its reflective, critical extension. The only cure for any perceptual illusion or error, as Merleau-Ponty so rightly pointed out, is more and better perception.

And that is why what is needed—indeed all across the spectrum noted—is a critical instrumental realism. That mode of realism is and should also be a phenomenologically critical realism such as is provided precisely by variational theory. Let us then return to a few of the examples above and note what variations, within the contexts noted, might show:

1) Beginning with the science cases, there is an almost deliberate attempt to practice variations. My colleague, Bob Crease, recently reported on biomedical imaging technologies in *Science,* where he shows how, by deliberately varying and comparing very different imaging processes, richer results are obtained. Different technologies are different processes aimed at the same target—coherence interferometry utilizes faint reflections of light, optical coherence tomography uses infrared radiation, MRI vibrates nuclei, etc.—and thus show nuanced differences, which, almost like classical eidetic phenomenology, let the phenomenon show itself. Here, to get to a truth claim, the variational use both seeks precision and yet comprehensive variations.

2) Note, now, how distant this is from the highly reduced "sound bite" culture of television if the analysis is left without variation. The Deaver manipulation of network news probably shows, underneath, the complicity of corporate politics with the media as much as anything, for what if the news had not "bought" the "working stiff" bit, but instead

showed Reagan nodding off while the cabinet was in the process of determining what bill would be vetoed? (Critical variation paralleling the science example is, of course, possible in analysis as well, and the TV viewer could read more extensive news analysis from any number of sources as well, but here we return to the problem of informed, critical communities once again.)

3) In the case of MTV, it could be said that the artifacts of the technologies themselves become fascinating. The possibility of magically transmogrifying images, collage juxtapositions, nonsense streams, etc. become the very stuff of the "play"—is MTV deconstruction embodied? It is at least the playful use of imaging in fictive mode, and in that retains the different kind of variation which belongs to creative and artful praxis.

I must, however, conclude: what I am suggesting through the examination of imaging technologies is that the roles of referentiality, perception, and bodies, are not without import, but must be seen in contexts very different from their classical situation in earlier epistemologies. Referentiality results properly only from critical and "socially constructed" results within a trained community employing variational investigations. Perceivability is polymorphic and is always both bodily and cultural—no perception without embodiment/no embodiment without hermeneutic context. And bodies belong to more than one dimension, both "biological," here used metaphorically, and "social," again in a metaphorical sense. The post-, a-, and non-Modern critiques thus call for a re-contexting of all of these problems.

Works Cited

Baudrillard, Jean. *The Gulf War Never Happened.* Bloomington: Indiana UP, 1995.

Capricorn One. Dir. Peter Hyans. Screenplay by Peter Hyans. Based on the novel by Peter Hyans (Lane Cove, N.S.W.: Doubleday Australia, 1978). Warner Bros. 1978.

Crease, Robert P. "Biomedicine in the Age of Imaging." *Science* 30 July 1993: 554+.

Derrida, Jacques. *Speech and Phenomena.* Trans. David Allison. Evanston: Northwestern UP, 1973.

Fox-Keller, Evelyn. *Reflections on Gender and Science.* New Haven: Yale UP, 1985.

Ihde, Don. *Instrumental Realism.* Bloomington: Indiana UP, 1991.

——. *Technology and the Lifeworld.* Bloomington: Indiana UP, 1990.

The Lawnmower Man. Dir. Bret Leonard. Screenplay by Bret Leonard and Stephen King. Based on the story in *Night Shift,* by Stephen King (Garden City, NY: Doubleday, 1978). New Line Cinema, 1992.

Moyers, Bill. *Living on the Edge.* Includes excerpts from Moyers' 1992 documentary, "Minimum Wages: The New Economy." Videocassette. Okapi Productions, L.L.C. WGBH Educational Foundation. Public Affairs Television, 1995.

Young, Iris. *Throwing Like a Girl and Other Essays.* Bloomington: Indiana UP, 1990.

II.

PERFORMATIVITY

5

UNSPLITTING THE SUBJECT/OBJECT:
LAURIE ANDERSON'S PHENOMENOLOGY OF PERCEPTION

Sam McBride

In the poem "Dog Show," from Laurie Anderson's massive performance piece, *United States,* we hear from a boy whose dreamy and subdued voice invites us to reflect upon his psychological construction. The boy dreams he is a dog in a dog show, and when his father comes to the show he, the father, remarks with approval, "that's a really good dog. I like that dog." When the boy's friends come to gaze upon him, the boy thinks, "no one has ever looked at me like this for so long." Clearly, the boy's dream reveals his desire to be accepted and admired, but there's more to it than that. Perhaps the son perceives his father's values, which are such that he appreciates dogs more than his own child. Further, "no one has ever stared at me like this for so long" can mean "it has been a long time since anyone has stared at me," which implies either a desire for or dread of being looked at. Conversely, the line can mean "no one has spent such a long time staring at me," implying a realization of a new and unusual experience.

More poignant still is the image of the child, a human subject, imagining himself as a dog on display. While dogs are living beings, humans have traditionally classified all non-human beings as more akin to objects for the very reason that they are not human and because we presume that they lack "innately human" self-awareness. Therefore, dogs are considered things to be compared, analyzed, displayed, and scrutinized, under the control of and for the benefit of human subjects. The story implies that for the son to gain the attention and admiration of the father, he must display himself as an object; that is, he must empty himself of subjecthood so that his father, a fellow subject, will notice him. Yet the boy narrates his own story, a story of desire, the story of a subject.

On another level, the story transfers some of the audience's experience of the boy onto Anderson. "Dog Show" is the penultimate event of *United States,* which is very likely the best known work of performance art; the final, full-length, four-part version of the piece, as much a concert as art, was viewed by more than 80,000 people throughout the United States and Europe. In contrast to the dog's assumed lack of consciousness and the child's desire (conscious or unconscious), Anderson has purposefully placed herself on display for her audience; and since *United States* is her longest performance work (and has been distributed throughout the word via various mediated forms including books, recordings, and videos), the same can be said of Anderson: no one has ever stared at her for so long. At the same time, "Dog Show" invites the audience to identify its own activity: objectifying Anderson as she displays herself.

At the very least, the piece complicates the easy categorization of humans as subjects and the supposed differences between subjects and objects—a strategy we find throughout Anderson's work, in pieces such as "Listen, Honey . . ." from a performance entitled *Empty Places*. Here Anderson (by whom we mean, here and elsewhere, the persona, "Anderson," who could be describing real or fictitious events) describes a protest march in front of a Playboy Club. When "one of the bunnies" asks Anderson about the purpose of the march, Anderson responds that she is there to protest the economic exploitation of women. The "bunny" then makes her own protest, telling Anderson that "this is the best job I've ever had," and that if she wants to "talk about women and money," she should take her protest down to the garment district, where women face real economic exploitation ("Why don't you go and march around down there?"). Anderson's response is "Hmmmmmmmmmmmmm . . ."

While open to the same psychological interpretations as "Dog Show," this piece clearly has more political scope. Anderson, according to her story, was herself engaging in a political action, a parade; she was protesting the Playboy Club's treatment of women as objects (or as Anderson's piece states, as animals, evoking "Dog Show"). It also points out that, while some groups within society may object to specific forms of sexual and economic exploitation of women, other (yet no less real) instances of sexual, economic and class exploitation may be overlooked elsewhere.

Clearly, however, by participating in a march, Anderson puts herself on display, turning herself into an object in order to accomplish her agenda. The twist is that while Anderson turns herself into an object in order to benefit a woman who is being treated as an object, the objectified Playboy bunny subjectifies herself; she speaks, and shows herself to be a thinking, self-aware individual, who does not perceive herself as being exploited.

As with "Dog Show," feelings generated from "Listen, Honey . . ." may carry over into the audience's understanding of Anderson. Just as the Playboy "bunny" (another animal) is putting herself on display for monetary gain in front of a group of men, so is Anderson benefitting monetarily from putting herself on display. Both Anderson and "the bunny" gain something from self-objectification. Anderson earned more than a million dollars, for example, from her 1981 recording of "O Superman" (which reached the Number 2 slot on the British pop charts), after a $400 investment (Dery 57). Then, as a result of that success, she signed a Warner Bros. recording contract which extended almost to the 21st century (Hochman F1), and she continues to sell out performances. After having worked as a college art history teacher, children's book illustrator, art reviewer, and museum director (Marincola 63), and then supplementing her income from government and foundation grants, Anderson can say along with "the bunny" that, at least financially, her current occupation (as "the closest thing to a pop star . . . in the performace art genre" [Hood]) "is the best job I ever had." At this point, perhaps, the audience should say "Hmmmmmmmmmmmmm"; the object witnessed on stage is actually a subject which thinks, reflects, and earns a living. Here again, the subject/object dichotomy is portrayed not as a neat split, in fact not as a dichotomy at all, but as simultaneity, or perhaps a continual, rapid alternation. "On again./Off again," as Anderson says elsewhere, "Always two things switching./One thing instantly replaces/another" ("The Language of the Future" in *United States*). With "Dog Show" and "Listen, Honey . . . ," Anderson is scrambling the subject/object divide, erasing the slash mark intended to keep subject and object separate.

Anderson is not the first performance artist to problematize the subject/object dichotomy. In fact, performance art as a genre, with its emphasis on placing human subjects on display (without the theatrical convention of characterization), appears well-suited for questioning the subject/object divide. "Happenings" artists of the early 1960s, for instance, often used human subjects as props, as purely visual elements in their events. These artists specifically sought non-actors for their works with the realization that professional actors would insert character—something the "happeners" didn't want. In some events "happeners" instructed their assistants to maintain a neutral expression, avoid personality and move with machine-like precision reminiscent of the robot dances of Bauhaus artist Oskar Schlemmer. Some Happenings exhibited a reverse strategy, presenting objects as subjects; Jim Dine's "Vaudeville Show" and Robert Whitman's "American Moon," for example, both sought to animate inanimate objects (cardboard cut-outs and puppets, respectively). Fluxus artists also toyed with subject/object relations, often, as in the case of Anderson, implicating the audience. La Monte Young's proto-Fluxus "Composition 1960 #6" instructs several performers to sit on stage and do nothing but gaze intently at the audience. As this piece was performed, audience members often became uncomfortable when confronted with performing objects who revealed themselves as subjects engaged in the task of objectifying the audience. In contrast, for one George Brecht piece ("Symphony #1," 1962) members of a "Fluxus Orchestra" reached their arms through life-size cut-out photos of themselves to play their instruments, in effect bringing to life the photo-objects.

The roots of this gesture can be traced to experimentalist musician and composer John Cage, who influenced both Happenings and Fluxus artists, and whose composition *4' 33"* is arguably less about silence than about the environmental noise that occurs in a concert hall, including that produced by the audience. Since the pianist is passive and silent, the traditionally passive and (not quite) silent audience is given the de facto role of performer. Among his influences, Cage has claimed the Futurists and Dadaists, two avant-garde groups who also engaged in redefining subjects and objects. The Futurists proposed a "magnetic theater" in which metallic objects would appear to move about on stage under their own power when animated by magnets under the stage (Blumenkranz-Onimus). Futurist founder Tomaso Marinetti transformed himself into pseudo-machinery in his "Zang Tumb Tuum," a sound poem mimicking the noises produced in battles of the first world war (Tisdall and Bozzolla Ch. 4). Hugo Ball similarly objectified himself in a 1916 dada performance at the Cabaret Voltaire of a gibberish poem, "Karawane"; Ball describes a special robot-like costume designed for the performance which made him look "like an obelisk" with wings (qtd. in Goldberg 61).

Performance artists of the late 1960s and early 1970s pursued gestures derived from this avant-garde performance tradition, though their assault on the separation between subject and object generally went further than those of Happenings and Fluxus artists. Some artists turned their own bodies into art objects: Chris Burden became a target (in contrast with Jasper Johns's obsession with painting targets on canvas) when he had himself shot in the arm with a .22 caliber rifle ("Shoot" 1973). About the same time he became street debris—lying under a tarp on a busy Los Angeles boulevard, with two burning flares his only safeguard ("Deadman" 1973). Significantly less macho is Elenor Antin's "Carving: A Traditional Sculpture." Over a five-week period, the artist each day produced four photographs of her nude body as she endeavored to lose weight and thus sculpt her figure into the "ideal" form. The body art tradition has continued into the early 1990s through the work of artists such as Matthew Barney and the S & M performances of Bob Flanagan.

Coincident with (and subsequent to) the body artists of the early 1970s were performers who practiced a conceptual strategy of blurring subject and object. Collette enacted a form of self-objectification when she developed her conceptual death (conveniently willing her estate to a new persona, Justine, who then became president of the Collette is Dead Co., Ltd.). Pat Oleszko explored the effect of costumes on her subjectivity, most notably as "Pat Kioski," a performance/persona for which the costume was a portable souvenir stand, from which Oleszko sold postcards. Bonnie Sherk enacted the objectification of animals (which Anderson alluded to in "Dog Show") by eating lunch in a cage at the zoo. Dennis Oppenheim moved from body art performances in the early 1970s to animating mannequins and mechanical puppets as stand-ins for the body.

Anderson's work encompasses both the direct use of her body as an object as well as the conceptual transformations questioning the subject/object split. Anderson's work is especially worth studying in this regard because, in contrast to most performance artists of her generation, she continues not only to perform, but to explore subject/object relations; questioning the boundary between subject and object has been a consistent theme in her performances for the past twenty-five years, even as her performance artist peers have returned to making art objects.

Anderson also differs from other performance artists in the extent to which she has been visible within popular culture. While most 1970s performance artists remained virtually unknown to all but those with connections to the avant-garde art circuit, Anderson has achieved a significant level of recognition within the pop music world (through the surprise success of "O Superman" and her subsequent Warner Bros. albums) while still maintaining her art world associations. A study of Anderson's strategies of blurring subject and object not only provides insight into those strategies but provides an opportunity to investigate whether Anderson's strategies have "crossed over," as she has, into popular culture.

The performance events cited thus far, those of both Anderson and her performance art peers, illustrate a tension between subject and object, an uncertainty that subjects are always and essentially subjects, and objects always objects. The same tension lies at the heart of the philosophy of Maurice Merleau-Ponty, whose theories of subject/object relations make a useful tool for analyzing these works. In *Phenomenology of Perception* (which, along with the same author's *The Visible and the Invisible* and Wittgenstein's *Philosophical Investigations,* Anderson read during her college years [Marincola 63]), Merleau-Ponty grounds all human experience within/as the body. He says, in effect, that my ability to foreground, to focus on something, is the gesture by which I label a perception, a sensory experience, as an object, something external from myself (67). Such an understanding of perception suggests a difficulty in traditional Western philosophy: the categorization of some sensory experiences as subjects and others as objects. Regardless of whether the perception on which I focus is animate or inanimate, animal or human, he suggests, the result is the same: the perception is posited as an object. Nothing about my initial experience of the bodies of fellow humans, therefore, suggests that they are somehow perceived as subjects. Furthermore, after analyzing relationships between what I perceive as objects, I come to think of my own body as an object within the world (70).

Yet, simultaneously, I think of myself as different from the rest of the world, since my body is the ground of my perceptions. For example, I note that, in contrast with other objects, I can move my body directly (or it moves itself), and I cannot gain a complete perspective of my body (since it is the ground of my perspective) (Spurling 21). When I *think* about perception, my thought is that physical objects such as eyes, ears, and nose, etc., are the tools of those perceptions; yet the very action of *thought* seems separate from, or more accurately, in addition to those objects and the objective world. This perception leads me to think of myself as more-than-object, as a subject.

While I think of myself as more-than-object, I also exist in relationship with those things I perceive as objects, in a system where those objects also exist in relationship to one another (Merleau-Ponty 68). While I focus on an object, Merleau-Ponty points out, I can perceive that object from a variety of angles, in part because I perceive other objects around and partially hidden by the primary focus. For example, while I focus on object A, I can perceive not only what I see, but also, to some extent, what object B, located behind object A, can "see." Objects, therefore, "form a system or a world, and . . . each one treats the others round it as spectators of its hidden aspects which guarantee the permanence of those aspects by their presence" (Merleau-Ponty 68). In other words, not only do subjects have the qualities of objects, all objects possess in some way the qualities of subjects; everyone and everything are constantly both one and thing, subject and object.

Anderson's performances enact several strategies which are illustrative of this indistinctness between subjects and objects. By the very fact that she appears before an audience, she is objectified within her performances. She is the "thing" the audience has come to see, just like any other art or entertainment object (a television, movie, or computer screen; a sculpture or a canvas). She enhances and emphasizes this quality by "de-subjectifying" herself in a variety of ways. In her concert film, *Home of the Brave,* she (and her assisting performers) first appears masked, her body and head completely covered by white linen, with a drawn-on smile and two dots for eyes. The same costume is used in the studio-produced video of "Sharkey's Day," but here Anderson's costume is all white except for the head, which is the same shade as the background. As a result the viewer sees Anderson's white body, as well as the eye dots and drawn-on smile and nose, but not her head; she looks like a two-dimensional effigy of herself. Similarly, in *United States* she has worn mirrored glasses, which don't allow her audience to connect with her eyes, the human being's primary organ of perception (her use of such glasses also indicates her complicity with popular culture, as they often form a part of the rock star's stage persona, most significantly in the case of Bono, lead singer for U2, the most "Andersonesque" of all rock bands in the 1990s).

While these activities serve to de-emphasize her subject qualities, at other times Anderson is more blatant about presenting her body as an object. In *Home of the Brave,* Anderson displays her head on a giant screen at the back of the stage. Disconnected from her body and enlarged one hundred times its normal size, the head appears like a magical object, floating in space. In "Reverb" (which appears in *United States* as well as *Home of the Brave* and *Collected Videos*), Anderson turns her head into a drum; a contact microphone embedded in the bridge of a pair of glasses picks up sounds transmitted through her cranial structure as she knocks on her skull and clicks her teeth. Similarly, in "Drum Dance" also from *Home of the Brave,* she turns her body into a trap set by Velcro-ing electronic switches to parts of her anatomy, then hitting those switches against herself to trigger electronic percussion sounds. Such actions emphasize the body's object qualities; and yet Anderson's self-objectification, when seen as a strategy, reveals the strategist as a subject. By speaking to her audience and originating actions, she further reminds her audience that the apparent "object" it witnesses is simultaneously a subject.

Anderson's interest in emphasizing the object-qualities of subjects has been important since her earliest performance work, such as "Automotive" (1972). This performance developed from Anderson's observations of outdoor musical concerts in Rochester, Vermont, where the audience remained sitting in their cars while listening to the music, much like drive-in movies. After each piece, instead of applauding, they honked their car horns. Anderson introduced a Fluxus-like reversal of the situation, putting a small audience into the gazebo where normally the musicians would sit, and arranging the cars to blare their horns on cue (Kardon 8). Here the audience (those persons sitting in the cars) became the performers in a more obvious, active way than in, for example, Cage's *4' 33"*; the participants were revealed as performing objects, while their awareness of themselves as performers would remind them of their subjectivity.

The opposite of this strategy is that of emphasizing the subject qualities of objects. One of Anderson's best-known inventions is the tape-bow violin (which followed the earlier, somewhat similar viophonograph and was later transformed by digital technology). This instrument features a playback head mounted where normally the bridge and strings would be. A bow strung with magnetic tape rather than horsehair is then pulled across the violin, allowing the recorded sounds to be played back. In pieces such as "Talk Show" from *Home of the Brave,* the sound recorded on the tape is a human voice (interestingly enough, the prime analog for the violin since its introduction). While we are accustomed to machines such as tape players *re*producing human sounds, we generally think of violins as *producing* musical sounds. The mixture of the two is startling: a violin appears to be speaking as a subject.

Anderson's interest in turning objects into subjects can be traced back to her earliest work, even before she began giving performances. Her *Handbook* (1972) centers a word or phrase on each right-hand page. The words and phrases join together to describe the reader's activities while reading the *Handbook.* Two pages, for example, say "the important thing is . . . turning," while two later pages say "by now turning . . . has become habit" (qtd. in Kardon 8). Such a technique draws attention to the reader's interaction with the book, suggesting both are engaged in a mutual exchange, an exchange of subjectivities.

Almost twenty years later Anderson produced (and this time mass marketed) another artist's book, *Empty Places,* which documents the performance of the same name. While most of the photos in the book are either of Anderson in performance, or "art" photos by Anderson (and other photographers), the "Contents" page and a special section titled "About Empty Places" are snapshots of what Anderson herself might see during a performance and while on tour. Photos include pictures of the audience applauding her concert, assistants behind the scenes, reporters in a press conference and radio interview, and fans waiting for autographs. All these photos are taken from what would be Anderson's perspective. Here Anderson turns the subjects who make up her audience (and who normally view Anderson as an object) into objects, reminding the reader that Anderson is a subject perceiving her environment even while performing. The photos emphasize that viewing her performance is a mutual exchange of subjectivities.

The strategies addressed thus far can be described as reversals, emphasizing subject qualities of entities traditionally classified as objects, and vice versa. The text of "Closed Circuit" from *United States* exemplifies another approach to blurring the distinction between subject and object: alterity or simultaneity, emphasizing both subject and object qualities of an entity at the same time. One verse of "Closed Circuit" describes some hula dancers who Anderson saw "just hula-ing down the street." A hula dancer is a subject who can willfully act to send a message with her body. At the same time, she is simultaneously an objectified woman intended exclusively to be looked at as a closed sign system. The hula dancer is both object and subject, objectified yet subjectifying. Earlier in the song Anderson whispers, "You're a snake charmer, baby; and you're also the snake," and later, "you're a shepherd, baby, and you're also one, two, three hundred sheep." This alludes to the power of being in the subject position; the subjects, the snake charmer and shepherd, manipulate and control the destinies and activities of the objects, the snake and sheep. At the same time, the objects are implied to have subject qualities; the snake can only be "charmed" if it has a mind (of its own). Furthermore, the desire of the subjects to control the objects reveals that the subjects acknowledge some degree of subjectivity within the objects, some degree of willfulness to work against their "masters," a resistance that makes mastery worthwhile. As masters, the snake charmer and shepherd will have conquered resistance, the resistance of a fellow subject. But Anderson combines both sides of this master/slave dichotomy into one entity: "you" ("You're a snake charmer [subject], . . . and you're also the snake [object]"). The entity "you" is simultaneously subject and object.

Hula dancers and snake charmers as subjects/objects within power relationships bring us again to Merleau-Ponty's assertion that all perception posits objects, yet the perception of one's ability to perceive leads one to consider oneself as being different from the surroundings; the perception, that is, of oneself as subject. Merleau-Ponty's term for human existence as both subject and object is incarnate subjectivity (Langer 50). This implies that while I can posit both mind and body, they exist not as independent entities fortuitously joined together within me, but as the two sides of one coin, merely different aspects of one thing (Barral 91). This notion is particularly apparent in sexuality. I may be sexually attracted to object A differently than to object B (Bannon 79). Sexual desire brings my body to my awareness in a new way (Langer 50); yet the difference between the two attractions cannot be accounted for only by my body. Sexuality implies the integral simultaneity (or perhaps alterity) of body and mind, or perhaps that body and mind are the same thing.

At the same time, while there may be a difference between my attractions toward objects A and B, part of what creates that difference is that I begin to perceive more than a simple physical difference between the two; this leads me to posit that the object toward which I am attracted (or from which I am repulsed) is not simply an object, but is itself an incarnate subjectivity. "Normal" sexual meaning, Merleau-Ponty asserts, exists only in dialogue, when my incarnate subjectivity is attracted toward another; this he labels "intersubjectivity"—an exchange of significance which occurs between beings (cf. Langer 50; Spurling 41; Barral 145-46). Because sexuality is such a fundamental aspect of human existence, intersubjectivity is an equally important corollary of human experience.

However, if humans are incarnate subjectivities engaging in intersubjectivity, patriarchal sexuality is fundamentally flawed. Men have traditionally objectified women, claiming that women really "are" only objects, while attempting to reserve subjectivity as their own. Merleau-Ponty acknowledges the possibility of patriarchal sexual relations when he discusses the shame which results from the realization that a subject has reduced me to an object through his gaze. The problem (for men) is that, because women too are incarnate subjectivities, they can (at least in theory) return the gaze, objectifying the men who have gazed at them. No body, then, and no gender, is purely passive or active, subject or object. Further, as Butler observes, Merleau-Ponty implies that the gendered body is an historical idea, dependent on "the incorporation. . . of cultural memory and knowingness" (154), which implies that gender is socially inscribed, rather than a natural phenomenon.[1]

Of course, a realization that gender is socially inscribed does not alleviate the discomfort felt when a body socially-inscribed as female is objectified by a body socially-inscribed as male. Anderson has described herself as a victim of such patriarchal objectification in her photo/text piece "Object/Objection/Objectivity." The piece focuses on men who overtly attempted to objectify her, in Anderson's interpretation, by giving "unsolicited comments (of the 'Hey Baby' type)" (qtd. in Owens 49, as below). Anderson chose, as Merleau-Ponty's theories suggest, to assert her subjectivity by gazing back at those men who sought to objectify her. To further empower herself, Anderson not only gazed back but photographed ten men who gave her "cat-calls," permanently and literally turning the images of those men into objects. The ten photos, along with texts describing the actions of the men, form the piece. But to further objectify the men (rather, I presume, than "to protect the innocent"), their eyes are blocked out in the photos.

Anderson specifically spoke of her actions in photographing the men as violent, as "assault." It was her way of "stealing something" from them, of "turning [them] into an object (subject matter)," of "shooting" them, all as a way of dealing with her anger over being objectified, the anger of a subject. At the same time, Anderson appears to seek more than revenge, and more than simply to objectify men (Morgan 81); if she sought only a simple reversal, she would have left the men as objects. Instead, her texts accompanying the photos not only tell of the actions the men took which motivated Anderson to photograph them, but also the reactions of the men to Anderson's gesture. Those reactions ranged from self-deprecation to further catcalls to (at least mild) anger. Most of the men, however, seemed "pleased and flattered by the 'honor'" which she bestowed upon them. By showing these reactions, Anderson, while objectifying these men, reveals that they also remain subjects; in other words, she re-subjectifies the men she has worked to objectify, revealing them as incarnate subjectivities. Furthermore, the piece opens with a story about a *woman* who saw Anderson in a restaurant and was convinced Anderson was a soap opera star; Anderson claims it was her anger over this experience that set her thinking about how *men* objectify her. The piece, therefore, is concerned with the problem of objectification by humans, male and female, not just by men; it shows an understanding that all genders are both subjects and objects.

For a PBS video art series, *Alive from Off Center,* Anderson created a striking example of work problematizing gendered subject/object relations. In one early scene she complains of being too busy to accomplish her work within a cultural system that requires artists to promote themselves by interacting with the media. To solve this problem, she claims she had herself cloned. The clone appears as an image of herself, but distorted via make-up and electronics to appear male, mustachioed, and a midget. This image is loaded with ambiguous, overlapping insinuations regarding sexuality and gender. Anderson has reproduced without the aid of male sperm. Yet when she reproduces within patriarchal culture, the result is a male. The deformed, midget size of that which Anderson reproduced, however, recalls Freud's analysis of the exterior female sexual apparatus, the clitoris, as a small, deformed, inadequate penis. Later in the program, "natural" male attitudes are lampooned when the clone, while shaving its/his/her hairless face, suggests to Anderson that producing a Rocky-meets-Rambo movie might be a good project for the two of them. Anderson is obviously dealing with gender differences and expectations in this piece.

Anderson comments within the video that she felt surprise at seeing the male clone, an alter image of herself, implying that to position herself as a subject within male-dominated culture, she must do so as a male (although later, when the male clone requires an assistant, he is cloned as a very large female, also a distorted image of Anderson). Most important here is that Anderson positions herself as a subject. She is obviously the more important member of the pair, while the clone is solely performing a support position (reversing the modern gender positioning of boss and secretary). Anderson speaks of the clone as an object, much as a patriarchal husband might speak of his wife. A later scene capitalizes on this husband/wife imagery by showing Anderson sitting in an easy chair reading the paper while the clone does the menial work of composing.

Yet Anderson is not content with such a straightforward gender reversal. One scene begins as a reversal, showing Anderson writing music (in the style of Beethoven, directly onto paper without recourse to a musical instrument to "test" the sounds she notates) and masterminding the duo's work, while the clone simply bangs on the drums to work out a rhythm. Here the image is one of artist/genius vs. technician/assistant, a scene which puts Anderson in charge, in a subject position, yet which does not necessarily place the clone into a traditional female role (though his role is certainly subordinate). But Anderson complicates this image by revealing the artificiality of the scene and the technology behind it. We hear the male voice of an off-stage director telling both Anderson and the clone what to do and where to appear; in fact, Anderson composes in the manner of Beethoven, not her usual practice, only because the voice of authority instructs her to do so. In other words, while the scene posits Anderson in a subject role, it simultaneously shows that both she and her male clone are objects being directed by something exterior. For Anderson, the subject/object qualities of men and women are very complex phenomena.

The foregrounding of gendered subject/object relations *à la* Merleau-Ponty apparent in Anderson's work has corollaries in the activities of her performance art peers. Several have pursued gender crossing in some manner. Elenor Antin donned a fake beard and costume as "The King" (in the style of 18th-century France, not Elvis), strolling along a San Diego beach speaking with her/his surprised "subjects." Paul Maurice Best became "Octavia," whose facial characteristics and dress vacillate from predominately male to predominately female. Colin Campbell enacted a video persona dubbed "The Woman from Malibu" (the artist cross-dressed as a woman while acting and speaking as "himself"). Thought Music, a performance ensemble of Laurie Carlos, Jessica Hagedorn, and Robbie McCauley, developed a drag parody of "The Tonight Show." These artists have used performance (live and mediated) to foreground their questioning of culturally inscribed gender codes, to blur the boundary between gendered subjects and objects.

But equally telling is the extent to which pop culture figures have been accepted by the public while enacting a reconfiguration of traditional gendered subject/object relations, often in ways notably parallel to Anderson's. The Artist Formerly Known as Prince has created a gender-confused symbol for use as his self-identification. Michael Jackson projects a macho image on stage, complete with *faux* military costumes and crotch grabbing, but exhibits an extreme passivity off-stage. His "Black and White" video recalls the gesture of Anderson's clone; through the power of computer morphing, males appear to transform with ease into females, and vice versa. Madonna allows objectification of her body in a variety of forms, yet much like Anderson, appears to exercise a significant level of control over how she is packaged and presented; Madonna echoes with even greater authority Anderson's "Playboy bunny" in "Listen, Honey . . ." as "the bunny" claims she is the primary beneficiary of her own exploitation.

Such gender-blurring has a lineage from rock musicians of Anderson's generation (Brian Eno and David Bowie, for example), yet the extent of recent public acceptance of this can be seen by contrasting work of two bands from different generations: The Rolling Stones and U2. For its 1989 "Steel Wheels" tour, The Stones hired Mark Fisher to design a huge, high-tech stage set vaguely reminiscent of the facade of Paris' Pompidou Center (with the addition of huge video screens, fireworks, and light show). The set was immediately labeled postmodern by architects and designers (cf. Arcidi; Fisher; Papadakis). Within three years, U2 also went high-tech, presenting a postmodern "Zoo TV" tour on a set with huge video screens, telephone hook-ups (for a moment when the band sought to telephone the United States president or some other political leader) and large-screen computer links. While the Stones' theme was a romanticization of post-industrial urban decay, U2's was multi-media chaos. Both, however, went beyond the common use of technology in rock concerts (e.g., light shows, massive sound systems, etc.) and created on-stage *environments* which foregrounded the technology; the technical apparatus was as much a performer as were any of the band members. Such environments show a debt to the high-tech performance spectacle Anderson developed in the early 1980s.

Yet the Stones' set served as a space for Mick Jagger and the band to strut and display their rock bad-boy, macho image, an image reinforced with erupting pyrotechnics and huge inflatable figures of voluptuous females. U2, in contrast, presented a multi-media blizzard which served to ironize and deflate the band's image as rock stars. Much as Anderson has maintained an ironic stance toward her own success (and a corresponding critical edge to her work), a stance based in part on an awareness of her own objectification, U2 played up the image of the rock-star persona, revealing that it is, indeed, only persona, a camp version of macho; lead singer Bono was as much Liberace as he was Elvis or Mick Jagger. While the Stones sought to portray themselves as straight-forward subjects, U2 presented themselves as subjects aware of their own (self-)objectification.

Rock musicians' and performance artists' interest in subject/object relations show that objectification of humans is more than simply a problem of men objectifying women. Instead, it suggests that in our society both male and female are objectified, or rather (since Merleau-Ponty suggests that all humans are indeed objects) de-subjectified, and yet that subjectivity is (or can be) re-asserted via intersubjectivity, a mutual exchange between two subjects which are simultaneously objects (or incarnate subjects). Anderson, for example, works to draw her audience's attention toward individual incarnate subjectivity in order to work against patriarchal modes of thinking and traditional male/female relationships, but just as important, and in a more general sense, to reconfigure the human subject, both male and female, away from the subject/object split of traditional modernist and earlier philosophy, and toward the model suggested by Merleau-Ponty. The extent to which the gendered boundary between subject and object is beginning to be questioned in popular culture suggests Anderson's work is having an effect.

Yet positioning Anderson as enacting the theorizations of Merleau-Ponty reifies the same gender trap (the male as seminal originator, the female as mere vessel for transforming abstract idea into physical form) which Anderson critiques in her clone video (*Collected Videos*). From the vantage point of Merleau-Ponty's theories, he and Anderson should be seen not in a one-way relationship, but engaged in intersubjectivity. Thus Anderson's work should be explored not simply for how it enacts Merleau-Ponty's theorization, but also for how it re-acts to it and acts upon it. Significant in this regard is the woman Anderson describes in *Object/Objections/Objectivity* who insists Anderson is a soap opera star and who first motivated Anderson to explore moments when she was objectified. Anderson's anger was kindled when one woman objectified another; only then did she choose to "shoot" the men giving her unsolicited comments. This motivating event implies that, though both men and women can objectify others, those others who are objectified are most commonly women. Equally important is the male director's voice of authority which objectifies Anderson and her clone. Anderson's lack of apparent authority over that male director (especially after having presented herself playing subject to the clone's object) suggests objectification remains primarily, or perhaps ultimately, "a man's job." The fact that Anderson's name is listed on the video's credits as the "real" director simply complicates even further these gendered relationships; Anderson apparently directed the male voice to sound as if it were directing her. These works suggest that, while using Merleau-Ponty's theorization that all humans are subject to objectification, Anderson also questions whether Merleau-Ponty perceives the extent to which women are the primary victims of objectification.

Rather than simply accepting the imprint of Merleau-Ponty on her work, Anderson uses Merleau-Ponty to reveal the inadequacy of his own theorization: his optimistic view of asserting one's subjectivity by returning the gaze is more efficacious for an incarnate subjectivity which is culturally inscribed as male than for one culturally inscribed as female. By pointing this out, Anderson is not merely "doing" Merleau-Ponty: she is doing something *to* him. She is working with his theorization, but also taking it to places where Merleau-Ponty probably wouldn't have gone: within the culturally inscribed realm of female subjectivity. Anderson's work posits a "yes" answer to the question, "would Merleau-Ponty's theory of subject/object relations have been different had he been born female?" This action can be read simultaneously as enacting the two-way directionality of Merleau-Ponty's theory of intersubjectivity, and simultaneously Anderson's invocation of her power as a subject to objectify his theories.

This idea of Anderson taking Merleau-Ponty to places he might hesitate to go has an analogy within Anderson's work. One of the most intriguing ways she has asserted her subjectivity has been in her work with William S. Burroughs. Anderson has identifed Burroughs as a mentor, doubtless because of his refusal to submit to any given category or media (at various times, he has been a writer, a painter, and a photographer) and because of his role as "a conjurer, a magician, an occultist intent on breaking the sacred vessels of normative perception" as well as his consistant attempts to "undo the cultural spell with which we've all been hypnotized" (Kaufman 77). Anderson speaks very respectfully (almost reverently) of Burroughs, and attributes "Language is a Virus" to him on a large-screen projection at the back of the stage during her performance of the song. His voice is the one recorded on the audio tape Anderson plays on her violin in "Talk Show." Further, Burroughs appears several times in the film *Home of the Brave,* once as a disembodied telephone voice, and again on-screen delivering a monologue about seeing himself reflected (as an object) in his listener's eyes. Anderson's admiration of Burroughs has even extended to her inclusion of Lawrence, Kansas (not the kind of urban venue that would normally attract a performance artist), on her tours in order to accomodate her artistic mentor, who was a local resident (Hood). Burroughs reciprocated this admiration, for besides their collaborative efforts—in addition to his appearence in *Home of the Brave,* the two, along with text/sound poet John Giorno, recorded an album together (*You're the Guy I Want to Share My Money With*)—he praised Anderson as "a remarkable per-former" (T. Morgan 569).

But as is the case with Anderson's connection to Merleau-Ponty, we should not take her relationship with Burroughs as being merely imita-tive: the misogyny that characterized both his work and his personal life demonstrates the absurdity of such a conjecture (although even here Bur-roughs' admiration for Anderson places his "reputation as a woman-hater" in question [T. Morgan 7-8]). The relationship, then, is neither imitative, nor is it submissive or passive, for in fact, Anderson has appropriated and objectified her mentor. This is perhaps best evidenced in his apperances with Anderson in *Home of the Brave.* Twice he dances across the stage with Anderson. The dancing is most interesting. Here Anderson has convinced a gay man, purportedly a misogynist, to appear with a woman in a traditional male role as lead in a tango. At the same time, because Burroughs appears old and slow, and because he's a poor dancer, Anderson actually appears to lead. This moment encapsulates the feminist potential of Merleau-Ponty's theory of intersubjectivity. Just as Anderson can borrow (from) Burroughs in order to take him where he would not otherwise go, so too can she borrow Merleau-Ponty's theory to lead it where Merleau-Ponty did not. As such, Anderson suggests a revision or addition to Merleau-Ponty's subject/object theories, based on a feminist understanding of the impact of culturally inscribed gender coding.

Note

1. There is an interesting dichotomy, drawn along gender lines, in the com-mentary/explication on Merleau-Ponty. Bannon (a man) insists that Merleau-Ponty develops a justification for the body as subject, rather than object; the body cannot be an object because it is "the *condition* for objects" (64). On the other hand, Spurling and Barral (women) interpret Merleau-Ponty's position as that "the body is in one sense an object" (Spurling 21); Spurling suggests this view reflects Merleau-Ponty's refusal to ground his philosophical discourse within a body/mind dichotomy.

Works Cited and Consulted

Anderson, Laurie. *Collected Videos*. Prod. Laurie Anderson. Videocassette. Warner Reprise, 1990.

——. "Dark Dogs, American Dreams." *Hotel*. New York: Tanam P, 1980. 107-31.

——. *Empty Places: A Performance*. New York: HarperPerennial, 1991.

——. *Home of the Brave*. Prod. Paula Mazur. Videocassette. Warner Reprise, 1986.

——. *United States*. New York: Harper and Row, 1984.

——. *United States: Live*. Prod. Roma Baran and Laurie Anderson. Recorded 7-10 Feb. 1983. LP. Warner Bros., 1984.

Anderson, Laurie, William S. Burroughs, and John Giorno. *You're the Guy I Want to Share My Money With*. LP. New York: Giorno Poetry Systems, 1981.

Arcidi, Philip. "Timely Adjustments: Retrofit Technology." Papadakis, 56-61.

Bannon, John F. *The Philosophy of Merleau-Ponty*. New York: Harcourt, Brace, and World, 1967.

Barral, Mary Rose. *Merleau-Ponty: The Role of the Body-Subject in Interpersonal Relations*. Pittsburgh: Duquesne UP, 1965.

Blumenkranz-Onim, Noemi. "The Power of the Myth: Electricity in Italian Futurism." *Electra: Electricity and Electronics in the Art of the 20th Century*. Ed. Frank Popper. Paris: Les Amis du Musee d'Art Modern, 1983. 148-62.

Butler, Judith. *Excitable Speech: A Politics of the Performative*. New York: Routledge, 1997.

Dery, Mark. "From Hugo Ball to Hugo Largo." *High Performance* 11.4 (1988): 54-57.

Dilliberto, John. "The Laurie Anderson Interview." *Down Beat* Oct. 1984: 22-24.

Fisher, Mark. "It's Only Rock 'n' Roll." Papadakis, 46-51.

Goldberg, RoseLee. *Performance Art: From Futurism to the Present*. Rev. ed. New York: Abrams, 1988.

Hochman, Steve. "Laurie Anderson Opts for a Creative Housecleaning." *Los Angeles Times* 8 Feb. 1990: F1.

Hood, Woodrow B. Review of Anderson, Laurie. "Stories from the Nerve Bible: A Retrospective, 1972-1992." Performed at the Lied Center, Lawrence, Kansas, Mar. 29, 1994. *Postmodern Culture* 4.3 (May 1994). http://dlo202.telia.com/~u222500056/laurie/texts/politics.htm

Kardon, Janet. "Laurie Anderson: A Synesthesic Journey." Kardon, 6-31.

Kardon, Janet, ed. *Laurie Anderson: Works from 1969 to 1983*. Philadelphia: Institute of Contemporary Art, 1983.

Kaufman, Frederick. "William S. Burroughs at the Los Angeles County Museum of Art: Pariah or Pope?" *Aperture* 146 (Winter 1998): 77-78.

Langer, Monika. *Merleau-Ponty's Phenomenology of Perception: A Guide and Commentary*. Tallahassee: Florida State UP, 1989.

Marincola, Paula. "Chronology." Kardon, 63-83.

Merleau-Ponty, Maurice. *Phenomenology of Perception*. New York: Humanities P, 1962.

Morgan, Stuart. "Laurie Anderson: Big Science and Little Men." *Brand New York* (Spec. Is. *Literary Review*). London: Institute of Contemporary Arts; Literary Review, 1982. 77-85.

Morgan, Ted. *Literary Outlaw: The Life and Times of William S. Burroughs*. New York: Avon, 1988.

Owens, Craig. "Sex and Language: In Between." Kardon, 48-53.

Papadakis, Andreas. "An Interview with Mick Jagger." Papadakis 52-55.

Papadakis, Andreas, ed. *New Architecture: The New Moderns and the Super Moderns*. London: Academy Group, 1990.

Spurling, Laurie. *Phenomenology and the Social World: The Philosophy of Merleau-Ponty and Its Relation to the Social Sciences*. London: Routledge and Kegan Paul, 1977.

Tisdall, Caroline, and Angelo Bozzolla. *Futurism*. New York: Oxford UP, 1978.

6

TOWARD A PHENOMENOLOGY
OF THE ROLE-PLAYING GAME PERFORMANCE

Daniel Mackay

Role-Playing Games and the Imaginary Entertainment Environment
With the release of Dungeons & Dragons in 1974, the role-playing
game became a full-fledged part of American popular consciousness.
Generally marketed in the form of rulebooks that provide, in addition to
the rules, advice to help players construct complex and interesting characters, these games are a non-technological performance form that serve
as the prime model for many new, very technological, mediated, online
games known as Multi-User Domains or MUDs. As the basis for emergent entertainment forms, the role-playing game provides the basic
guidelines from which these more recent games are constructed. The traditional role-playing game, which is the object of this study,[1] invariably
takes the form of collaborative story-creations in which up to a dozen
players sit at a table and enact fictional personas through which they
interact with one another and the Game Master.

Because the role-playing game performance is itself an archipelago
of other art forms with longer and deeper histories, it requires what I call
an "imaginary entertainment environment" for its setting—an imaginary
mise-en-scène that is created to persist and adapt itself through a number
of different media. The imaginary entertainment environment is a fantasy world that grows and changes due to the contributions of pre-existing forms of expression, such as acting, game-playing, and narration.
Although existing long before the role-playing game in the different
modes of expression that comprise religion (oration, singing, chanting,
parable-writing, and so on), the imaginary entertainment environment is
first identified with the role-playing game because the role-playing game
performance is an entertainment form (unlike religion, which, while it
might entertain, is not an entertainment form) that has a number of different modes of expression built into it from the very beginning. The
very first role-playing game setting, a medieval fantasy realm for the
D&D game called "Blackmoor," was, even with its appearance in 1971,

an imaginary entertainment environment because it was a fictional setting created out of the interaction of game play, narration, and acting, all bound up in the performance of the game. Today, the phenomenon of the imaginary entertainment environment dominates the comic book, role-playing game, collectible card game, computer and video game, and fantasy/science fiction paperback markets, and has a strong presence in the television and film markets. These fictional settings change over time as if they were real places and are published in a variety of media (e.g., novels, films, and role-playing games), each in relation to the others and each contributing to the growth, history, and status of the setting. Because they appear in so many media, imaginary entertainment environments are always collaborative. In fact, often their brand names become more important than the author, director, or game designer; this can be seen in the prominence of names such as *Star Wars, Star Trek, Babylon 5, Forgotten Realms, Dragonlance, DC Comics, Marvel Comics, Thieves' World,* and *The World of Darkness*—all of which take precedence over the name of the contributor or author. Indeed, in imaginary entertainment environments the setting itself, through its imposition of strict conventions and tropes, functions as a co-author of the work.

In the case of *Star Wars*—truly a multimedia experience—the same imaginary entertainment environment is referred to in movies, novels, short stories, children's fiction, graphic story albums, radio plays, comic books, computer and video games, model kits, action figures, poster art, live-action and animated television shows, the "Star Tours" ride at Walt Disney World, news groups, web pages, and hundreds of undocumented tabletop, live-action, computer, and online role-playing games. Deborah Fine's mammoth coffee table book, *Star Wars Chronicles,* as well as Allan Kausch's "Star Wars Timeline," which was included in the 1997 Winter edition of *Star Wars Insider,* both situate the multimedia interfaces to *Star Wars* in relation to one another. *Star Wars Chronicles* draws on them in order to paint a consistent vision of a singular fantasy world, into which each of these forms taps. Kausch's timeline furthers that project by situating twenty-one different comic book mini-series, sixty-two novels and children's books, three graphic story albums, thirteen computer/video games, and six feature films (two of which are yet to be made) into a single timeline spanning some 5000 years before the events of the first *Star Wars* movie, and forward twenty-three years into the future.

What the imaginary entertainment environment has contributed to various media is a breaking of the hermeneutic approach that sees a setting as a mere background for one work or set of works (e.g., a trilogy or series of films) which take the setting into oblivion with it when the final work is published. The imaginary entertainment environment has outlets among all media and interfaces. Every time a new product is published it acts as an update sending a "chronicle of actual events" from that world into our world. "The medium itself is no longer identifiable as such" writes Baudrillard, "and the confusion of the medium and the message (McLuhan) is the first great formula of this new era. There is no longer a medium in the literal sense: it is now intangible, diffused, and diffracted in the real, and one can no longer even say that the medium is altered by it" (30). Due to both the multiple modes of expression associated with each of the role-playing game's performance spheres and role-players' need for consistency in order to suspend disbelief about a fantasy world, the role-playing game is the harbinger of the now ubiquitous imaginary entertainment environment—invented fifteen years before "multimedia" became a catchword.

The goal of the game system is to actualize a certain kind of performance, and indeed, a certain kind of performer, the role-player, out of the shared experience of the game. These games generate complex spheres of identity—both diegetically (in-the-game) and non-diegetically (in-the-real-world)—i.e., the social identity of the player, created during and around the narrative's performance, and the fictional identity of the player-character, created within the performance. As such, an understanding of the role-playing performance requires an analysis of the structure of these games and of the phenomenology of play within that structure.

Spheres and Frames: The Structure of the Role-Playing Game

Richard Schechner's theory of performance provides a good start for an understanding of the environment of the role-playing game performance. Schechner defines performance as "ritualized behavior conditioned/permeated by play . . . a specific coordination of play and ritual." He then makes this definition more meaningful by placing it in the context of five discrete yet porous concentric spheres, which are, from smallest to largest—*Drama, Script, Theater, Performance, and Ritual:*

Drama is tight, verbal narrative; it allows for little improvisation; it exists as a code independent of any individual transmitter; it is, or can easily be made into, a written text. A script—which can be either tight or loose—is either a plan for a traditional event . . . or it is developed during rehearsals to suit a specific text as in orthodox western theater. The theater is the visible/sonic set of events consisting either of well-known components . . . or of a score invented during rehearsal. . . . To some degree the theater is the visible aspect of the script, the exterior topography of an interior map. Performance is the widest possible circle of events condensing around theater. The audience is the dominant element of any performance. . . . [finally,] ritualized behavior extends across the entire range of human action, but performance is a particularly heated arena of ritual, and theater, script, and drama are heated and compact areas of performance." (*Performance Theory* 91-95)

Applying these five spheres to the role-playing game, we see that the rulebook is analogous to *Drama*—a "tight, verbal narrative . . . code independent of any individual transmitter." There are significant differences between a traditional dramatic text and a published role-playing game—for example, Schechner's drama "allows for little improvisation," while the role-playing game is a performance system which requires improvisation. In any case, the rules establish a flexible yet invariant structure that provides role-players with an initial sense of security. "Play," Schechner asserts, "is dangerous and, because it is, players need to feel secure in order to begin playing" (*Future* 26). At conventions and local gaming centers, it is most often the rules that bring a group of role-players together. At this stage, the players begin to form what Gary Fine calls an "idioculture"; i.e., a "system of knowledge, beliefs, behaviors, and customs peculiar to an interacting group to which members refer and which they employ as the basis of further interaction [and to] construct a shared universe of discourse" (*Shared* 136). When security has been established and the idioculture has taken primary shape and play is well underway, players become more adventurous, for "risk, danger, and insecurity are part of playing's thrill" (Schechner, *Future* 27). In keeping with this, after a narrative has formed around a specific rules-system, the players will often proceed to make changes to the system in order to accommodate their own innovations, which reflect both the contributions of individuals and the group dynamic.

The *Script* of the role-playing session is an inflated sphere of influence which includes the *Drama,* but adds the contributions of the narrative's individual players. Whereas the script in Schechner's model is either a "plan for a traditional event" or a plan developed during rehearsals specific to a dramaturgical production, the role-playing game's narrative script is the result of the Game Master's various preparations for each episode coupled with the players' hopes, plans, concerns, and ambitions for their characters, as prescribed by the game system. According to one player, ". . . the rules [for Dungeons & Dragons] are like Aristotle's *Poetics*. . . . They tell me how to put together a good play. And a [Game Master] is the playwright who reads these things and puts his play together" (Fine, *Fantasy* 88). What this role-player is identifying, in Schechner's terms, is the creation of the role-playing game session's script, or plan of action, from the drama and his contributions as Game Master.

In addition to creating the scenario for each session, the Game Master is responsible for creating and role-playing all non-player characters with whom the player-characters meet and interact. Preparing for the game session often requires a great deal of writing. Players must compose not only episode plot outlines, and maps, but also descriptions of non-player characters, vehicles, equipment, spells, monsters, and alien races. Players may also be asked (or may volunteer) to write background material about their characters or maintain logs of what happened during prior sessions. Sometimes, a player may even share some of the world-building chores by writing, drawing, or mapping a description of her hometown, her spaceship, or her homeworld (depending on the setting and scope of the game). While most communication during the game is oral, note-passing between players, or between player and Game Master, is common. Game Master, game designer, and writer Aaron Allston coined the term "blue-booking" for his method of having players use college exam booklets to record private dialogues with the Game Master and other players during the session. Blue books were also used to record what a character might do in between sessions (Fannon also notes that e-mail is taking over this last function [238]). In any case, it is important to note that the role-playing game script is not solely in the Game Master's hands, for he does not determine what the characters will do and where the characters will go in the fictional world—this is largely determined by the player-characters themselves.

It is difficult to separate this third sphere of *Theater* from the fourth of *Performance* due to the absence of performer-spectator division. Normally, role-playing games do not include observers who remain apart from the action. The distinction between performer and spectator is, however, inherent in Schechner's separation between these two categories. One might be tempted to say that these two spheres merge in the role-playing game; a useful distinction, however, can be made here. In the role-playing game, the *Theater* is the "visible/sonic set of events" (and sometimes written—in the form of notes passed between players or between player and Game Master) that occurs around the game table and that is available only to the player-characters and the non-player characters (controlled by the Game Master). The *Performance,* on the other hand, is the set of events available to the players themselves and the Game Master, which includes all of the characters' interactions (*Theater*) as well as out-of-character remarks and events.

To pursue this further, we must shift our analysis from Schechner's spheres to another useful model—Fine's appropriation of Goffman's system of frame analysis to identify "finite worlds of meaning" within the role-playing game performance (*Shared Fantasy* 181). According to

Fine, there are three main frames of reference operating within the role-playing game performance: 1) The Social Frame inhabited by the person; 2) The Game Frame inhabited by the player; and 3) The Gaming World Frame inhabited by the character. Like Schechner's spheres, these perceptual frames are fluid, shifting, and porous. Fine likens them to laminations that support the subsequent layering of one frame upon the other, each incorporating, but not invalidating, the others. Within a role-playing game session, players, generally responding to a change in communicative protocol, constantly switch frames, often in mid-sentence.

In the course of a game, I could operate in the social frame and address a fellow player by name, perhaps asking him about something that happened to him on his way to my house. I could also address that player *qua* player, asking him how many hit points his character had remaining before he fell unconscious after suffering a wound, or how many spells his character could memorize at one time. Third, I could address that player in-character. Fine provides, for example, an account of a group of players discussing various games they had participated in. When one player asked another, "where were you?," the reply was, "in Detroit," to which the first player replied, "no, in the game," and with this clarification, he finally got an appropriate response: "over by some huts" (*Shared* 201).

Fine identifies the function of engrossment as a motivating principle behind the role-players' switching (or not switching) between frames: games are "engrossable" to the extent that players become "caught up" in the game; such engrossment, however, has an intermittent quality—it depends on events that occur in the game world (*Shared* 196). Fine demonstrates this principle through the account of a game player who says:

". . . I would guess that as the game gets more and more interesting people do less and less talking out of character. . . . I'm sure that there are times when [talking out of character] can be very, very frustrating to referees, 'cause like I was reffing a game once, and the players kept making comments about the room and how the water didn't taste very good. . . . I would suspect that as the game got more and more intense, people would stick more and more to the game itself." (qtd. in *Shared* 197 f.)

This player's observations corroborate my own experience as a player. I have found that the most memorable and meaningful moments were those in which all players were in-character, when it didn't matter how the water in the room tasted because no one was reaching for a drink. This applies to my own duties as Game Master as well: I had the most fun, and felt the closest to my players, when I was having conversations with them in-character as a non-player character. Note that this is not the same as describing the action of another character I was in control of as Game Master: it is only true when I was pretending to be that character, speaking their words and addressing those words to a specific character in our group.

This suggests some further distinctions with which we can refine Fine's model, particularly with reference to his third frame, that of the "game world" in which the player is "in character." Actually, the player's role in the game world is not merely that of playing a character, because it takes on three specific forms based on modes of address. Fine's third category accurately describes the player's activity in the first-person mode of address—the role-player is in-character, speaking in the first person as the character. A player is in this frame when he speaks as a character. We can imagine a character saying something like, "I'll not cross that river until after sunset." In this frame, when the player speaks, the character lives. Unlike dramaturgical theatre, however, a player's body is not generally seen as being synonymous with the character's body. In a role-playing game, there are no casting considerations—there is no limit to the kind of role you can play, other than the limits prescribed by the subjectivity the role-playing game rulebooks create, for the events of the role-playing game occur within the imagination of the players.

But there is also a frame that is characterized by third-person address, in which role-players and Game Master assume a story-teller, or *raconteur,* relationship to their characters via narrating their characters' actions and possible actions in the third-person. A player would be in this frame if he told me, "There's no way my character's gonna swim across until it's dark!" The player's speech act is not the character's.

There is also a second-person mode of address. Borrowing the concept of the "constative utterance" from J. L. Austin's work on the performative possibilities of language, the constative frame is marked by what I call "the address" and occurs when the Game Master describes settings and situations to the players in-character and in the second person. I provide the following fabrication as an example:

You walk into a room filled with a damp, mold-stench. The light filters through in rays from angled windows a dozen feet above your heads on either wall. In these white rays the visible puffs of air that are your breaths can be seen intermingling and rising into invisibility in the absolute darkness of the space above the sunlight. This space, indeterminately tall, is plumbed only by your redolent expirations—now detached from any nerve center with which you might gauge the height of the ceiling that you can feel looming over you, but in blackness remains completely unseen.

This frame is a descriptive one; it is usually the province of the Game Master, although players may lapse into it when describing their character's actions. The notes that are sometimes passed between players and Game Master are most often written from the constative frame: "you see . . . ," "you hear . . . ," "it occurs to you. . . ." Although all frames are unstable—and players are constantly flickering between them as Fine describes—the constative frame is particularly unstable because in being addressed in the second person players sometimes forget that they are being addressed as their character, not as their social selves. The constative frame is an out-of-character frame, yet, it remains in the realm of what Fine identifies as the "game world."

The above distinctions, then, reconfigure Fine's three frames into a five-frame model of the role-playing game performance: 1) The Social Frame, which is inhabited by the person; 2) The Game Frame, which is inhabited by the player; 3) The Narrative Frame, inhabited by the *raconteur;* 4) The Constative Frame, inhabited by the addresser; and 5) The Performative Frame, inhabited by the character. Taken together with Schechner's spheres, these frames indicate the complexity of behavior within the role-playing game.

Finally, we need to consider all of the above with reference to Schechner's fifth and largest sphere, that of *Ritual.* Role-playing games constitute a specific kind of ritual, one efficacious for the small group of role-players. The ritual of role-playing takes place, as all ritual does, within a larger cultural sphere; however, it is embodied—put into practice—at an idiocultural level, i.e. among a small group of friends.

The Phenomenology of Play in the Role-Playing Game

Play within the role-playing game's imaginary entertainment environment is one of simulation rather than imitation; as such, it is best described by what Baudrillard calls simulacra, a milieu in which "Simulation is no longer that of a territory, a referential being, or a substance. It is the generation by models of a real without origin or reality: a hyperreal. The territory no longer precedes the map, nor does it survive it" (1). The concept of the simulacra is found earlier, in Barthes' "The Structuralist Activity," in which he first establishes that the reality status of the object in question is irrelevant: "It is of little consequence," he writes, "whether the initial object liable to the simulacrum activity is given by the world in an already assembled fashion . . . or is still scattered . . . [or]

whether this initial object is drawn from a social reality or an imaginary reality" (1129).

The "structuralist activity" is one in which *homo significans*—humankind as "defined not by his ideas or his languages, but by his imagination" (1128)—reconstructs an object

in such a way as to manifest thereby the rules of functioning (the "functions") of this object. Structure is therefore actually a simulacrum of the object, but a directed, interested simulacrum, since the imitated object makes something appear which remained invisible, or if one prefers, unintelligible in the natural object. Structural man takes the real, decomposes it, then recomposes it. . . . [B]etween the two objects, or the two tenses, of structuralist activity, there occurs something new, and what is new is nothing less than the generally intelligible. (1128)

This activity corresponds to two different operations within the role-playing game performance. The first level is the formal structure of the game itself: the one in which the "object" that is reconstructed is the fantasy world of the imaginary entertainment environment and its characters. Such reconstruction begins with the decomposition of the object, a fragmentation into meaningless or context-less units which are grouped according to a specific pattern (called a "paradigm" in linguistics). It is from this paradigm, what Barthes likens to a reservoir, that "one summons, by an act of citation, the object or unit one wishes to endow with an actual meaning" (1129). For example, in the role-playing game's formal structure, role-players use the rules in order to simulate reality by dissecting their perception of reality, with all its fluid subjectivity, into units appropriate for quantifying a character. In the Advanced Dungeons & Dragons game (1978), for example, the game's rules determine that a character is structured from a paradigm that includes six attributes (strength, dexterity, constitution, intelligence, wisdom, and charisma) and four orientations (warrior, wizard, priest, and rogue). Additional paradigms include moral alignments and proficiencies.

The second level of the structuralist activity in the role-playing game performance is the social structure of the idioculture and subculture: the one in which the objects that are reconstructed are the role-players themselves, not their fictional characters, but the actual subjectivities and self-identities of the players as they operate within the role-playing game performance and larger spheres (e.g., *Ritual*). Here, the role-player's own identity is reconfigured according to the rulebook. This level of the structuralist activity entails the creation of identity and, subsequently, community, both based on the text of a role-playing game as it is embodied during social interactions.

In *The Act of Reading,* Wolfgang Iser makes the fundamental observation that while the reader organizes the text in order to create meaning, the text, conversely and simultaneously, organizes the reader. The paradigm of the reading process Iser identifies as the "blank"—the all-important arrangement of unspecified spaces within the text, which the reader's imagination fills in so as to create the story. The blanks in the text are filled with the reader's images, and in this way, the written code of the text uses its blanks to create a text-specific reader—an act of identity creation dependent upon the string of images the blanks evoke in the reader (203).

The role-player who reads a role-playing game text (either a rulebook, sourcebook, or work of fiction that the reader associates with a particular role-playing game) is created by that text. The role-player's everyday quotidian self (which itself is created by the quotidian environment and the repetitious interactions of day-to-day affairs) is reconfigured into a reading-self, a series of images culled from the same reservoir of experiences shared with the quotidian self, but restructured according to the written code and blanks of the text. Sometimes the reading-self transcends the reading experience for a few moments until the everyday reality reconfigures the reading-self back to the quotidian self. During such moments, the player-as-reading-self is coming from the same perspective as when she was ordered by the symbolic code of the text. In such circumstances, the player-as-reading-self is that much more likely to see correspondences between what she read and her experiences in her extrinsic environment.

During the decompositional operation of the process, the reading-self is merely a succession of images drawn from the paradigm of textual blanks, or as Iser says: "a clash of images that keeps separating us from our own products" (Iser, *Act* 188). The reading-self is nothing more than fragments of an imagination, just as the role-player's character, in the formal structure of the game, is nothing more than a series of quantified fragments loosely coalesced around game system-determined paradigms.

The second of the structuralist activity's two operations is the act of assemblage, of creation, from the decontextualized fragments and units that were dissected from the object during the first operation of the process. "What is happening, at this second stage of the simulacrum activity," Barthes writes, "is a kind of battle against chance; this is why the constraint of recurrence of the units has an almost demiurgic value: it is by the regular return of the units and of the associations of units that the work appears constructed, i.e., endowed with meaning" (1129). Within the social structure of the role-playing game, the game's text keeps the string of images within the player's "reading-self" from being more than an effect of chance. The reader is reduced to a sequence of images—structured according to the text's paradigmatic blanks—which remain scattered until the reader's own experience and activity provides a sense of unity to the experience.

We see this happening in the way a player constructs a character. It is this character concept that, ideally, renders intelligible the fragments with which the character is defined. In one particular performance of a role-playing game (AD&D system) for which I served as Game Master, a player named Wesley created the character Dom Ixhil Contelliat. Within the *Drama* sphere of the game, Ixhil Contelliat was defined as being a fifth level neutral evil dom (warrior priest) with a 16 Strength, 8 Intelligence, 15 Wisdom, and 13 Charisma. Within the *Script* sphere of the game, however, Wesley assembled these units into an intelligible character concept: Ixhil was raised since his boyhood as a slave in Scornubul. There, growing from boy to adolescent to man as a manual laborer (high Strength), Ixhil contemplated his lot, comparing himself to the free men he saw stepping forth from the shadows of the marketplace: merchants and thieves hungry for power and cutting deals to get ahead in a world with little hope for peace. Ixhil grew strong but learned to disdain material comforts and rewards; he grew wise in the ways of men (high Wisdom), but vowed to serve his god Myrkul, the god of death, by sending Him souls, and thereby relieving miserable mankind of its burden of pain and desire. Ixhil spent his time seething at his captors— and he regarded everybody as his captors. Yet he learned control and could manipulate people to his own ends (moderate Charisma). He was ambivalent about earthly law and chose to enslave himself to his evil god only when he was finally freed of his terrestrial enslavement (neutral Evil), becoming a dom in his service. Ixhil, however, had never received school lessons in basic disciplines, could not read, practice arithmetic, nor successfully debate (low Intelligence).

The character concept is the point of origin for a character, but the words the player speaks in-character, in response to the constellation of addresses that occur during a session, become the inborn character concept that the player could not have identified when he first set himself upon the task of creating a character. Merleau-Ponty has observed a similar phenomenon during any form of speech-giving:

The orator does not think before speaking, nor even while speaking; his speech is his thought [. . . .] The orator's "thought" is empty while he is speaking and, when a text is read to us, provided that it is read with expression, we have no thought marginal to the text itself, for the words fully occupy our mind and exactly fulfill our expectations, and we feel the necessity of the speech.

Although we are unable to predict its course, we are possessed by it. The end of the speech or text will be the lifting of the spell. (*Phenomenology* 180)

In a sense, a player's in-character speech or gesture is a form of sensory reception—the player acts the part of the character, and upon reflection, makes an object of himself through utterances such as: "I just said this" or "I just did that, hmm that's uncharacteristic of me." The player's thought is emptied and a sensory receptivity occurs—gesture is sensory reception. As Merleau-Ponty observes:

Just as the sense-giving intention which has set in motion the other person's speech is not an explicit thought, but a certain lack which is asking to be made good, so my taking up of this intention is not a process of thinking on my part, but a synchronizing of my own existence, a transformation of my being (*Phenomenology* 183 f.)

In becoming a gesturing-percipient (a perceiver who perceives through action), the player empties himself of thought and becomes receptive to the acoustic, physical efficacy of his own gesture (once again: "we feel the necessity of the speech") as he plays the character. This gesture, becoming receptive to its own "spell" (to use Merleau-Ponty's term), sets itself up as a self-generated address for the player to perceive. As he perceives his own gestures (as the character) as an object, the circuit of role-playing is continued, for the role-played gesture continues the alterity of the player: in effect, the player, through the role-played gesture, addresses himself as an other within the imaginary *mise-en-scène* of the game. By addressing himself as "other," the player merely has to respond as "other" (in the role of the character), and the circuit of imaginary personas is perpetuated. The player perpetually addresses himself through gesture and speech, thereby becoming the object of his own address.

We should also note here that the creation of character in the game is not a solitary act but is significantly influenced by the idioculture that forms around the game and the interactions of the players. Thus, it was not only Wesley's proactive desire to role-play Ixhil Contelliat that elicited a performance of that character: it was equally his reaction to his being addressed as Ixhil that encouraged Wesley to stay in character—in the performative frame. This demonstrates the unique aspect of the role-playing game I have called "the address"—player-characters address themselves from a first-person performative basis to each individual character on a per-character basis, usually in the second person (constative frame). The address is the adhesive that fixes characters in their roles: in addressing a player as another character, not only are you encouraging him to react to that address by remaining in-character, but his in-character response to you will be an address that will stabilize your performative experience in the theater of the game. Furthermore, during Wesley's performance, he may engage in the frame-switching we have already described. He may, for example, switch between the *raconteur* frame and speak of himself in the third person (e.g., Wesley says, "Ixhil waves his hand over the city in a doom-foreshadowed gesture of contempt") or, during a speech act or gesture, employ a first person perspective (e.g., Wesley, as if he were Ixhil, waves his arm before him, within inches of another player who, grinning, sits next to him).

This process of fabricating a character can, in turn, render the player's own subjectivity and self-identity intelligible in a world in which people are archived according to credit ratings, income tax returns, I.Q. tests, student exams, on-the-job evaluations, and consumer habits. In other words, after going through the process of creating a cohesive character from fragments and bits, players can carry this experience over to their own lives. Role-playing game groups usually form when a critical mass of like-minded role-players congregate because of a shared experience with a role-playing game or games. In such circumstances, all the players exhibit reading-selves that have been ordered by a common set of role-playing game texts; those reading-selves, furthermore, persist during the players' ventures into gaming culture (whether it be at a convention, recreation center, local gaming club, etc.). In this way, the players' experience with the role-playing game text and the *Drama* sphere shapes not only their character creation process (*Script* sphere), but their own self-identity and group identity (*Ritual* sphere). A shared experience with the written word allows players to communicate more deeply than mere cultural reappropriation and fantasy sharing; it allows for players to transform the giddiness and excitement associated with product art (the anxious arousal advertisers stir up in consumers) into a basis for human relations founded upon trust and respect—indeed, a basis for a new social network. I have observed this process many times among my role-player friends, many of whom confess to experiencing a sense of unity underlying the chaos and fragmentation of everyday reality. The structuralist activity "highlights the strictly human process by which men give meaning to things. Is this new?" Barthes asks. He then answers:

Of course the world has never stopped looking for the meaning of what is given it and of what it produces; what is new is a mode of thought (or a "poetics") which seeks less to assign completed meanings to the objects it discovers than to know how meaning is possible, at what cost and by what means. Ultimately, one might say that the object of structuralism is not man endowed with meanings, but man fabricating meanings. (1130)

Perhaps this is why, in the United States, much of the hostility and aggression against the role-playing game has come from the religious right. Accusing the role-playing game of being an avenue to satanic worship and occult practices, what the religious right is really at war with is an alternative social world, in which "men give meaning to things" and, moreover, try to render intelligible the process behind creation. The role-playing game narrative and the imaginary entertainment environment are manifestations of this search. And, unendowed with the grace of the Divine Spirit to enlighten their imaginations, role-players—left to look outward to popular culture and inward within themselves for their images and meaning-construction—have rattled the shepherds of the lost flock.

Note

1. This essay is a drawn from Mackay's master's thesis, "The Dolorous Role: Toward an Aesthetic of the Role Playing Game" (New York University, Tisch School of the Arts, 1997), which provides a much more detailed analysis of the role-playing game performance (Eds.)

Works Cited and Consulted

Austin, J. L. *How to Do Things with Words*. Cambridge: Harvard UP, 1962.

Barthes, Roland. "The Structuralist Activity." 1964. *Critical Theory Since Plato*. Rev ed. Ed. Hazzard Adams. New York: Harcourt Brace Jovanovitch, 1992. 1128-33.

Bateson, Gregory. *Steps to an Ecology of Mind*. New York: Ballantine, 1972.

Baudrillard, Jean. *Simulacra and Simulation*. 1981. Trans. Sheila Faria Glaser. Ann Arbor: U Michigan P, 1994.

Cataldi, Sue L. *Emotion, Depth and Flesh*. Albany, NY: SUNY P, 1993.

Fannon, Sean Patrick. *The Fantasy Role-Playing Gamer's Bible*. Rocklin, CA: Prima, 1996.

Fine, Deborah, and Aeon Inc. *Star Wars Chronicles*. San Francisco: Chronicle, 1997.

Fine, Gary Alan. *Shared Fantasy: Role-Playing Games as Social Worlds*. U of Chicago P, 1983.

Goffman, Erving. *Frame Analysis*. Cambridge: Harvard UP, 1974.

Iser, Wolfgang. *The Act of Reading: A Theory of Aesthetic Response.* Baltimore: Johns Hopkins UP, 1978.

———. *The Implied Reader: Patterns of Communication in Prose Fiction from Bunyan to Beckett.* Baltimore: Johns Hopkins UP, 1974.

Kausch, Allan. "Star Wars Timeline." *Star Wars Insider* 35 (1997): (insert).

Merleau-Ponty, Maurice. *Phenomenology of Perception.* New York: Routledge, 1982.

———. *The Visible and the Invisible.* Evanston, IL: Northwestern UP, 1968.

Schechner, Richard. *Between Theater & Anthropology.* Philadelphia: U of Pennsylvania P, 1985.

———. *The Future of Ritual: Writings on Culture and Performance.* London: Routledge, 1993.

———. *Performance Theory.* New York: Routledge, 1988.

7

THE SPELL OF THE SENSUOUS:
CASINO ATMOSPHERE AND THE GAMBLER—AN EXPANSION

Felicia F. Campbell

David Abram's book of ecological philosophy, *The Spell of the Sensuous: Perception and Language in a More-Than Human World*, draws on personal interviews with shamans from around the world as well as Husserl's phenomenology and Merleau-Ponty's radicalization of phenomenology. In this study of the shamanic experience, Abram comes to define perception as an "an open activity . . . a dynamic blend of receptivity and creativity by which every animate organism necessarily orients itself to the world (and orients the world around itself)" (50). This has broad applications: the shaman in the jungle who enters into a relationship with nature in which he loses a sense of individual identity by merging with the greater whole is not so different from the gambler who enters into a relationship with the virtual or artificial reality of the casino, propelling him into the altered state of the "action."

As we are all aware, our physical perceptions are limited to our five senses; thus we can never fully comprehend an object. For example, we can see only the part of a slot machine immediately before our eyes, and cannot view the back, sides, top and bottom at the same time we see the front. Neither can we see the mechanics of the machine without opening it, nor can we discover the molecular structure without destroying the object as a whole. Perception of those parts of the machine that we do see changes with each gaze because of shifts in lights, dust or age. Each object presents facets which catch the eye while simultaneously hiding others. When the body responds to this presentation, the thing that it is responding to answers in kind by inviting us to focus our senses on it. Perception then, as Abram echoing Merleau-Ponty points out, is "this reciprocity, the ongoing interchange between my body and the entities that surround it. . . . a sort of silent conversation that I carry on with things, a continuous dialogue that unfolds far below my verbal awareness—and often . . . *independent* of my verbal awareness . . . an impoverished duet between my animal and the fluid, breathing landscape that it inhabits" (52-53).

It is this reciprocity between object and observer that the casinos exploit so expertly, creating their very special environments for the gambler to traverse as he seeks the altered state that is "the action." Make no mistake, casinos, for good or ill, are, for many, power places where they enter an altered state to test their favor with the gods of chance. As the shaman enters the jungle or desert, so the gambler may well begin his journey to an altered state at McCarran airport, moving from the gate, through banks of slot machines arranged under surreal metallic palm trees and onto the moving walkway where unseen voices of celebrities speak, exhorting him to stand on the right to allow those walking to move past him on the left. Inside the terminal, more metallic palm trees and glitzy shops compete with scale models of casinos in progress to begin to define the geography of this special place. Huge ceiling-hung television screens in the baggage area beckon him to the delights of the Strip, as the real world is left behind.

By his very perception of these new elements of environment, he is, as Abram would say, entering "into relation with it," experiencing "a living interaction with another being." Referring to nature's trees, he notes that referring to trees as inert objects denies "the ability of a tree to inform and even instruct one's awareness, is to have turned one's senses away from that phenomenon" (117). By analogy, the same may be said of interactions with the metallic trees which are part of the landscape that serves to plunge our voyager more deeply into this alternate reality.

Consider the gambler, now sniffing the air of the Strip, first deciding which casino calls to him, then after selecting and entering it, looking for the table or machine with his name on it. Something will draw him to his "lucky" table or machine and he will insist that there is a kind of communication between himself and the object.

Of course, gaming paraphernalia is designed to foster this "communications." All kinds of slot machines, of course, have one to one relationships with their players, even though the players would argue that there is something special about a particular machine in a bank of seemingly identical machines that call to them. Early slot machines were ornately engraved, drawing the eye to their nonlinear artwork. Some were the carved upper torsos of western characters such as cowboys or dance hall girls with the machines set into their chests. Early slot machines required that the player interact by pulling a handle and the player was rewarded by the sounds and feel of innards of the machine as the reels clinked into place. Today's electronic machines attempt to reproduce the illusion of control that players had with the older machines by giving them the choice of pulling a handle, pushing a button or placing a finger on the screen. Really "in" gamblers are initiates of the casinos' various clubs and ritually insert their electronically encoded cards into the machines, amassing points as they win or lose, and leaving a profile of their play encoded in casino files.

Pack Schmidt, anti-hero of Edward Allen's comic novel, *Mustang Sally,* is a third-rate professor at a third-rate university in the midwest, where he feels life is being leached out of him. A devoted but low-roller gambler, he finds a kind of rebirth in Las Vegas and expresses his reaction to the Vegas scene this way:

But it's not just the games; it's the whole town, something I can feel in the back of my jaw every time I see a picture of the Strip on television, the way the town bathes itself in light, the way you can just walk into it and get lost and nobody will come chasing you with papers to grade. . . . after one of these trips, when I go home again to my office, and the house. . . . everything goes better for a few weeks. I stride from office to parking lot, my briefcase swinging briskly at my side and I feel perked up and cleaned out, like a man who has just had a session on a kidney dialysis machine. (14-15)

Clearly there is a reciprocity, a give and take, between Schmidt and the overarching environment. That it's possible to sit on the Bellagio's balcony watching the multicolored play of waters on an ersatz Lake Como and view the Eiffel Tower at the same time, or stand outside of Caesar's Forum and listen to the whistle of an old time Riverboat moored next to the Imperial Palace, adds to the surreal nature of the journey. Perhaps as Abram believes . . . "the human intellect (is) in, and secretly borne by our forgotten contact with the multiple non-human shapes that surround us" (49). Again referencing Merleau-Ponty, Abram suggests that the world of perception involves "attunement or synchronization" between one's own rhythms and the rhythm of the thing perceived. The way we dress, the way we walk, the way we wear our collars; all are ways of synchronizing ourselves with our environments. All are part of a "ceaseless dance between the carnal subject and its world" (54). Things beckon to us as we interact with them.

Pack Schmidt, our very small-time gambler who refers to himself as "The Hero with a Thousand Dollars," sniffs Las Vegas and remarks, "Everything sits out in front of me, unspoiled like a new deck of cards, like fresh pins in a bowling alley, though I don't bowl anymore" (12), and sees the night laid out in front of him like "a big toy" which reactivates all of his favorite superstitions, which include wearing for luck a herringbone jacket, missing a decorative button on one cuff (17). Clearly, he is preparing himself for engagement with the gods of chance, as a shaman will ritually prepare himself for engagement with the spirits.

He finds it odd to think that when he isn't present "these lights flash just as frantically for everybody else" (25).

Of course, he's wrong, as a gambler in her mid-sixties said to me, "When I come to Vegas, it's as though the whole city were putting on a huge party and it's just for me. I blend with it and while I'm walking through deciding where to play and during all the time I'm playing, I'm not my usual self but someone entirely different who is part of the whole wonderful whole." Another gambler described coming to Las Vegas like starring in a movie, completely leaving the mundane world behind, something made easier by the theming of casinos which allows him to select from various scenarios and landscapes. What happens to gamblers like them and the fictional Schmidt is what Abram describes in terms of the natural world when he explains that "In contact with the native forms of the earth, one's senses are slowly energized and awakened, combining and recombining in ever-shifting patterns" (63).

Those of us whose affinities lie with and have spent any length of time in the natural world as compared to the technological world are aware of the soothing and invigorating nature of chaotic landscapes in which eternal patterns exist, yet are never repeated in exactly the same fashion. Turbulent streams, jagged mountain peaks, desert dunes, irregular forests, all speak to us in a way that the harsh linear geometries of the contemporary cities, factories and offices in which most of us are imprisoned cannot. Our economy is based on convincing us that fulfillment lies in our interactions with newer-model houses or cars or pairs of athletic shoes, but, as Abram points out, manufactured items from milk cartons to washing machines have a certain life, but are *constrained* (italics mine) by the specific functions for which they were designed, thus are limited in what they can teach us, and reiterate without variation, requiring us to "continually acquire new built technologies, the latest model of this or that if we wish to stimulate ourselves." He goes on to discuss the stultifying nature of "the superstraight lines and right angles of our office architecture" which "make our animal senses wither even as they support the abstract intellect" causing "the earth-born nature of the materials" to be lost "behind the abstract and calculable form" (64.) These linear objects lack the lure of the fractal.

Casinos, while linear in their function to take as much money as possible from the gambler, blur their linearity by becoming on the surface labyrinthine fantasy worlds. While manufactured, like works of art, they are built to speak to us, to lure us, to stimulate us into merging with them, and to convince us that they are ever-changing, drawing us into other worlds, illuminated by countless, flashing multicolored lights. The topography of the casino eliminates as many linear reference points as possible through mirrors, blinking lights on everything from the slot machines to the earrings of the cocktail waitresses, non-linearly patterned carpeting in bold colors, clustered groups of slot machines contributing to the absence of straight aisles. As Pack notes, the casino "rings and churns" as he attempts to find an exit hidden so that "you will get lost and find yourself at the tables again and lose all your money" (82). This planned disorientation contributes to the altered state.

The smashing of time also contributes to this state. Linear time stops inside a casino where there are neither clocks nor windows to give the usual sensory clues dealing with the passage of time. Absorption in the action, as absorption in any creative activity, makes the usual passage of time seem to disappear and this is exacerbated by the marked absence of clues. For table players time is marked only by the regular rhythm of changing of dealers as they go on their breaks. Machine players lack even this marker.

The point is that, in some strange way, the constantly changing features of the gaming casinos seem to make up the other end of the spectrum of the chaotic landscapes of nature in which patterns constantly iterate, or repeat, yet are never exactly the same, leading to the altered state of consciousness which I am paralleling with the shamanic state.

Looking along the two and one-half miles of the Las Vegas Strip, the gambler sees a dream landscape where the Sphinx vies for attention with the Eiffel Tower and the St. Louis Arch. Here a piña-colada-scented volcano erupts on schedule like Old Faithful in front of the Mirage, while a pirate ship and a Spanish galleon do battle in front of Treasure Island. While masses of tourists stand gawking, the true gambler passes through part of all he surveys.

Our fictional Schmidt uses the imagery of nature to describe the Strip. "From the darkness of the valley floor," he rhapsodizes, "hotels rise in a soft light, like tropical shells. . . ." As he gazes at the massive shapes of huge hotels, he "can almost hear the casino sound, an ocean of bells and of buzzers. . . . I can't wait to let that sound wash all over me. To let it rinse away the musty smell that collects in my office when it's too cold to open the window" (20). In another spot, he refers to "the casino sound, like a thousand cash registers and a thousand video games all jumbled together in a kind of musical surf of bells and wheels and coins dropping into metal pans" (24). We get the definite feeling that he reacts far more strongly to the casino environment than he would to the sea to which he compares it.

A sense of smell is, of course, a large part of our sensory experience, and the odor of casinos is distinctive. While some casinos have found that spraying aromas, such an apple scent, increases wagers, for

Schmidt the normal casino smell is enough to transport him. Neither clean nor dirty, mixed with substances from tobacco to sweat, perfume and halitosis, he says casino air "is blended and softened to produce something warm and round and lived-in" (24). This is for him an essential part of the experience, and so important to him that he gambles only at tables where people are smoking. Even though he is a non-smoker, he feels that non-smoking tables are unlucky, the smoke somehow part of the ambiance. Thus, as Merleau-Ponty explains, at the heart of even our most abstract thoughts is "the sensuous and sentient life of the body itself" (45). The body in this sense is not the mechanized body of sinews and bones, but the body as it actually experiences things. This eliminates the dichotomy between body and soul in terms of sensate experiences. As Abram puts it, "the body is my very means of entering into relation with all things" (47).

Recognizing a tenet of chaos theory that everything is connected to everything else, the gambler, like the shaman or magician, may draw heavily on superstition or magic. Schmidt never uses the word win and believes it is good luck to be polite even to machines (29). He can "feel the presence of luck, like a ghost hanging over the huge signs, over the excited flowery torch of the Flamingo," over everything. Even the wind joins in as it blows down the Strip, a sign of good luck. Like the shaman or sorcerer, Schmidt has entered into the altered state by shedding the accepted perceptual logic of his culture. Like the shaman, Schmidt has "the ability to readily slip out of the perceptual boundaries that demarcate his particular culture—boundaries reinforced by social customs, taboos, and most importantly, common speech or language, in order to make contact with, and learn from, the other powers in the land" (10).

He is not alone. Gamblers' rituals are too numerous to catalogue here, but some typical behaviors of gamblers may help to illustrate. I'll begin with machine gamblers. One is the Lover whose hands move softly over the machine as though it were a beloved other, trying to lure it into spewing its riches into his hands. Not for nothing is gambling parlance studded with sexual terms like betting "the come" or the "don't come." The Patter, a variation on the Lover, softly pats the sides of the machine all the while talking to it. The Pleader maintains a constant dialogue with the machine, usually referring to it as "baby" as he begs for its favors. Thumpers beat a rhythmic tattoo on the side of the machine while Ragers are almost always male and literally pound the machines with their fists, seeming to believe that they can force them into submission. Prayers sit silently with constantly moving lips. Singers, usually out of tune, and Whistlers are the most annoying to other players. All, however, regardless of their annoyance factor are totally absorbed in "the action" within the world of the machine, largely unaware of anything going on around them and often of their own behaviors. Many gamblers have a set of lucky numbers they constantly bet on keno and some male craps players refuse to bet if a woman is shooting.

When he is in Las Vegas, Schmidt recognizes his place in the scheme of things. Chaos theorists know that everything affects everything else, and so does Schmidt, who realizes that timing is everything: ". . . See a penny, pick it up, change the world—walk in the front door of the Riviera one second later, one second earlier, and the world is transformed" (17). Later, "every time I turn my head I cause myself to step up to the crap table a second later, every step I take changes the world. What a responsibility" (71). Like the shaman, Schmidt alters the common organization of his senses to enter into rapport with the non-human sensibilities that animate the local landscape (Abram 9).

Here in the neon jungle, Schmidt achieves a kind of vitality and rootedness that he cannot find in his normal environment and is unlikely to search for in nature. He likes fur, but on women, not animals (21). He has isolated himself from nature, but not from a need for sensate experience, an experience that for good or ill moves ever closer to virtual reality. Casinos even present a kind of in-house camaraderie. A fellow feeling exists for card players that is not present in the real world. At the blackjack table, players all face the same odds whether they are betting $5 or $500 and have a common adversary in the dealer. Here cultural and racial differences disappear during the action, often to be replaced after the players leave the tables.

Clearly everything about casinos is designed to assist gamblers in slipping the perceptual boundaries of their worlds. Linear time and space are smashed. Themed casinos representing diverse historical eras and geographical settings destroy the concept of an orderly, linear timeline and traditional geography and our gambler is well aware that like Dorothy, he is not in Kansas anymore.

Schmidt sums up his experience, saying, "Oh, my town, Vegas, my new plaything, merciless and soft. Sometime when I get drunk I am going to bend over, with my ass toward Mecca, and kiss the shampooed carpeting of my motel room, because this has been a difficult year" (27). He is a small-time gambler, but high rollers who seldom breathe the same casino air as small-time gamblers are just as ritualistic, their journey to the action on a different path. They will not pay for their luxurious suites which could rent for as much as $200,000 were anyone foolish enough to pay for one, nor the limousines that ferry them to and from the airport or around the city. They will play in special rooms protected from the hordes below. When they arrive, host casinos will designate special personnel to make sure that their every whim is satisfied; a casino is aware of the preferences of the high roller from wine to entertainment and sets out to create an out-of-this-world environment. Cultural differences are taken into account; thus a casino would not send a white limousine for an Asian high roller for whom it would have a negative association.

The same quest for the altered state that comprises the action calls both the high roller and Pack Schmidt. In neither case is greed the motive. In both cases, it is the slipping of ordinary perceptual bounds and moving into the intensity of another reality.

Perhaps this is why the Wizard of Oz theme failed at the MGM. It's difficult to imagine either the high roller or Pack Schmidt on the Yellow Brick Road to the Emerald City Bar. The shamanic gambler may neither want to identify with Dorothy, nor discover the man behind the curtain manipulating everything.

Works Consulted

Abram, D. *The Spell of the Sensuous: Perception and Language in a More-Than-Human World.* New York: Pantheon P, 1996.

Allen, E. *Mustang Sally.* New York: Norton, 1992.

Merleau-Ponty, Maurice. *Phenomenology of Perception.* Trans. Colin Smith. London: Routledge & Kegan Paul, 1962.

8

THE PRACTICE OF PERCEPTION:
MULTI-FUNCTIONALITY AND TIME
IN THE MUSICAL EXPERIENCES OF A HEAVY METAL DRUMMER

Harris M. Berger

In this article I will argue that musical perception is best understood as a kind of practice and explore some of the broad consequences of this orientation for music research. I use the term practice in the dialectical sense elaborated by writers such as Pierre Bourdieu and Anthony Giddens. In their writings, practice (or human action) has been considered as the underlying social reality from which seemingly intractable opposites such as "the individual" and "society" are derived. The central insight of practice theory is that practice is always the individual's active achievement, but that active achievement is always constrained and enabled by past and present social contexts. In this view, "agency" (the subject's active intervention in the world) and "structure" (the order of society in which the subject is surrounded) are a duality, as inextricable as two sides of the same coin (Giddens, *Central Problems*). In this paper I will apply these ideas to the issue of musical perception. Many ethnomusicologists have revealed underlying, culturally specific systems of perception in music; others have observed that the same object in perception can be experienced in different ways. My aim is to show that perception is both profoundly influenced by the perceiver's social context and nevertheless is open-ended and actively accomplished by musical participants. In short, perception is a kind of practice.[1]

As a case study in the practice of perception, this paper offers some tentative hypotheses to explain how a heavy metal drummer actively shifts the focus of attention among temporal levels in musical perception in order to achieve various musical goals in nightclub performance. While the musical example explored in this paper is simple, the perceptual practices applied to it are not; in fact, they serve as key elements in the repertory of heavy metal perceptual practices. Although it is always difficult to abstract broad conclusions from limited ethnographic data, I believe the practices examined here may be common to rock and metal drummers in general and hope that future research will explore the applicability of these ideas to other areas of American popular music.

I will begin my examination of the data by introducing John Ziats, a heavy metal drummer, and providing background on the research project in the context of which our interviews took place. In the next section I will lay out my theoretical orientation and present the content of my interpretive dialogues with Ziats. In the following two sections I will examine Ziats's musical experiences in terms of Roman Jakobson's idea of multifunctionality and Edmund Husserl's ideas on time consciousness, respectively. I will conclude by showing how perception is a kind of practice and suggesting some of the wide avenues of ethnomusicological research opened up by this approach. As a case study in the perception of drumming, it will be best to begin this examination by looking briefly at contemporary work on temporal issues.

Recent Examinations of Rhythm in Music Scholarship

In the last twenty years ethnomusicologists, music theorists, musicologists, perception psychologists, and cognitive scientists have paid increasing attention to the topic of rhythmic perception. Sophisticated research and powerful insights have emerged from this attention, and many of these insights can be enriched and developed by viewing perception as a kind of practice.

In music theory, for example, large-scale rhythmic units have become a focus of interest. While theorists disagree about whether large-scale patterns of strong and weak beats (or "hypermeters") operate as macro-level analogs of traditional meters (e.g., Schachter; Smyth; Brower), no one can doubt that the debate has revealed previously unexplored levels of structure in Western art music. Other theorists have examined complex new forms of temporal organization on smaller scales, such as Elizabeth West Marvin's discussion of rhythmic contours or John Roeder's exploration of pulse streams. While many of these writers (for example, Carl Schachter) make reference to musical perception as the ultimate court of appeals for the validity of a given interpretation, none operating outside of the disciplines of cognitive science or psychology make the analysis of the act of the perception a central part of their academic method. Many powerful insights into the nature of musical structure have emerged from this research, but this scholarship could only be enhanced if the theorists would explore the act of musical perception by listeners in performance events, rather than undertaking decontextualized analyses of their own musical perceptions, however highly trained they might be. Apart from the occasional reference to the concrete perception of musical sound by particular listeners, the effect of much of this work is to treat music as a decontextualized musical text with autonomous musical structures. This is not to say that the musical structures explored in this way are mere fictions or that the research is without merit, but rather that the emphasis on musical structure rather than the perceiving subject obscures the subject's role in constituting those structures in experience.

By synthesizing approaches from cognitive science and psychology with the methods of music theory, other writers have come closer to grounding musical structure in the acts of the perceiving subject. Candace Brower, for example, explains that substantially different kinds of processing occur in sensory, short-term, and long-term memory, and uses these basic psychological concepts to shed light on the debate about the perception of large-scale metrical structure. David Smyth applies cognitive scientific notions of top-down versus bottom-up processing to shed light on similar issues. Focusing on perception rather than the musical sound *per se,* this research moves us closer to grounding the study of musical structure in the living experience of listening subjects. While this research provides numerous rich insights, none of these scholars centrally concern themselves with the effect of musical culture or the immediate situational context on perception.

Such criticisms of music theory and cognitive psychology are, of course, common among ethnomusicologists. As a discipline, ethnomusicology excels in constructing detailed studies of musical experience that show how perception, meaning, and aesthetics are culturally specific. Research on areas as diverse as South Africa (Blacking), Papua New Guinea (Feld), and Native America (Vander) implicitly or explicitly juxtaposes underlying systems of "native" musical perception with the norms of Western art music to display all musical perception as culturally based. Those ethnomusicologists specifically focused on temporal issues have shown how basic cultural assumptions about time and the organization of events affects rhythmic perception (Maceda; Stone [*Let the Inside; Dried Millet*]; Merriam). Their work does not merely reveal musical structures unknown to the Western European tradition (although it often does that); more fundamentally, it shows how the musical structures themselves are in fact artifacts of culturally specific systems of musical perception.

While such scholars are successful in pursuing this program, the systems of perception they posit are presented as descriptions of "the native's perspective," an idea that is problematic in a number of ways. The difficulty is not merely that all ethnography after Claude Lévi-Strauss's *Tristes Tropiques* and James Clifford's *Predicament of Culture* must account for the blurring of boundaries between self and other, the "native" and the "ethnographer." More fundamentally, the notion of native perspective leads the scholar toward a search for underlying cognitive machinery that produces experiences, thus obscuring the active role musicians and listeners play in constituting their perceptions; such an approach also makes invisible the complex differentiation of perception among the various participants in any given event. And while some cognitive scientists working in tandem with music theory or ethnomusicology have observed that a listening subject can perceive the same musical sound in several different ways, none of these scholars have taken the manipulation of perception as a central theme of research.[2] My goal in this article is to show that the active organization of perception is a basic aspect of performance, and that discussions of musical structure can only be enriched by attention to the practice of perception.

A Heavy Metal Drummer in Akron, Ohio

The data I will present here must be understood as a first step toward an ethnography of the practice of perception among rock and metal musicians. As distinguished from rock, heavy metal refers to a range of highly dramatic musical genres that first appeared in the late 1960s and early 1970s in Britain and the United States; metal emphasizes extremely distorted electric guitars, elaborate group arrangements, and individual virtuosity, and frequently depicts grim or aggressive emotions. While the study of popular music is a burgeoning area, little work has been done on the musical sound itself. Robert Walser's excellent book *Running with the Devil* is an exception to this general trend. But while Walser's book is unique and commendable for exploring musical sound in metal, he treats that music as a cultural object that has direct rhetorical and emotional effect on the listener. Analyzing transcriptions in the manner of a musicologist approaching a piece by Bach or Beethoven, Walser does not account for the fact that musicians can and do organize experiences of musical sound in a wide variety of ways. Thus, the various and complex practices of musical perception among heavy metal musicians are left unexamined.

Like most humanistic ethnomusicologists, my goal on entering the field was to share as much as I could of my informants' experiences of the music. I began my research in northeast Ohio in November 1992, and within a few months I had selected four distinct musical communities in which to work. One of these communities was the "underground" metal scene in the metropolitan Akron area. I began regularly interviewing musicians from two local metal bands—a small but respected death metal band named Sineater, and a progressive metal band called Winter's Bane that had just begun to leap from local to regional status and had signed a contract with an independent German label.[3] I met Sineater's drummer, John Ziats, in early 1993; by August, we had had five interviews and a number of informal meetings. In our first interviews Ziats and I discussed the broadest contours of his musical life, including his early interest in metal, his vision of the local music scene, his history as a member of local bands, his development as a drummer, and his aims and purposes in music making. In our next interviews we explored how Ziats organized his experiences of the diverse elements of the performance event.

With these points established, we finally focused on interpreting his experiences of particular songs. Sineater had broken up a year before I got to Ohio, and all of its former members agreed that the last song they had worked on together, "The Final Silencing," was their finest effort; the song became the focus of study for a total of twenty hours of interviews among three of the six members of the band. In our fifth interview, we discussed the general form of the song and the first few sections. The sixth interview covered the third major section of the song (see Example 1), and it was in this interview that Ziats and I came to some unique understandings of musical perception in time.

After listening to a demo tape of the song and listening again to the part in question, Ziats began to share his experiences of this section of the song with me. My goal was to understand how he grasped the part and made it emerge in his experience: What was essential and what was unimportant about the part? What aspects were foundational and what were embellishments? Where did the interest and "action" lie in the part? How was the part organized in the ongoing form of his experience? As we began to interpret Ziats's experiences of his drum part, the common ethnomusicological ideas of additive and divisive time became indispensable to our inquiry. To understand Ziats's musical experiences, I will need to explore critically the ideas of additive and divisive time.

Example 1. Bridge drum part to "The Final Silencing."

A Theoretical Framework: Protension, Retention, and the Living Present

The ideas of additive and divisive time are powerful but problematic concepts. Uncritically applied, they can lead the scholar to obscure the agent's active participation in perceptual experience. To guide inquiry into the temporal dimension of musical experience and clarify these ideas, a theoretical framework is needed; my approach emerges from the related, foundational insights of Henri Bergson, Edmund Husserl and Alfred Schutz.[4] The essential ideas of this school have been cogently explained in numerous locations (Ihde 84-103; Smith; Stone, *Dried Millet*), but because the term phenomenology has been so consistently misunderstood, and because these ideas are so integral to my argument, I will review them here and apply them to the more familiar concepts of additive and divisive time.

The naïve view of time perception is neatly captured in the image of the sweep second hand of the conventional wristwatch. Understood through the metaphor of that thin metal prong, the present is conceived of in daily language as an infinitely thin moment, endlessly gliding forward and turning future into past. (What time is it? It is one ten and five seconds, six seconds, seven seconds . . .) Like all phenomenological research, the phenomenological inquiry into time perception begins with a rigorous examination of the lived experience of time, or, more accurately, the lived experiences of change, procession, and stability. When we set aside our common reflective prejudices about what time is and return to the lived experience, Husserl's basic insight becomes clear and manifest: the present is not some infinitely thin moment rushing ever forward, radically separate from the future and the past; on the contrary, we live in the *thickness* of a living present in which the as-yet-unfulfilled expectations of the near future and the just-past-certainties of the recent past form an undivided whole. Though constantly changing, the anticipated near future and lived recent past exist simultaneously and constitute the lived reality of present experience.[5]

Some samples from language will illustrate the point. As I speak or listen, I am not merely aware of the words I say at the moment that I say them. As I hear or read one word, I am also simultaneously aware of the previous words spoken and have anticipations of the words to come. In Husserl's useful terminology, experiences of the recent past continuously experienced in the thickness of the living present are called retentions; anticipations of the near future extant in the thickness of the living present are called protentions. If we lived only in the infinitely thin present moment—that is, if we did not retain and protend—we could only be aware of the present word; complex sentence-level concepts would be an impossibility, because it is the experienced conjunction of the words across the moments that is responsible for the lived meaning of the sentences.[6] Quite immediately and concretely, if the mere awareness of the individual words of the previous sentence—"if," "we," "lived," and so on—are taken by themselves and not retained, there is no possibility that the meaning of the sentence as a whole will emerge. It is only when each new word is conjoined with the retentions of the previous word and all are conjoined in the thickness of the lived and experienced present that the meaning of the whole sentence emerges.

It is important not to confuse retention with memory. To remember an earlier part of the sentence means to make a phenomenon that was once present (but is now absent) part of the living present once again; to retain an earlier part of the sentence means to continuously hold the earlier words in experience. Thus, to experience and understand a sentence, the reader does not merely glance back—with eye or memory—at the first words or clauses; on the contrary; understanding a sentence means to retain past experiences of past words and clauses, to let their meaning lurk in retention and let their conjunction with the new, incoming words provide added sense and meaning. A momentary failure of retention will illustrate the difference between memory and retention in the clearest fashion. Reading a long sentence, I may become confused and have to actively remember or glance back at previous words or clauses. Here, I do not understand the sentence because I have failed to retain the first words in the thickness of my living present; I engage memory to bring those first words and clauses back into the living present in the hope that I may now retain them while I re-read the latter phrases and thus make sense of the sentence as a whole. Thus memory is being used to refresh retention, returning old experiences back into the protentional/retentional structure of the living present. Retention is an indivisible aspect of the living present; distinct from memory, retention is necessary if experience is to occur at all.

We can further this understanding by observing that experience does not merely have a protentional/retentional structure; the structure of the living present is organized and can be managed along a number of parameters. In all experience, protentions and retentions may be differentially foregrounded or backgrounded, and the span of the living present may be expanded or contracted.[7] To the issue of the span of the living present: reading Bourdieu after an exhausting day, I may have difficulty keeping all the parts of his long sentences present in retention; in such a case, we might say that the concrete dimensions of my living present are cramped, and I am only able to focus on a narrow temporal width. Alternatively, while in a state of calm attentiveness, I may be able to hold all of the nested clauses of Bourdieu's aggressively complex sentences in retention, conjoining them with the incoming clauses and thus broadening the temporal width of the living present. Don Ihde speaks to the issue of foregrounding or backgrounding experiences in retention or protention: while anxiously waiting for a telephone call, I may focus attention on the leading edge of the living present, protending and anticipating the sound of the bell and almost ignoring the retentions of all sounds that pass beyond the now-point. Alternatively, listening calmly but intently to a piece of music, I may languorously enjoy each note, allowing their continuity and retention to remain in experience and fore-grounding the retained moments and their continuity.

We can both better understand these ideas and prepare for our return to the interpretation of Ziats's experiences by applying them to the concepts, so familiar to the ethnomusicologist, of additive and divisive time. It is a commonplace of past ethnomusicological discourse to hold that time in West African music is perceived in an additive fashion while time in European music is perceived in a divisive fashion.[8] Not even addressing the post-modern recognition of blurred cultural boundaries, it is necessary to examine these ideas closely and see exactly how they might describe lived experience. At first the notions seem quite clear: additive music is music that is constituted by adding small temporal units together. For example, one way in which the so-called standard pattern of West African music can be understood is as a musical idea composed by adding together—or, more precisely, placing in series—five small groups of beats: one, two; one, two; one, two, three; one, two; one, two, three. Divisive music is constituted by taking a larger span of time and dividing it into equal units; common four/four time in Western art music is understood as a unit of time (one bar) divided into four quarter notes, four equal divisions.

Beyond the common but obviously flawed conflation of divisive versus additive time with even and odd meters, even before employing Husserl's concept of the living present it is apparent that the same piece of music could be perceived in an additive or divisive manner. A listener may hear the same beats in a piece of music either as composed of a series of small units added together or as a larger temporal unit divided into parts. (For example, in *Drum Gahu: An Introduction to African Rhythm,* David Locke urges the reader to explore both additive and divisive approaches in hearing the rhythms of Ewe drum ensembles [17-19]). Nothing inherent in the sound dictates that we hear it as beats added up or a unit of time divided, and the distinction between the two is a distinction in the listener's culturally based organization of their experience, not in the vibrations of the air itself. (In fact, there is more complexity here, but I will return to this point below.) Phenomenologists refer to perception as a process of constitution; unlike construction (the whole-cloth creation of ideas from imagination), in constitution we actively engage with the world and make it emerge in experience. In the language of phenomenology we may say that we are free to constitute the perception of a series of beats in an additive or divisive fashion.

Addition and division are two of many ways in which a listener may organize protentions and retentions of musical experience in the thickness of the living present. In the following discussion I will ground the notions of additive and divisive time in the rigorous analysis of lived experience. This exploration will provide us with the intellectual tools needed to understand the heavy metal data and enable us to draw further conclusions about the role of agency in perception and the differentiation of perceptual practices within a culture.

What is the structure of the living present when we perceive time in a divisive manner? Because of the complexity of the issue, let us take an extremely simple case: the experience of four beats heard as a series of quarter notes in four/four time. At the moment that the first beat is sounded, if the listener is to hear it as a division of a larger temporal unit, he or she must concretely protend the other beats of the bar; that is, the listener must experience, in the temporal "space" of the near future, three more beats while he or she is hearing the present beat in the now-point. (Further, the listener is likely to protend future units of four linked beats, but this brings us to the topic of larger levels of temporal organization, which is beyond the present moment in the argument.) When the second beat is sounded, the listener must conjoin this new beat with the retention of the first beat and the protention of the two upcoming beats. Likewise, the listener must conjoin the third beat with the retention of the first two and the protention of the fourth; similarly, the listener will conjoin the fourth beat to the retentions of the first three and actively disjoin these beats from the beats of the new bar emerging now in immediate protention. It is this dynamic and ongoing structure of retention and protention that constitutes the experiences of hearing four beats as divisions of a larger temporal unit. We can observe more broadly that throughout the period, attention is constantly focused on the level of the bar as it moves from pure protention to pure retention and that, as each beat emerges in the focal point of the "now," it is experienced as a figure against the ground of those moving protentions and retentions. In fact, it is this figure/ground relationship between present beat and the protended and retained beats that constitutes the experience of any beat as a quarter note and as a division of the bar.

Now, what is the structure of the living present when we perceive time in an additive manner? Let us again take a simple case: a pattern of two beats plus three beats.[9] As above, when the first beat is sounded, we protend the upcoming beat as part of the same temporal unit; similarly, when the second beat is sounded it is conjoined to the retention of the first. When the third beat emerges, it appears against the ground of the protended fourth and fifth beats; similarly, the fourth beat emerges against the ground of the retained third beat and the protended fifth; when the fifth beat finally emerges, it is conjoined with the retentions of the third and fourth beats. We must additionally observe here that, while the first two beats are sounded, the third, fourth and fifth are still protended, and, similarly, as the third, fourth and fifth beats are sounded, the first and second of the first repetition of the pattern are also protended.

The critical point here is that beats one and two are tightly conjoined as they pass from protention through to retention, just as beats three, four and five are tightly conjoined as they proceed through the living present. Of course the two small temporal sub-units are also conjoined to form the pattern, but their conjunction is of a higher order—a conjunction of units of beats rather than a conjunction of beats themselves.

With this in place, we are finally in a position to come to an explicit and concrete description of the difference between additive and divisive time. Further, we can begin to see the first glimmerings of the connection between these specific issues in temporal perception and the broader argument about perception as social practice. Additive versus divisive time refers to methods of organizing experiences in the processual, temporal thickness of the living present. In divisive time, the large temporal level of the bar is the ongoing background against which each beat emerges; in additive time, each beat emerges against the background of smaller two- or three-beat units, which themselves are conjoined to form larger units.[10] The difference between the two methods of constituting perception is that the listener engaged in divisive time places individual beats against the background of the bar as a whole, while the listener engaged in additive time places the individual beats against the background of small sub-units, which in turn are placed within the context of the pattern as a whole.

The critical distinction lies in the relationship of the immediate beat to larger levels of protention and retention. Both the additive and divisive processes of constituting perception requires the listener to experience large units at the level of the bar-as-a-whole or the pattern-as-a-whole. The two differ with respect to which level of protention and retention the immediate beats are related to most intensely. In the divisive process, each beat emerges intensely locked in a figure/ground relationship with the retained and protended notes of that bar. In our example, the third beat is tightly conjoined with the protention of the fourth beat and the retention of the first two beats; it is merely a division of the larger unit and is illuminated by its relationship to the numerous protentions and retentions of the larger temporal whole. In the additive processes, however, the beat emerges more tightly conjoined with the others of its small sub-unit, and the pattern as a whole is more deeply backgrounded. In our example, beat four is tightly conjoined with the retention of beat three and the protention of beat five; of course, beats one and two of the current iteration of the pattern are still retained and beats one and two of the upcoming iteration of the pattern are still protended, but they are protended less intensely. Further, it is each sub-unit as a whole, and not the individual beats taken by themselves, that constitute the pattern. Thus, for divisive processes, the primary and defining relationship is between the immediate beat and the protentions and retentions on the level of the bar-as-a-whole; for additive processes, the primary and defining relationship is between the immediate beat and the protentions and retentions on the smaller level of the sub-unit, which in turn are secondarily related to protentions and retentions on the level of the pattern as a whole.[11]

The reader will of course have noted that in this section I have shifted from speaking of additive or divisive time to additive or divisive processes of perception. It should be apparent that the issue here is the listener's method of grasping the world and making it emerge in experience. My goal in the rest of this article is to suggest that the issues at stake in ethnomusicological studies of perception are not of underlying cultural schemes that produce perception but rather practices of perception—practices grounded in the participants' social pasts and situational goals, differential across the participants within the event and open to the possibility of creative manipulation or failed execution. Such practices need not be either guided by explicit thoughts or reflexively understood, but there is no reason that they may not be. In either case, they are at least partially the outcome of the musical participant's agency; to borrow a phrase from Giddens, this is the case because, engaged in practice, the participants "could have acted otherwise" (*Central Problems* 56).

Initial Exploration of Ziats's Musical Experience:
An Interpretive Dialogue

With this theoretical orientation in mind, we can turn to my sixth interview with Ziats and begin to garner some important insights about his musical experience and the practice of perception. Earlier interviews had revealed that the snare drum (usually accenting beats two and four in rock musics) and the bass drum (usually falling on beats one and three) were often linked, and it took little time to establish that the snare and bass drum parts formed one unit in Ziats's experience;[12] similarly, the flow of sixteenths played on the high hat or "sock cymbals" formed a separate but related unit. Attempting to understand the relative importance and functions of the various units, I then asked Ziats which part (snare and bass, or high hats) he would play if he was only allowed to play one; Ziats said that independent of which drum he would use, he would play the flow of sixteenth notes because it formed the foundation of the drum part. A rock musician myself, I had always understood the accents on two and four as central to the music. To my surprise, additional conversation strongly confirmed that Ziats heard the flow of sixteenth notes as the basis of the part. To him, the snare and bass drums were merely accents in the flow of sixteenths.

Ziats was not at all surprised that I heard two and four as foundational to the part. The audience hears the snare first, said Ziats; the other band members tap out the quarter notes, but drummers build up their parts from small units. Ziats then explained how the song was put together in rehearsal. Guitarist and main song writer Dann Saladin composed a series of sustained power chords for this section.[13] In rehearsal Ziats had to compose a drum part to go along with Saladin's guitar part and, in his aural imagination, conjured a flow of sixteenth notes, much in the style of Queensrÿche drummer Scott Rockenfield; immediately after, he decided to add the snare and bass parts as a layer on top of the high hat's foundation. Most importantly, this method of composition—building up parts by layering larger temporal units above smaller ones—paralleled the manner in which he structured his listening in performance. Ziats explained that while the audience usually focuses on two and four and the guitar players tap out the flow of quarter notes with their feet, Ziats himself would focus on the sixteenth notes to keep the time both metronomic and flowing. If a player just "listened to the air" (that is, the huge silences) between two and four, he or she could easily get lost, said Ziats; focusing on the sound of the flow of sixteenth notes and the feelings of his arms articulating those parts, he said, helps him perform evenly and with authority.[14]

Engaging Ziats with ideas from my training, I explained the common ethnomusicological (nonphenomenological) notions of additive and divisive time perception, and I asked Ziats if he felt that his focus on the sixteenth notes was an example of the use of additive time. Ziats agreed heartily, and to hammer home the point, he described a part he had recently composed for a song his current band was writing. The part was formed by adding together three smaller rhythmic fragments—two seven stroke rolls shared between the bass and snare and pattern of five short pulses. Ziats was emphatic that he composed the part using an additive approach. Had the interview ended here, the simple conclusion would be that Ziats's scheme of perception followed the additive pattern. Given more supportive data, the conclusions one would draw would fit into the general form of traditional ethnomusicological inquiry: the people from X culture perceive musical sound in Y manner. Further conversation, however, revealed the problem of such a interpretation.

Ziats and I applied the notions of additive and divisive time to other drum parts, and we began exploring this part in more detail. Ziats's drum kit was unavailable during our interview, but he did have a pair of drum sticks with him; at one point I asked him to play his drum part on the surfaces available in the room. Like the metal (and rock) guitar players I had interviewed, Ziats tapped out the quarter notes with his foot. After I pointed this out to him, Ziats explained that in an abstract sense, the quarter notes were the most basic and foundational level of the time; the bars were composed by adding quarters together and the sixteenth notes composed by dividing the quarters into four parts. I began to suspect that the conclusion that Ziats perceived the part in an additive fashion might be premature, and I wondered if the idea that one temporal level was always perceived as a rhythmic foundation might be an abstraction from the concrete practice of playing and perceiving music. In fact the more important question was not which level was more foundational but which level stood in the foreground of the living experience of musical performance, when, and for what reason. Examining different scenarios and types of events, Ziats and I concluded that if he wanted to get into the smooth grooving feel of the part (the usual case) he would focus on the flow of sixteenth notes as he first indicated; however, if the band was not tightly coordinated with the drums or his time was especially poor, he would focus on the quarter notes (that is, the first of every four sixteenth notes on the high hat); if the band was well coordinated and he wanted to connect with the audience, he could focus on the beats that they heard most strongly—two and four.

Before turning to broader points in the discussion, it is important to note heavy metal (like many rock-based musical genres) is rich in rhythmic complexity, and the apparent simplicity of this example should not lead the reader to misunderstand the sophistication of heavy metal drummers. Changes in tempo and groove, complex fills and all manner of compositional and performance techniques give metal its diversity and power. By exploring the creative organization of attention in this one simplified example, my goal is to display musical perception as an active process. The organization of awareness in the perception of more complex parts, the shifting of attention to different instruments in the ensemble, the musicians' attention to non-aural aspects of the performance event and the partial sharing of experience between musicians and audience members is the focus of several chapters of my dissertation. While this paper has focused on the active organization of experience in the narrow confines of this one simple musical example, the possibilities of creative social perception in the full range of elaborated musical structures and situated contexts is immense.

Interpretation of the Musical Experiences I:
The Concept of Multi-Functionality

At this point in the interview, it became apparent to me that focusing attention on different temporal levels in musical perception involved the same principle of multifunctionality that Prague school semiotician Roman Jakobson had suggested for language, so I explained the idea to Ziats. Jakobson argued that all verbal interactions involve six distinct dimensions, each with its own function; all six dimensions and functions occur at once, but in different interactions some functions may be emphasized more than others. For example, two of the dimensions are channel and reference: channel refers to the physical media by which the communication is established, and reference refers to the denotations and meanings of the words. Both channel and reference are a part of every communication, but the context and the interlocutor's goals determine which dimensions will be foregrounded and which will be backgrounded. Talking on the phone when the line is clear, for example, I may forget about the complex technology that enables our conversation and focus on the meanings of my interlocutor's words. Here, reference is foregrounded, but it must be understood that channel is present as part of the background. By the mere act of talking, the speaker implicitly confirms the fact that he or she assumes the channel is still operative and the other is listening; otherwise, he or she would not be conversing but merely talking to him- or herself. Alternately, if static obscured the line, the precise meanings of the other's words would become of secondary importance. As both speakers shouted "Hello? Hello?" the dimension of channel would be quickly shifted to the foreground. In its broadest sense, to say a sphere of experience is multifunctional is to say that it has numerous simultaneous dimensions, each of which is always operative and each of which may take the foreground of attention at any moment.

Speaking about rock and metal in general as well as this song specifically, I suggested to Ziats that the focusing of attention on different temporal levels in music perception was multi-functional. It was clear from the interview that focusing on any one level had certain consequences and could be used to serve a particular purpose in the performance event. Thus, the sixteenth notes flow by in a swift and uninterrupted fashion, and by focusing on these the drummer can enter into the flowing groove of the music. The quarter notes exist as a mean between the swiftly flowing sixteenth notes and the widely spaced two and four; they are also the level that the other band members tend to tap out. By focusing on these, the drummer may coordinate more tightly with the other band members. Finally, because the heavy accents on two and four are what draw the audience's attention most intensely, a focus on this level is useful in helping the drummer project his part out to the crowd and draw them into the music. Ziats explained that, if on a given night his tempo was not consistent or the band was not well coordinated, he would focus on the quarters. If the basic coordinations were not a problem, as was usually the case, he would let his attention drift to the level of the flowing sixteenth notes and let the groove roll along smoothly. Alternatively, he could focus on two and four to connect more directly with the crowd.

But the various temporal levels are not merely functional; they are multifunctional in Jakobson's sense. That is, all of the levels occur simultaneously, as do all the functions. As Ziats attends to the rolling flow of sixteenth notes, he is also simultaneously playing the quarters (as articulated by the accented first note of every four on the high hat) and the snare and bass on two and four; likewise, he is simultaneously coordinating his part with those of the other band members and the gestures and body movements of the audience. All of those functions and levels occur, and the foregrounding of any one level (and subsequent backgrounding of the other two levels) is achieved to serve Ziats's needs in that particular performance event. Discussing the idea of multi-functionality and its application to the issue of temporal focus in performing this part, Ziats agreed that Jakobson's notion did indeed describe his musical experiences and that he would shift his attention from flowing sixteenths to solidly spaced quarters depending on his needs in the event.

Interpretation of the Musical Experiences II: Protention and Retention

We can use this data to understand musical perception as a kind of practice; indeed, the outlines of that argument should be clear to the reader at this stage of the analysis. But the phrase "the focusing of attention at different temporal levels" is broadly stated, prone to misinterpretation, and reveals little about the musician's experiences and the manner by which he or she constitutes them. The notions of additive and divisive time provide some help, but, as I have shown above, these ideas are still much less explicit and revealing than one would like. How, for example, does a listener constitute additive or divisive perception in particular situations and what are the concrete differences in experience between the two? To explicitly and systematically understand the temporal dimension of musical experience, we must examine the anticipation, emergence and retention, the continuity and discontinuity, the foregrounding and backgrounding and the dynamic play of presence and absence in the experiencing of musical sound. In fact, the "focusing of attention at different temporal levels" refers to processes of organizing musical sound in the living present. My goal here is to use the intellectual tools from phenomenology to provide an explicit description of the experience of this processual organization. Unlike the above discussion of Ziats's experience, these descriptions have not emerged in the fieldwork dialogue and therefore must be seen as tentative hypotheses in the phenomenological ethnography of heavy metal and rock.

The differences between "focusing on the sixteenths" and "focusing on the quarters" most closely parallels the differences between additive and divisive time explored above and will thus serve as a starting place. Let us begin with the experience of the sound of the high hat. Following my earlier discussion, it is clear that "to focus on the level of the quarter notes" means to hold all the quarter notes intently in experience as they process through the narrow center of the living present. Thus, on beat one, the high hat stroke in the now-point is highlighted or foregrounded. Simultaneously, the other fifteen sixteenth notes of this bar are protended as well, but the sixteenth notes falling on the downbeats are foregrounded, while the other twelve (the notes falling on the "e," "and," and "ah" of beats one, two, three and four) are grasped more lightly and are held in the defining background.[15] The same foregrounding and backgrounding relationships take place as the notes are protended, performed and then retained in the trailing thickness of the living present. On the "and" of three, for example, the high hat strokes on the first three downbeats are foregrounded in retention, while the upcoming high hat stroke on the downbeat of four is intensely protended. Likewise, the sixteenth note divisions of the first two beats and the "e" of beat three are retained, while the "ah" of beat three and the three off-beat sixteenths of bar four are protended. However, these notes are grasped less intensely and are thus less vividly central in experience; they act as a defining temporal background to the foregrounded retention and protentions of downbeats in the same way that the irregular white center acts as a defining spacial background to the two silhouette-shaped black patches in the famous Rubin's goblet drawing.

In sum, the foregrounding of the high hat strokes on the downbeats as they process from protention to retention is the concrete, experienced reality that the term "focusing on the quarter notes" imprecisely describes. The presence, in the background of experience, of the three notes of equal duration dividing up the silence gives the part its sixteenth-note "feel."

In fact, there is even greater complexity and richness here that these descriptions elide. The previous discussion did not examine the relative foregrounding and backgrounding among the notes on the downbeats. Such factors as the note's distance from the now-point, its presence in protention or retention, and its status as a strong beat or weak beat (understood from the subject's perspective, of course) all would play a role in determining the intensity with which it is grasped compared to the other notes falling on the downbeats. While there is no doubt that all experiences of musical sound occur in the thickness of the participant's living present, and while it is clear that the focusing on different levels of time is achieved by organizing sound in the living present, the richness of lived experience always transcends our descriptions of them; further, descriptions based in theoretical generalizations and not returned to the fieldwork dialogue are most subject to error. Therefore, these descriptions must be understood as hypotheses to be explored in future fieldwork. This does not mean that these descriptions are mere speculation, and I hope that they will guide the way to more nuanced conversations between myself and Ziats, as well as between other researchers and musicians.

Having examined the organization of the living present necessary for "focusing on the quarters," it will be easier to explicate the organization necessary for "focusing on the sixteenths." First of all, it is not clear from the context of the interview whether the phrase "focusing on the sixteenth notes" was meant as "focusing on the sixteenth notes as heard in groups of four" or "focusing on the ongoing flow of sixteenths;" I will thus handle each case separately. The former case is not very different from my initial examination of additive time. Focusing on the sixteenth notes as groups of four, the drummer will foreground the present note and tightly conjoin it with the other notes in their emerging four-note unit. Thus, for example, as the second sixteenth of beat three emerges, it is tightly conjoined with the retained sixteenth note on the downbeat of three, as well as the protentions of the sixteenth notes on the "and" and the "ah" of three. Just as the sounds in a word are not merely heard as separate entities but grasped together to form a synthetic whole, these sounds will be grasped together as they process from protention, through the now-point and into retention. These four-note units are then conjoined to form the bars at a higher level; just as a sentence is experienced as groups of phrases and not merely serial strings of sound, the bar as a whole is experienced as groups of four-note units and not merely strings of individual notes by themselves.

Given the context of the interview it seems that the second case, that of "focusing on the sixteenths as an ongoing flow," is more likely what Ziats intended when he referred to "focusing on the sixteenths." This situation would be marked by a less intense contrast of foreground and background than was present in the earlier cases. Rather than strongly foregrounding the notes that fall on the downbeats and strongly backgrounding the notes that fall on the off beats as they process through the living present (the case of focusing on the quarters), the listener focusing on the sixteenth notes grasps the notes more evenly, flattening out the difference of intensity between the vivid foreground and the vague background. The result is the experience of an ongoing flow of sixteenth notes continuously processing from protention to retention rather than of a series of quarter notes emerging against the background of a sixteenth note "feel." When focusing on the flow of sixteenths, the present note is foregrounded against a ground of ever-approaching protentions and ever-receding retentions.

It should be clear that a smooth continuum exists between the two cases of focusing on the sixteenths. Thus, the more tightly conjoined the adjacent groups of four within experience, the more they are heard as a flow of four-note units emerging across the span of the section; the more loosely the groups of sixteenth notes are conjoined, the more the high hat part sounds like an endless string of sixteenth notes. It should also be clear that both situations are sharply distinct from a focus on the quarters, which present the notes on the downbeats as sharply foregrounded against a background of sixteenth note divisions; the distinction between "focusing on the quarters" and "focusing on the sixteenths" is precisely the same as the elaborated phenomenological descriptions of the distinction between additive and divisive time.

While all of this takes us a long way toward a more explicit understanding of the concrete differences between focusing on the quarters and focusing on the sixteenths, we must recall that we have neglected the place of the snare and bass drum parts in the experience; returning it to the discussion will not be difficult. It was clear and explicit from this and previous interviews that Ziats heard the flow of sixteenth notes as one coherent unit and the bass and snare drum parts as another coherent unit.[16] Like a part hocketted between a soprano and a bass or a simple two-note melody, the snare and bass parts are tightly linked with one another and form a unit sharply distinct from the flow of sixteenth notes on the high hat.[17] With each maintaining its own internal foreground and background relationships in experience, the two parts also fall into a foreground/background relationship with one another: when "focusing on the quarters" or "focusing on the sixteenths" the snare and bass part form an ongoing background to the foregrounded high hat part. It is important to recall here that backgrounded experiences are not absent from experience; on the contrary, they are present in a vague form and often are a key part of the lived experience as a whole. Just as a quiet, inner melody in a complex, multi-part piece of counterpoint informs and colors the more obvious and foregrounded upper voice, so do the ongoing snare and bass part, taken as a unit, become a defining background for the foregrounded high hat part.

And just as a listener may shift attention between the melodic lines in a piece of counterpoint, so may Ziats shift attention from the hats back to the snare and bass. Such a spatial and timbral adjustment of attention is precisely what is meant by "shifting focus" from "the level of the sixteenths" or "the level of the quarters" to "the level of two and four." This ability is not obscure, and a variety of such selective attention is well known in perception psychology as the "cocktail party effect." Just as an individual holding a conversation in a loud party may foreground her or his interlocutor's words and background the general din of the affair, or let the interlocutor's words slip into the background to eavesdrop on another speaker's words, Ziats may foreground either the snare and bass or the high hats, while allowing the other to slip into the defining background of his experience. Because of the accents in the snare and bass part (and because the norm in rock and metal is for the snare to heavily accent two and four), a spacial and timbral shift of attention to the snare and bass means that the protended and retained notes on two and four become the most foregrounded; thus, "the level of two and four" becomes the de facto focus of attention.

Conclusions and Future Directions:
The Organization of the Living Present
as a Practice of Perception

The primary purpose of phenomenological ethnography in ethnomusicology is to describe the musical experiences of others. Musical sound is not merely present in the world; it is an artifact of an individual's grasping of the world in perception. People with different social histories and cultures grasp the world, and thus experience it, in very different ways. By reading an ethnography that describes how those with different social histories grasp their music in perception, a person can come to understand a music that might otherwise be incomprehensible. As cross-cultural translation, phenomenological ethnography in ethnomusicology is not much different from early ethnomusicological work that sought, as I suggested above, to garner "the native perspective."

However, my goal in this paper has not been merely descriptive. A basic tenet of the phenomenology of perception is that perception is actively and socially achieved by the participants. Studies that focus on musical sound alone carry with them the implicit assumption that perception is universal and that what varies from culture to culture are the types of artifacts produced; phenomenological approaches assume that both the music perceived and the act of perception are specific to each musical culture.[18] While structuralist approaches often recognize that perception varies with social history, such approaches seek to unearth unconscious systems that generate experiences for the musical participants; phenomenological approaches, however, assume that there are at least some aspects of the constitution of perception that are accessible to the participants and over which those participants have some level of control. Further, as a kind of modernism, structuralist approaches assume that there is one underlying scheme of perception in each culture and implicitly or explicitly take as their study object an ethnomusicological variation of Chomsky's ideal speaker/hearer in the homogeneous speech community; phenomenological approaches take the concrete individuals and diversity of their experiences as a study object, and one result of this is to discover complex and reciprocal relationships in the practices of perception of the participants in each event.

In sum, phenomenology takes perception to be a kind of practice or action. As such, the broad generalizations about practice developed by such theorists as Bourdieu and Giddens also apply to the act of perceiving. Thus, as practice, each act of perception is dependent on the individual's social experiences and the broader social history that led up to them; such a social history influences but does not determine perception, and each act of perception depends on the individual's active and agentive engagement with the world. To the musician who has spent long hours learning to hear complex chord changes or subtle nuances in pitch or tempo, the idea that one's perception is grounded in one's social history but at the same time actively achieved should be easy to accept. Further, as practice, perception is oriented toward the agent's goals and intentions in the performance situation, and yet such acts have a range of consequences some of which often run counter to the actor's intent. For example, in small ensemble jazz (and many other musical styles) different performers see different members of the rhythm section as the rhythmic foundation of the group, and subtle difference of tempo are crucial to the band's rhythmic cohesion. On a small scale, the present vision of intentions and consequences should be comprehensible to the jazz soloist who has studiously followed the tempo of the drummer throughout a performance, only later to discover (upon listening to a recording of the performance) that the rest of the band was following the bass's tempo. My goal in presenting this detailed description of the organization of the living present is to show the rich data and insights that emerge when we treat perception as practice.

First, it should be clear from this discussion that perception is never simply a mirror of the world, though neither is perception mere fantasy. "Focusing on the sixteenths," "focusing on the quarters," "focusing on two and four"—the discussion of the organization of the living perception showed that there are numerous ways in which Ziats's drum part may be grasped in perception; in fact, the part is open to an almost endless variety of possible combinations of foregrounding and backgrounding, conjoining and disjoining for a listener willing to experiment with perception. Second, and perhaps more important, the data show that it is simple and comprehensible acts (foregrounding and backgrounding, conjoining and disjoining) that determine how the part will be perceived. Choosing among an open-ended range of possibilities of perception, John Ziats is no cultural dupe whose experience of the world is generated and determined by unconscious structures; on the contrary, he is an agent constituting perception. Further, the structure of his experience is manifest in the event itself, and the practices by which he constitutes those experiences are accessible to him, both in private reflection and in the dialogue of the ethnographic interview. Third, and related, the selection between different ways of organizing the living present is not arbitrary or capricious but rather geared toward the participant's musical goals in the performance event. Further, by "focusing on the sixteenths," a phrase we now can use to mean an explicated method of organizing musical sound in the living present, Ziats can enter into the groove of the music. By "focusing on the quarters" Ziats can correct any basic tempo problems that might occur, and "focusing on two and four" can be used to draw the audience into the performance. Fourth, perception is not something that is achieved identically by all the participants in an event. For example, almost all of the heavy metal and commercial hard rock guitarists I spoke with said that the drummer was the player most responsible for the tune's overall groove; as a result, the guitarists explained, they mainly focus on the level of the quarter notes and would follow the drummer's tempo almost anywhere it led. The audience members have no responsibility to stay synchronized, and they generally grasped as most central the loudest and most obvious part of the music— the snare accents on two and four. As such, Ziats's perceptual practices do not merely serve individual ends but are oriented toward others in the event. Finally, displaying precisely how these particular perceptual practices are tied to the long term events in Ziats's musical life, as well as the history of heavy metal and American music more generally, is a crucial project best accomplished by cross-cultural comparison and a comprehensive social history of musical perception; such a study is clearly beyond the scope of this article.

Having viewed Ziats's perception as fulfilling narrow musical goals in the context of the event, we have almost reached the end of the discussion. But it must be remembered that all narrow situational goals— musical or otherwise— are connected to the actor's larger plans and projects, and that these have consequences that always exceed the actor's intentions. Thus, the narrow musical goal of presenting a tightly coordinated and aggressively grooving band may seem unremarkable and prosaic, but this is not the case when placed within the broader context of the purposes and consequences of heavy metal more generally. As such, perceptual practices should not merely be of interest to those who study musical sound but also to those who study music's role in society, history, and politics writ large. It is only when we understand even the largest-scale social and musical movements as actively constituted by the social actions of individuals that we can view society and history as meaningful and living experience.

Notes

1. For a fuller exploration of practice theory and its applicability to the ethnomusicology of perception, see Berger, especially chapter one.

2. Bringing cognitive science approaches to music theory, Fred Lerdahl and Ray Jackendoff, for example, suggest that the musical score may imply more than one musical structure and posit "preference rules" to account for the possibility of differing interpretations. Brower (24) voices similar observations. Bringing cognitive science approaches to ethnomusicology, Ulrich Wegner also notes that musical structure can be construed in varying ways.

3. The term "underground" refers to the varieties of heavy metal that exist largely outside or on the margins of the mainstream music industry and receive little commercial airplay. Death metal is a subgenre of underground metal that began in the mid-eighties and is primarily characterized by deep, growly, unpitched vocals. When used to modify the name of a variety of rock or metal, the adjective "progressive" is used to indicate that the band employs complex musical structures. Sineater could be described as a kind of progressive death metal, employing growly unpitched vocals and highly elaborated song structures; Winter's Bane was closer to the commercial end of the underground metal scene, but the band's songs were sufficient in length and complexity to make their music "progressive metal."

4. In many ways Jacques Derrida's early critiques of Husserl's ideas on time (esp. 60-70) share common features with Husserl's thought, and an interested reader might find his work relevant to this discussion as well.

5. Christopher Hasty has recently applied this basic Husserlian insight to show that even the most apparently discontinuous contemporary Western art

music is in fact experienced in the thickness of the living present (61-62). Brower has also connected similar observations from William James with music research (22).

6. The terms "conjunction" and "disjunction" were most fruitfully applied to the relationships between and within experience by William James (esp. 44-52). By "conjunction" James meant the lived connections of experiences across phenomenal space and time while "disjunction" was used to refer to the lived separation of experiences. While Husserl never uses precisely those terms, we can understand the ongoing continuity of protention and retention in the living present as a kind of temporal conjunction. On the compatibility of Husserl's phenomenology and James' radical empiricism, see James Edie.

7. I am using the terms foreground and background here in an abstract, general, and descriptive sense. When an entity in experience is foregrounded, it is experienced with greater emphasis, detail, and clarity; entities backgrounded in experience are not "less experienced" by the subject. They are, however, less emphasized, and are present to the subject with less detail and clarity. I am using these two words as technical terms to describe the lived organization of experience, not as visual metaphors for sound experiences. I intend the same abstract, descriptive organizational approach with the use of the term "temporal level," which I develop below.

8. While some writers maintain this idea (e.g. Small 269-273), recent ethnomusicological work on Africa has surpassed the simplistic equation of additive time with West African music and divisive time with Western European music (cf. Kaufman; Stone "In Search of").

9. It is important here to realize that odd versus even meters must not be conflated with additive versus divisive time. One can perceive a pattern of four repeating beats in either an additive or a divisive manner. I use the example of a simple pattern of two plus three because such patterns are commonly associated with additive time, but no necessary connection exists.

10. Considering musical experience from a very different perspective, auditory perception scholars have also explored the grouping of sounds across time into coherent rhythmic units and the existence of multiple levels of temporality. A good overview of this literature can be found in Handel (383-419).

11. As always in phenomenological research, my goal is to set aside previous philosophical presuppositions, return to the lived experience itself, and describe that experience as effectively as possible. My aim here is not to dictate the organization of experience in additive or divisive perception but to describe these methods by which listeners organize their perceptions. While the reader may feel that my descriptions are more or less accurate, it should be clear that this is in no way intended as a prescriptive account, nor is this section ethnographic.

12. In fact, the snare and bass parts in the section we were discussing are slightly unusual for this genre. In rock and metal, the norm is for the snare drum

to strongly accent two and four. This fact was supported by interviews with other drummers, and throughout our interviews Ziats and I regularly conflated the temporal level of two and four with snare parts in general. As such, these remarks are relevant to both Ziats's experiences as a whole and those of most metalheads.

13. In many forms of American popular music, the term "power chord" is regularly used to refer to a chord composed of the root, the perfect fifth and the octave. Power chords are sometimes composed of the root, the fourth and the octave; on occasion the power "chord" is limited to the interval of the fourth or fifth. These forms are common to most forms of rock and metal.

14. In the contemporary discipline, a body of writing has emerged examining the subtle, positive discrepancies between the musicians' performances and the metronomically precise underlying pulse (most recently, Keil; Prögler; Alén). These authors view playing "ahead" or "behind" the beat, and myriad other "discrepancies," as the basis for the experience of "groove" or "swing" in music. This important work reveals new dimensions of rhythmic organization, and Ingrid Monson's recent comments suggest that performers actively manipulate this dimension of musical structure in performance. As a dimension of structure, groove, swing, and participatory discrepancies are all subject to perception, and future research might focus on the active organization of perception at the micro-level and the effect of perception on the groove or swing of a performance.

15. By the syllable "e" I mean to indicate the first sixteenth note after the downbeat; by "and" I mean to indicate the sixteenth note falling in the middle of the beat, and by the syllable "ah" I mean to indicate the last sixteenth note of the beat. This syllable usage is common among drummers in many Western traditions, including rock and metal.

16. Approaching musical experience using different methods, auditory perception scholars have also noted similar effects. The grouping together of the snare and bass in experience would be referred to as "streaming"; the separation of the streamed-together snare and the bass sounds from the high hat sound would be referred to as "streamed segregation" (cf. Bregman and Pinker; Handel 185-218).

17. Ziats said in our interviews that, while the bass and snare parts are almost always taken together to form a coherent unit, this relationship can be understood in a number of other ways (for example, as a rhythmic call and response). Walser has also observed what he calls a dialogic interaction between bass and snare drum parts (personal communication, 1995).

18. The standard example of this insight from the field of phonetics revolves around the phonemes "r" and "l." It has been repeatedly observed that speakers whose native language does not contain these phonemes do not merely have a difficulty producing the English sounds "r" and "l;" they are frequently

unable to perceive them as well. Using rather different approaches from phenomenology, phonetics has also arrived at the insight that the act of perception is deeply dependent on learning.

Works Consulted

Alén. Olavo. "Rhythm as Duration of Sounds in Tumba Francesa." *Ethnomusicology* 39 (1995): 55-72.

Berger, Harris M. "Perception in the Moral Continuum of History: An Ethnography of Metal, Rock and Jazz in Northeast Ohio." Diss. Indiana U, 1995.

Bergson, Henri. *Time and Free Will: An Essay on the Immediate Data of Consciousness.* 1889. Trans. F. L. Pogson. New York: Macmillian, 1916.

Blacking, John. *Venda Children's Songs: A Study in Ethnomusicological Analysis.* Johannesburg: Witwatersrand UP, 1967.

Bregman, Albert S., and Stephen Pinker. "Auditory Streaming and the Building of Timbre." *Canadian Journal of Psychology* 32 (1978): 19-31.

Brower, Candace. "Memory and the Perception of Rhythm." *Music Theory Spectrum* 15 (1993): 19-35.

Bourdieu, Pierre. *Outline of a Theory of Practice.* Trans. Richard Nice. Cambridge: Cambridge UP, 1977.

Clifford, James. *The Predicament of Culture: Twentieth Century Ethnography, Literature, and Art.* Cambridge, MA: Harvard UP, 1988.

Derrida, Jacques. *Speech and Phenomena and Other Essays on Husserl's Theory of Signs.* Trans. David B. Allison. Evanston, IL: Northwestern UP, 1973.

Edie, James M. *William James and Phenomenology.* Bloomington, IN: Indiana UP, 1987.

Feld, Steven. *Sound and Sentiment: Birds, Weeping, Poetics, and Song in Laluli Expression.* Philadelphia: U of Pennsylvania P, 1982.

Giddens, Anthony. *Central Problems in Social Theory: Action, Structure and Contradiction in Social Analysis.* Berkeley: U of California P, 1979.

——. *The Constitution of Society: Outline of a Theory of Structuration.* Berkeley: U of California P, 1984.

——. *New Rules of Sociological Method: A Positive Critique of Interpretive Sociologies.* 2nd ed. Stanford: Stanford UP, 1993.

Handel, Stephen. *Listening: An Introduction to the Perception of Auditory Events.* Cambridge, MA: MIT P, 1989.

Hasty, Christopher F. "On the Problem of Succession and Continuity in Twentieth-Century Music." *Music Theory Spectrum* 8 (1986): 58-74.

Husserl, Edmund. *The Phenomenology of Internal Time-Consciousness.* 1905. Trans. James S. Churchill. Ed. Martin Heidegger. Bloomington, IN: Indiana UP, 1964.

Ihde, Don. *Listening and Voice: A Phenomenology of Sound.* Athens, OH: Ohio UP, 1976.

Jakobson, Roman. "Closing Statement: Linguistics and Poetics." *Style in Language.* Ed. Thomas A. Sebeok. New York and Boston: Wiles and Son and Technology P of MIT, 1960. 350-77.

James, William. *Essays in Radical Empiricism.* 1912. Gloucester, MA: Peter Smith, 1967.

Kauffman, Robert. "African Rhythm: A Reassessment." *Ethnomusicology* 24 (1980): 393-415.

Keil, Charles. "The Theory of Participatory Discrepancies: A Progress Report." *Ethnomusicology* 39 (1995): 1-20.

Lerdahl, Fred, and Ray Jackendoff. *A Degenerative Theory of Tonal Music.* Cambridge, MA: MIT P, 1983.

Lévi-Strauss, Claude. *Tristes Tropiques.* Trans. J. and D. Weightman. London: Jonathan Cape, 1973.

Locke, David. *Drum Gahu: An Introduction to African Rhythm.* Crown Point, IN: White Cliffs Media, 1967.

Maceda, José. "The Concept of Time in a Music of Southeast Asia (A Preliminary Account)." *Ethnomusicology* 30 (1986): 11-53.

Marvin, Elizabeth West. "The Perception of Rhythm in Non-Tonal Music: Rhythmic Contours in the Music of Edgard Varèse." *Music Theory Spectrum* 13 (1991): 61-78.

Merriam, Alan P. "African Musical Rhythm and Concepts of Time-Reckoning." *African Music in Perspective.* New York: Garland P, 1982. Monson, Ingrid. "Response." *Ethnomusicology* 39 (1995): 87-89.

Prögler, J. A. "Searching for Swing: Participatory Discrepancies in the Jazz Rhythm Section." *Ethnomusicology* 39 (1995): 21-54.

Roader, John. "Interacting Pulse Streams in Schoenberg's Atonal Polyphony." *Music Theory Spectrum* 16 (1994): 231-49.

Schachter, Carl. "Rhythm and Linear Analysis: Durational Reduction." *Music Forum* Vol. V. Ed. Feliz Salzer. New York: Columbia UP, 1980.

——. "Rhythm and Linear Analysis: Aspects of Meter." *Music Forum* Vol. VI, Part 1. Ed. Felix Salzer. New York: Columbia UP, 1987.

Schutz, Alfred. *The Phenomenology of the Social World.* 1932. Trans. George Walsh and Frederick Lehnert. Evanston, IL: Northwestern UP, 1967.

Small, Christopher. *Music of the Common Tongue: Survival and Celebration in Afro-American Music.* London: J. Calder; New York: Riverrun P, 1987.

Smith, F. Joseph. *The Experiencing of Musical Sound: Prelude to a Phenomenology of Music.* New York: Gordon and Breach, 1979.

Smyth, David H. "Large Scale Rhythm and Classical Form." *Music Theory Spectrum* 12 (1990): 236-46.

Stone, Ruth M. *Dried Millet Breaking: Time, Words, and Song in the Woi Epic of the Kpelle*. Bloomington: Indiana UP, 1988.

——. "In Search of Time in African Music." *Music Theory Spectrum* 7 (1985): 139-48.

——. *Let the Inside Be Sweet: The Interpretation of Music Event among the Kpelle of Liberia*. Bloomington, IN: Indiana UP, 1982.

Vander, Judith. *Songprints: The Musical Experience of Five Shoshone Women*. Urbana: U Illinois P, 1988.

Walser, Robert. *Running with the Devil: Power, Gender and Madness in Heavy Metal Music*. Hanover, NH: UP New England, 1993.

Wegner, Ulrich. "Cognitive Aspects of Amadinda Xylophone Music from Buganda: Inherent Patterns Reconsidered." *Ethnomusicology* 37 (1993): 201-42.

III.

SPECTATORSHIP

9

ZOÖPTICON:
INSPECTING THE SITE OF LIVE ANIMAL INFOTAINMENT

Ralph R. Acampora

Despite being a common feature in cities throughout the world, the zoo remains a morally troubling institution. Usually the controversy is framed in these terms: either the zoo is (primarily) a sanctuary for animals or else it is (primarily) an exhibition of animals—if the former, then it appeals to laudable conservation ideals; if the latter, then it panders to lowly amusement values. Thus the ambivalent nature of the zoo's identity—between refuge and circus—marks it as a site of ethical contest. In fact, there are question marks surrounding its purpose and function even within each of the characterizations mentioned. If the primary purpose is conservation, which goal is paramount: preserving species (abstract entities of genetics) or protecting animals (qua individuals)? If the primary purpose is exhibition, then the question is do zoos educate people ecologically beyond "mere" entertainment? Or, less dichotomously, what is the quality of its "infotainment" agenda?

Negative answers to questions such as these have led skeptics to take a decidedly dim view of zoological establishments. Dale Jamieson, for example, has analyzed the putative justifications for the zoo as an institution. He considers the major arguments in defense of zoos and finds them far from compelling, arguing that amusement seems a rather frivolous compensation for captivity; similarly, education in the zoo does not appear to happen very often or very well; research activities there, are, for the most part, far-fetched, circular, redundant or trivial; preservationist breeding programs "save" animals only "in the thinnest biological sense," sacrificing real individuals' quality of life for the benefit of abstract species (291ff.).

What is interesting about this sort of critique is not the intermediate results (which, for the record, I believe are largely sound); the rationale for reaching an ultimate recommendation of abolition is instead the illuminating facet on which I wish to focus. One of the critical pivots employed by Jamieson is (an appeal to) a moral presumption against keeping wild animals in captivity. Yet, we may ask, on what experiential ground is such a presumption based? "It is surely true," Jamieson claims, "that in being taken from the wild and confined in zoos, animals are deprived of a great many goods" (292). Surely true, I would say, for an audience already disposed by somaesthetic encounter and somatological reflection to care about the bodily or behavioral ramifications of other animals' losing their liberty! Precisely at this juncture we will see how a phenomenological approach, especially one that focuses on the lived patterns of animate bodies, is helpful in understanding what is wrong with zoos.

Brave New Zoos: Illusions of Biotopia

Lately, many zoos have been reforming their exhibition design into greater conformity with their captive animals' original (wild) habitat (cf. Page; Richardson). Instead of being housed in mausoleum-style buildings subdivided into small rooms with cage bars, many of today's zoo inhabitants are kept instead in microcosms of quasi-wildernesses, planned and set up with decidedly more biological parameters in place. This is certainly the case with the Zoo Atlanta, which, under Terry Maple's direction beginning in the 1980s, transformed itself from one of the worst municipal menageries into a highly naturalized environment that is comfortable and engaging for animals and visitors (Maple and Archibald). This change of circumstance has occurred in tandem with the implementation of behavioral enrichment features (first initiated by Heini Hediger, this century's international dean of zoo supervision and Maple's chief source of inspiration)—apparatus and activity ranging from toy-like mechanisms for relief of boredom to actual predation as a near-facsimile of hunting in the wild (Markowitz).

Yet, such reforms remain on the level of the virtual: almost natural, but not quite—they are, in other words, always only artificial attempts at achieving at most asymptotic verisimilitude. The problem is not merely one of degrees, of technical shortfall in the reproduction of reality (in fact, state-of-the-art reconstruction has progressed to the point where entire ecosystems have been assembled and stocked by the creators of Montreal's Biodome). Rather, the difficulty is structural: as one expert admits, even "good" zoos—just in virtue of their being zoos—"must reduce nature to the extent that they make residents visible to visitors" (Markowitz 12). This reduction means that even the best practical examples of zoological naturalization are condemned, on principle, to provide sites/sights of simulacra. Zebras and tigers are not beings whose nature it is to laze under the gaze of human observation; usually, if we got too close, they would avoid or attack us (more on this point below). Thus zoos face a dilemma of dishonesty: as they improve environmental realism to impressive heights, with proportionate poignancy they increase the sense that animal preservation is being simulated (i.e., not actually accomplished). Our suspicion is aroused: can tigers or zebras exist in the zoo, or do only "tigers" and "zebras" reside there? Perhaps the ultimate creature of naturalized presentation is an artifact of somatological hyperreality, a disembodied entity reincarnated as a nicer replica of its former self—what certain postmodern critics would call the "real fake"(cf. Baudrillard; Eco).

Still, a defense of zoo-keeping might dismiss such criticism as beside the main point of genetic conservation of species. As for the living individual organism, one apologist allows that "if an animal lives as a member of a social group that is proper for its species, feeds from natural vegetation, finds its own mates and rears its own offspring, it does not seem to matter overmuch if it is also protected from predators, or is amenable to human observation" (Tudge 256). After all, so the argument goes, we have rescued the animal from endangerment in its external environment. Or have we? Consider a limit case described by Neil Evernden in *The Natural Alien* (referring to condors):

A singular bird, certainly, but one which can be regarded as saved only by accepting a limited, biological definition of a bird as the physical manifestation of coded genetic information. Were it regarded as the manifestation of embodied limits and therefore the functionary of a particular "place," the fact that we have expertly exterminated that place makes nonsense of any claims that the bird has been saved. (151)

At stake, here, is the bodily being of animality—whether it is properly reducible to objective corporeality (matter in the form of genetic development), or must also somatically incorporate its ecological habitat and natural history (on the phenomenal plane of lived experience). Since the former reduction overlooks the latter condition, an incomplete description of the animal body results; hence we have good phenomenological reason to doubt the adequacy of zoological preservation, whatever its rationale may be from the vantage of "scientific management."

Under the lens of this skepticism, I would add that we can criticize the whole salvational tone of zoo rhetoric. The dream of the most "progressive" zoological conservators, Tudge asserts, is to return future generations of their presently endangered keep into the circumstance of wilderness, "to take them back to the wild at some future, more relaxed and more enlightened time" (255). Geopolitically, however, the prospects for economic relaxation and ethical enlightenment are not very encouraging. On the contrary, dedication to an international ethos of growth and greed has become the strongest force of our times, overwhelming pleas for a steady spirit of sharing: as Melle, following Peter Sloterdijk, notes, under modernity's aegis, "science, technology, production and consumption, fashion, [and] mass media . . . are all dominated by the kinetic imperative of accelerating acceleration" with little or no regard for qualitative value (107). What then becomes of the utopian visions that are held to be the highest justification of zoological parks and gardens? One answer is that they are birthed from, and aligned with, a dubious faith in the promise of biotechnology. For instance, if it should take centuries instead of decades for the enlightened epoch of zoological paradise to arrive, we will (so they say) ride out the extended time by freezing the seminal and embryonic material of those species threatened with extinction (Tudge 170). Eventually, come Releasement Day, biodiversity will be resurrected in its full beauty and splendor—if not here on Earth, then on the surface of some suitably geo-engineered planet (e.g., Mars with its ice caps melted down for water). This caricature, incidentally, is not so far from the mark, for zoo ideology has a tendency to wax Noachian: see philosopher Jacques Dufresne's Biodome encomium, in which he refers to "technology in the service of life" under a "Rainbow Covenant" (6-12).

In any case, it should be obvious that futuristic planning of this sort presumes socio-ecologic stability over a very long term. Yet those measures necessary to prevent collapse of society and biosphere—human population control and sustainable lifestyle—are also precisely the factors that would most contribute to habitat preservation and species conservation in the wild to begin with! The unavoidable answer to mass extinction, then, behind all biotopian dreams of intervention and re-education (training in wilderness survival skills is necessary for reintroduction of zoo animals [Tudge 233-40]), is *self*-limitation.

Captive Animals and Docile Bodies: The Somaesthetics of Visiting

Doubly paradoxical, the zoo conceals much about nonhuman animality, and reveals at least as much about humanity: as Mullan and Marvin put it, "interpreting the presentation of wild animals in the zoo reveals much more about the variety of the cultural expression of human identity than it does about the zoological nuances of the animal universe" (xvii); and, using Foucault's *Discipline and Punish,* they extend this observation by claiming that "zoos are about humans, for zoos tell us stories of human power, the exercise of control and domination" (45).

How, then, does this insight refract upon the medium of the human body itself? As Merleau-Ponty and others have pointed out, the lived body is existentially larger than the anatomical unit; it incorporates a live space of potential motility and sensory engagement. For the prison guards, asylum wardens, and zoo keepers of centuries past, living their carcerally institutional bodies meant adopting carnal duties and corporal stances that assumed "the techniques of force and fear are appropriate to the management of 'brutes'" (Mullan and Marvin 37). Various reforms in the twentieth century have cast a more humanitarian atmosphere over these places. Yet, even today, the visitors who come to see the (human or animal) inmates are constrained by the layout of architecture and the routine of policy to experience their bodies as having outer horizons shaped by an analytical arrangement of space (primarily and paradoxically conducive to inspection at a distance). Circumscribed separation and continual surveillance interrupt natural processes of trans-species sociality and etiquette (including, ironically, avoidance); the space of interface cannot be negotiated neutrally into the zone of existential equilibrium ordinarily established amongst free-ranging animals.[1] Under these conditions, Mullan and Marvin note, the visiting body unconsciously becomes a locus of hierarchical observation, oscillating between the poles of voyeuristic removal and prying proximity (31; 34: cf. Phelan). In these ways, then, the zoo retains its morally problematic status—even when viewed through the alternative lens of hermeneutic phenomenology of body.

The typical zoo precludes most if not all forms of somaesthetic relationship. Certainly, the potential for association between visitors and inhabitants is severely if not entirely curtailed: "nowhere in a zoo," argues John Berger, "can a stranger encounter the look of an animal. At the most, the animal's gaze flickers and passes on. They look sideways. They look blindly beyond. They scan mechanically. They have been immunized to encounter" (26). Putatively, there may be some sort of partnership at work between keepers and the kept—but even that possibility has a patronizing profile.[2] It would seem, then, that at the zoo one is led either toward indifference or toward pity. Whichever the case may be, respect is not realized because its ground of admiration is removed from the scene. By proceeding on a phenomenologico-hermeneutic path of praxiology, one discovers that the zoological "garden"—despite or even through its peaceful park-like image—is predominantly an institution of power the specific functions of which are to display and preserve its keep. Notwithstanding the lack of punitive or penal intent on the part of its organizers, the zoo nonetheless may be considered an artificial space of enforced occupancy and demonstration, an island of constraint within the series of social(izing) establishments that Foucault termed "the carceral archipelago" (297; cf. Morris).

To some, this characterization might seem too harsh or unfair. In fact, zoos have been defended against such (or, as we shall see, merely semblant) judgment. For example, zoologist and philosopher Stephen Bostock responds in the following fashion:

The urge to dominate, to show one has power over others, is doubtless an important part of human nature, and equally, no doubt, this urge sometimes motivates the capture and keeping of animals. But to regard this as the major motivation behind all wild animal keeping is a wild exaggeration! (63)

This sort of deontological remark can counter criticism only on the level of intention, however. It enables one to argue that some such keeping is not motivated by a drive-to-dominate or that what is so motivated is not primarily so. Further, moving onto a consequentialist level, it allows one to make the charge that the original critique is itself a form of genetic fallacy: even if misotherist tyrants founded zoodom from an imperial impulse toward biocolonial oppression, it does not follow that there would necessarily be anything wrong with the eventual fruits of their ill-intentioned work—in fact, in spite of doubts regarding their once being reduced to a collection of living trophies, we can rest assured that today's zoo inhabitants reside unmolested in truly wonderful, homey habitats (or so the argument might run).

Yet, notice that my largely Foucauldian criticism of carcerality at the zoo remains untouched by this response—because the critique is not based on a genetic or motivational thesis at all, pursuing instead structural observation. Whatever the motives of any zoo director, the nature or pattern of zoological exhibition abides. The zoo's lifeworld is structured around holding and showing wild animals in captivity and violating their status as free beings; somatologically, this structure ensures the production of docile bodies (or dead ones) (cf. Foucault 135-69). Such production of docility, in and of itself, constitutes and demonstrates a relation of powerful dominion (captor over and above captive, the carceral shot through the carnal). Carnality here refers to the boundary-breaking force of organic or fleshly excess—of swellings and peelings, of turgidity and atrophy, of pumping circulation and oozing excretion, in short of the alternately invisible and visible flow and ebb of embodied vitality's drives and impulses; "the carceral," by contrast, designates the boundary-building power of mechanical or technical containment—of limited access, constant rigidity, fixed passage, and panoptical surveillance. That relation, regardless of what any keeper has in mind, derives from and stays in place—zoo as enclosure and stage: animal archive at the least, conservation circus at its extreme.

Show(ing) Animals: The Scene and Structure of Zooptical Zeal

The doyen of zoo philosophy, Heini Hediger, once commented that animal specialists and criminologists share in common certain methods of professional practice (3). Indeed, and further, what he said about holding animals captive both foreshadows contemporary zoological sentiment and has been eerily echoed by paternalistically progressive calls for prison reform: "One wants the inmates to feel as comfortable, as snug, and as much at home as possible" (18). Whatever our impression of efforts at "humanizing" imprisonment (of our own species), it is hard to deny that improvements in zoo conditions have actually occurred over the past few decades.[3] Does this mean, I ask in closing, that the carceral comparison is now misplaced?

I do not think it is—certainly not if Foucault is right to suggest that carcerality has productive effects going beyond simple suppression. Visibility is a key concern here. Bentham's prison design, the Panopticon, was "to induce in the inmate a state of conscious and permanent visibility that assures the automatic functioning of power" (201). There is also in the zoo a nexus of power and vision, but with the roles reversed: the function of controlling the animals' placement and diet is to habituate them to tolerate indefinite exposure to the visive presence of humans.[4] Flattening Merleau-Ponty's world-fleshly dialectic of the visible and the invisible, the "zoöpticon" is a kind of panopticon turned inside out—similar principles are at work, and, although they are arranged in opposite vectors of force, over the long term they tend to produce the same result: an institutionalized organism, one largely incapacitated for life on the outside. More insidiously still, whether originally human or nonhuman, the transformed product is often a monstrous animal all too ready for the carceral milieux that have socially and ecologically colonized the (no longer quite so) external world.[5]

Another axis of Foucauldian critique reveals juxtapositions of epistemic activities and political interests, particularly as these configure bodies and inscribe flesh. In the zoological park practices of knowledge and power do intersect. Hediger's life-long enterprise, for instance, was to re-establish the zoo on a biological basis (*Wild Animals in Captivity* 3; cf. Foucault, *Birth of the Clinic*). His program was to be pursued in the style of systematic science, and it was held to empower its practitioners somatologically (i.e., with hermeneutic control over bodily behavior): "The [animal's] whole body is like an open book, to be read by those who know how" (*Psychology and Behavior of Captive Animals* 148). This is similar to what Foucault said of prison organizers: "They were [to be] technicians of behavior. . . . their task was to produce bodies that were both docile and capable" (*Discipline and Punish* 294). The same comment can be made in respect to zoo personnel's duty. Docile bodies are capable of conservation and demonstration, and so their production is at a premium. As Hediger puts it, "There are three reasons for stressing the need for tameness in as many animals as possible in zoological gardens: tameness is attractive; tameness is healthy; tameness is expedient. . . . Trained animals have more show value than raw [!] animals" (*Wild Animals in Captivity* 157; 161).

Inexcusable menageries once upon a time, zoos have developed into cultural institutions of infotainment capable of defending themselves on scientific grounds—that is, by appeal to aims of conservation and education. Yet such defenses are not strong: the former appeal is weak because heroic rescues to save species by removing specimens from the wild (and holding them or their descendants or genes "on reserve" indefinitely) are inefficient and incoherently utopian; the latter appeal is superficial in that it rests on bad faith (i.e., inauthentic presentation of captive animals as truly wild ones). Incarcerating animals in the name of science does not then appear justifiable, evolution beyond discredited forms of entertainment notwithstanding. A "moral physics" of confinement is operative in the zoological park: corporeally, the zoo is to serve as a repository of genetic material; somatically, it is to function as a conservatory of whole body conduct (Tudge ch. 7). Despite the best intentions, efforts, and achievements toward making these forms of confinement more comfortable for the inhabitants and more palatable to the visitors, zoos still partake profoundly in a pattern of prison-like institutions partially constitutive of late-modern civilization. Violent seizure, forced captivity, thorough exhibition, programmed feeding and breeding, commodified exchange—all these activities testify: to display animals is already to discipline them; to preserve species it is necessary to punish individual specimens (qua representative inmates). When we go to the zoo, we visit animals not only in the sense of "meeting" them (inspection by ocular survey), but also in the archaic sense of affliction, through imposition and interposition of power (mastery/control). Visiting here, we watch the keep with inquisitive eyes and all the vim of salvation. What we are looking at is unclear: Do we actually see animal others? Do we spy upon a dark and distorted mirror? Or do we stare simply into a visual vacuum?

In closing, although I have submitted zoo-going to structural critique, I do not wish to condemn zoo-goers personally—because we (I count myself) go to the zoo primarily from pre-rational need. How better to satisfy the evolved yearning for authentic animal encounter in a largely urban culture is precisely the problem toward which practical zoologists and philosophers of culture should now direct their combined attention and energy. Field preservation is coming back into a priority position with conservators and deserves our renewed support. "Not a way to achieve harmony with the natural processes of our world," explains William Weeks, "Zoos and botanical gardens and deep-cold technology will not be substitutes for *in situ* conservation—conserving organisms in context, where they live" (55). Penguin Parade, at the tip of southeast Australia (Victoria), is an example of a site dedicated to combining this strategy with allowance for human visitation. Part of the Phillip Island Nature Park, this reserve is designed to protect and promote awareness of blue penguins (previously called fairy penguins) and attracts some 500,000 visitors a year. At sunset virtually every night of the year, tourists wait along the boardwalks and in the viewing stands to watch the penguins cross Summerland Beach as they return from their coastal fishing waters on the way to their sand-dune burrows. The result is not only a close yet unobtrusive encounter with the birds but, via the admission fees and profits from souvenir sales, a self-funding reserve dedicated to protecting the penguins ("Phillip Island").

Notes

1. On the notion of inter-species etiquette, see Anthony Weston's *Back to Earth,* esp. chap. 7. For Weston "elementary politeness" toward animals means at least "working in their media, as it were, not primarily ours, and going to them in a way that allows them to break off the encounter whenever they wish" (13). Cf. Hediger's admission that "friendship between animal and man, in the sense of intimate positive relations, can only be achieved by unforced, voluntary approach on the part of the animal, and not through the irresistible force of contact" (*Wild Animals in Captivity* 165).

2. Cf. Wilson: "In a culture in which hunting has become a sport, jet fighters are named after birds of prey, and an animal-rights movement has interjected previously unspoken questions, all relations with our animal companions on this Earth have been thrown into crisis. That crisis is present at the zoo in the very glances traded between animal captives and their human keepers" (248).

3. After animal collector Peter Batten made an investigative tour of United States zoos about twenty years ago, his book-length report constituted a damning expose of the institutions' lack of attention even to biological basics. See his (and Stancil's) *Living Trophies.* Following his lead in zoo evaluation (q.v. esp. chap. 12), I have visited Zoo Atlanta periodically over the past decade to assess its changing conditions. In fact, this particular site has seen noticeable change for the better—to the point where eighty percent (and maybe more) of Batten's own condition checklist appears to be met (as of March 1995).

4. Ironically, because it beats down instincts of alertness and avoidance, this habituation itself undermines the possibility of really meeting animals— face-to-face, or better yet, body-to-body. The irony, somaesthetically speaking, is that over-exposure is tantamount to disappearance. Berger puts this anti-phenomenon starkly: "The zoo to which people go to meet animals, to observe them, to see them, is, in fact, a monument to the impossibility of such encounters" (19). This is the pornographic moment of zooscopy. Cf. C. Adams' *Neither Man nor Beast,* esp. ch. 2.

5. Cf. Birch 3-26. So-called reintroduction programs must monitor the movements of the released, frequently by remote electronic equipment; parole boards have already borrowed similar tracking devices as Foucault scholar Thomas Flynn points out. Animals "paged" while on parole? Convicts reintroduced "into the wild"? Would there be plausible distinctions anymore—ultimately and most poignantly, then, between freedom and imprisonment? This is the sort of fear motivating Birch's analysis, namely the suspicion "that there is no wilderness [free otherness] anymore in the contemporary world, in the technological imperium" (10).

Works Cited and Consulted

Acampora, Ralph R. "The Body Beneath Bioethics: Somatic Bases of Inter-Species Morality." Dir. Thomas Flynn. Diss. Emory U, 1996.

Adams, C. *Neither Man nor Beast.* New York: Continuum, 1994.

Batten, Peter, and D. Stancil. *Living Trophies.* New York: Thomas Y. Crowell, 1976.

Baudrillard, Jean. *America.* London: Verso, 1988.

Berger, John. "Why Look at Animals?" *About Looking.* New York: Pantheon, 1980. 1-26.

Birch, Thomas. "The Incarceration of Wildness." *Environmental Ethics* 12.1 (1990): 3-26.

Bostock, Stephen. *Zoos and Animal Rights.* London: Routledge, 1993.

Dufresne, Jacques. "The Meaning of Biodome." *Quatre-Temps* 16.2 (1992): 6-12.

Eco, Umberto. *Travels in Hyper Reality.* San Diego: Harcourt Brace Jovanovich, 1986.

Evernden, Neil. *The Natural Alien.* 2nd ed. U Toronto P, 1993.

Flynn, Thomas. Personal Interview. 1996.

Foucault, Michel. *Birth of the Clinic.* New York: Vintage, 1973.

——. *Discipline and Punish.* Trans. A. Sheridan. New York: Random House [Vintage], 1979.

Hediger, Heini. *Studies of the Psychology and Behavior of Captive Animals in Zoos and Circuses.* Trans. G. Sircom. London: Butterworths Scientific, 1955.

——. *Wild Animals in Captivity.* London: Butterworths Scientific, 1950.

Husserl, Edmund. *Collected Works.* Vol 1. Trans. T. E. Klein and W. E. Pohl. The Hague: Martinus Nijhoff, 1980.

Jamieson, Dale. "Against Zoos." *Reflecting on Nature: Readings in Environmental Philosophy.* Ed. Dale Jamieson and Lori Gruen. Oxford UP, 1994. 291-99.

Maple, Terry, and E. Archibald. *Zoo Man.* Atlanta: Longstreet, 1993.

Marietta, Don E., Jr., and Lester Embree, eds. *Environmental Philosophy and Environmental Activism.* Lanham, MD: Rowman and Littelfield, 1995.

Markowitz, Hal. *Behavioral Enrichment in the Zoo.* New York: Van Nostrand Reinhold, 1982.

Melle, Ullrich. "How Deep Is Deep Enough? Ecological Modernization or Farewell to the World-City?" Marietta, 99-123.

Morris, Desmond. *The Human Zoo.* New York: McGraw Hill, 1969.

Mullan, Bob, and Garry Marvin. *Zoo Culture.* London: Weidenfeld and Nicolson, 1987.

Page, Jack. *New Zoo.* Washington, DC: Smithsonian Institute P, 1990.

Phelan, Shane. "Intimate Distance: The Dislocation of Nature in Modernity." *In the Nature of Things.* Ed. J. Bennett and W. Chaloupka. Minneapolis: U of Minnesota P, 1993. 44-62.

"Phillip Island Nature Park Penguin Parade." May 12, 1999. http://www.labyrinth.net.au/~penguins/penguins/pages/reserve/page1.html#start

Richardson, Nan, ed. *Keepers of the Kingdom: The New American Zoo.* Charlottesville, VA: Thomasson-Grant & Lickle, 1996.

Sloterdijk, Peter. *Critique of Critical Reason.* Trans. M. Eldred. Minneapolis: U of Minnesota P, 1987.

Tudge, Colin. *Last Animals at the Zoo.* Washington, DC: Island P, 1992.

Weston, Anthony. *Back to Earth.* Philadelphia: Temple UP, 1994.

William Weeks. *Beyond the Ark: Tools for an Ecosystem Approach to Conservation.* Washington, DC: Island P, 1997.

Wilson, Alexander. *The Culture of Nature.* Cambridge: Blackwell, 1990.

10

A PHENOMENOLOGIST IN THE MAGIC KINGDOM

H. Peter Steeves

Vacationing at the Happiest Place on Earth

Her name is not really Joanna. You would not know it to talk to her—to hear her claim it, saying the name as if she has said it her whole life. Soon we are discussing options and I try to remember my Birnbaum's Official Guide: "finding the best package means first deciding what sort of vacation you want and studying what's available." I have studied. I know, for instance, that her name is not Joanna. Disney Travel Company agents may not use their real names on the phone. I also know that she will only tell me about a couple of packages, although many more might be available. This, too, is a rule. I have studied by contacting the AAA and reading about their "Minnie Vacation" and "Everyone's a Kid Again" packages for comparison. I have some True Rewards points accumulated from the phone company which I might put toward a special offer made available by Disney through AT&T. I have travel books and price guides, and I am ready to do business. "Happy hunting!" says the Birnbaum's.

But there is no hunt. I wonder who Joanna really is. I even feel bad calling her and asking about vacation packages at Disneyland as if I already had not done extensive research. It feels like cheating—she has no idea what she is facing, how much I already know and thus can use to my advantage. I hesitate and contemplate, thinking of the significance of it all as I recite my credit card number over the phone.

What does it mean "to buy a vacation"? What transformation does one undergo in order to "become" a tourist? Both questions point to a particular form of foundational consumption. Being on vacation consumes vacation days that I have been given by (earned from?) my employer. A vacation is a vacating, a move from production to consumption. Whether I take my vacation at home or use it to travel the world, I am vacating my place of work and using up a commodity: my free time. Indeed, the concept of a vacation requires the commodification of time as well as labor. It assumes a distinction between work and leisure, between work and life. Only when I am not in possession of all of my time does the concept of free time have any meaning: it is a question of ownership, not idleness. Given such a social context, buying a vacation makes perfect sense. For my free time to have meaning I must not, in fact, be idle; rather I must consume. And today, experience is the commodity of choice—this much we have in common. From the rich couple cruising the Caribbean, to the ten-year-old cruising the Internet, we are all consumers of experience.

This is different from saying that we all have experiences or that we all enjoy new experiences. A culture that consumes experience has turned experience into a thing. Susan Willis is right in maintaining that there is "something sad in this: the quest for experience . . . [the] scurrying about in desperate attempts to have experiences deemed more meaningful than the sort that happen every day" (45). Once reified, experience can be bought and sold, and thus over- or under-valued. "Everyday experience," a commodity in abundant supply, is subjected to market forces and thus deemed of lesser value.

Experience also becomes an object of scrutiny, and this ushers in a rather strange parallel between tourism and phenomenology. Both involve a shift in attention; both move from the world to our way of taking up the world, from experience to the experience of experience. In the phenomenological reduction, the passing parade of experiences is itself the object of scrutiny. Normal, everyday life is made up of multiple experiences—the words you are reading and the piece of paper on which they are printed, for instance—but the phenomenologist attempts to focus attention on the experience of the paper rather than the paper itself, thus uncovering the structure of experience. The tourist is engaged in a different yet nevertheless similar reduction. The Main Street Electrical Parade at Disneyland was not fully described by noting its colors, shapes, and sounds, etc. It was not just an event. Tourists experienced it because it was an experience; they experienced it *as* an experience. This is not simple perception—not within the realm of what Husserl calls the Natural Attitude—although simple perception is not put out of action by such reductions. After performing the phenomenological reduction it is the same world—the same paper—that I am experiencing, only now I have bracketed the things that I experience, neutralizing the common beliefs about their natures, attributes, etc. Thus my convictions about the world remain, but they are set aside or "transvalued" so that I might begin phenomenological analysis of the experience itself (cf. Husserl § 31).

"Transvalued" is somewhat of a strange term here, though, because the epoché itself is valued. The knowledge gained after the reduction is worth having. Similarly, the "Tourist's Reduction" leaves me with the same world—the very same parade—only now the standard beliefs within the Natural Attitude are set aside and I can experience the experience of the parade. As a consumer, such experiences are worth having.

I do not wish to make a great deal out of this parallel. Undoubtedly there are greater dissimilarities between phenomenology and tourism in the long run. But I do want to maintain that there is something peculiar about tourism in its purest form, and that we might be able to get at that peculiarity through analysis of experience. In less phenomenological terms, Dean MacCannell proposes something in the same spirit when he points out that

[b]ecoming a scientist or a politician means, in part, learning and adhering to, even "believing in," the standards and techniques of one's profession. The process of becoming a tourist is similar. . . . Everywhere in the minutiae of our material culture, we encounter reminders of the availability of authentic experiences at other times and in other places. . . . [But] it is not possible simply to buy the right to see a true sight . . . [and] at Disneyland . . . where the tourist is made to pay for what he sees, the sight always seems to be faked up and "promoted." (135; 148; 156)

Disneyland, MacCannell argues, is different from the Golden Gate Bridge because the latter will continue to exist without the tourist in search of its experience. This is not necessarily true, but we can at least admit a difference. Disneyland's purpose is to be experienced (in order to generate profit). Consequently, an analysis of the Disney experience holds the promise of a special kind of knowledge—knowledge of who we are and how we are.

I would like to consider two overarching topics along the axes of experience, meaning, and being. First, what is the experience of a trip to Disneyland like in terms of perceptions, illusions, and reality? Is the Natural Attitude disengaged at Disneyland, and what significance is there to the constructed nature of the experience? Second, how does Disneyland construct identity and thus affect our being both in terms of an individual and a participant in a collectivity? What is the meaning behind Disneyland's value-system? Is Disneyland a utopia, a dystopia, or neither? Along the way, and toward answering these questions, we will want to consider brief narrative sketches of particular moments and attractions within Disneyland as well.

As Joanna assured me: "this is gonna be the happiest place you've ever been!"

In or Out of the Cave?

The immediate reaction of some visitors to the park parallels that of MacCannell: everything seems "faked up." The truth is that very little at Disneyland is what it appears to be, and this was Walt Disney's intention. Even his famous Disney signature is a fake—a stylized and engineered symbol built for public consumption—and Walt, we know, had to be taught how to reproduce the signature in case someone should ever ask for his autograph.

The question of truth at Disneyland, however, goes far deeper than the problem of the chasm between experience and reality. It is true that there are varying degrees of outright lies at the park. Linguistically, these run from the bold (e.g., on opening day there were several areas without grass or other plants—just bare, exposed earth—so Walt Disney ordered his grounds keepers to remove weeds from the parking lot, plant them inside the park to cover the bare areas, and attach labels to each with "long, horticultural-sounding names" [Koening 19])—to the subtle (e.g., Disneyland's well-known "Disneyspeak" in which customers are guests, employees are cast members, crowds are audiences, and police guards are security hosts). Experientially, lies populate the park with greater frequency than truths. There are by far more audio-animatronic animals than real animals, and within each of the attractions, more audio-animatronic people than real people.

For these reasons Disneyland has been criticized as one massive lie—a faked up environment that represents the popular triumph of artistic falsehood and representation over reality. Klugman addresses this point on the level of epistemological theory and competing notions of truth by making reference to Plato's Allegory of the Cave; she came to the point when she saw a man videotaping a monitor screen at Disney World and wondered about the resulting product:

If the video camera were recording only the monitor screen, it was possible that the original and the copy would be identical. A guest could take home not just the memory of a Disney experience, but the experience. . . . The world is falling deeper and deeper into a vortex of simulacra, I mused. Worse than being trapped in Plato's cave, we are now stuck in Pluto's doghouse. (Project 28)[1]

It is easy to see why Plato would not have allowed Walt a zoning permit to build EuroDisney near Athens. Poets, we know, are barred from the Republic because their product moves us further from the truth. The tree outside my office window is once removed from the Form of the Tree, but a painting of that tree is twice removed. The massive Swiss

Family Robinson Treehouse's tree is a similar copy of a copy. Entering Disneyland, then, is like going even deeper into Plato's cave—perhaps like entering a shadowy cave within that cave. Regardless, we are even farther from the light of Truth.

I would like to suggest an alternative reading, however. Such critiques work, I submit, on virtual reality where the experience truly is of a copy of a copy. Even within individual attractions at Disneyland, there is some merit to this Platonic criticism. The Star Tours exhibit, for instance, meticulously creates a faked environment that attempts to stand in for the real thing. At least partially. The problem is that the overall Disneyland experience is not of a fake world, but rather a *better* world. Disneyland is presented as a window out of the cave, a peek into the realm of the Forms. Thus the critics have it backwards: the lesson of the Disney experience is that our world is cave-like, but Disney's world is truer, better, and a way out.

The evidence for this interpretation is ample. It is clear that Disney intended his park to be another world. The plaque that greets each visitor upon entry reads: "Here you leave today and enter the world of yesterday, tomorrow, and fantasy." The Disney realm of the Forms is not bounded by space or time or even imagination. "I don't want the public to see the real world they live in while they're in the park," Walt Disney once remarked, ". . . I want them to feel they are in another world" (qtd. in King 121). The presentation of this world is not as a watered-down copy of the real thing, but as an idealized version of how the world should be.

Main Street U.S.A. is an excellent example. Most commentators get it wrong. Birnbaum's official guide says that "this pretty thoroughfare represents Main Street at the turn of the century. You remember—'the good old days'" (63). The standard critical response is that no, we don't remember; Disney's representation is no good—he sanitized it and "Disneyfied" it until it all became a lie. In this spirit, Richard Francaviglia writes:

The main question . . . ought not to be whether the ritualized Main Street experience is a good or a bad one, but rather a much larger issue stemming from that concern: 1) What was the small town American Main Street of the past really like? and 2) What did Disney and his fellow artists/designers choose to emulate?. . . . It goes without saying that returning to a real small town Main Street at about the turn of the century would be a sobering experience for anyone who believes that Disney created the real thing. . . . Main Street was liable to be dusty in dry weather, soupy in wet; or what one critic has called an "equine latrine." (144)

Francaviglia goes on to describe the "real" Main Street experience—complete with photos to document his case. He concludes, however, that Disneyland's Main Street is a success architecturally even if it is not an accurate representation of real Main Streets. Indeed, he calls it "one of the most successfully designed streetscapes in human history . . . with nearly perfect visual/architectural homogeneity" (148).

The point is that Disneyland is not supposed to be a copy of the world; rather it presents the world as a copy of Disneyland. "This is the way Main Street should have been," writes Koening (41). "[This is] not an imitation of a Main Street anywhere in the U.S., but a kind of 'universally true' Main Street—it's better than the real Main Street" concurs Margaret King (129-39). Yes, Main Street is paved and the horses never mess the street. Was your Main Street different? Is your Main Street different? The problem is that they are imperfect copies of the Disney Form. It is true that there are no recycling bins along Disneyland's Main Street, but the point is not to criticize Disneyland for this from the perspective of an "environmentally aware visitor" (cf. Project 195). The point is that people shouldn't have to recycle—they shouldn't have to think about the problems of trash and diminishing resources. Perhaps, your Main Street is filled with homeless people, crime, and run-down buildings, but this is not how Disney says it should be. It is an easy ideal to buy into.

On opening day, actress Irene Dunne christened the Mark Twain Riverboat by smashing a bottle containing waters taken from each of the largest rivers of America. The water fell into the river—the River of America—like a soul escaping the body and returning to the eternal realm of the Forms. The presentation tells us: this is *the* river of America, not a copy of the Mississippi or the Missouri. This is just how real rivers should be—calm and virtually free of life, a money-making resource, a waterway for human transportation, no flooding and no dry-spells.

And what of the celebrated use of audio-animatronics at the park? Louis Marin, in his landmark article "Disneyland: A Degenerate Utopia," understands these machines and technology in general as not just an ideal for our future, but as a presentation of truth. "Nature," he writes

is a wild, primitive, savage world, but this world is only the appearance taken on by the machine in the utopian play. In other words . . . the Machine is the truth, the actuality of the living. Mechanism and a mechanistic conception of the world, which are basic tenets of the utopian mode of thinking from the sixteenth century until today, are at work in Disneyland. . . . (63-64)

Disneyland prides itself on being a realm of fantasy and imagination. I have been arguing, though, that this fantasy is presented at the park as a Formal truth. This is possible because the kind of fantasy to which Disney is referring is a specific, fantastical worldview *within* the larger worldview of science. That is, Disneyland is imbedded in the scientific worldview to an extent deeper than most visitors or cultural critics imagine.

It is easy to see how technology and fantasy become mixed at Disneyland. From the crude but inventive gadgets in the Swiss Family Robinson Treehouse, to Tomorrowland, where submarines, spaceships, holograms, and hi-tech modes of experiencing (e.g., the "Honey, I Shrunk the Audience" show) are presented as our finest future, the scientific worldview pervades Disneyland. The point I am attempting to draw out now, though, is deeper. It is to say that within the scientific worldview, the world and everything in it is a machine. It is the higher truth. The problem is that we are forced to live in the material world which is but a shadow of its Formal reality. In the material world machines don't operate correctly—they break down, and they hide their true nature. In Disneyland we can experience the Truth. There the environment clearly is mechanical, the animals and people clearly are machines. An audio-animatronic Indiana Jones can be Indiana Jones in a way in which Harrison Ford can only dream. And an audio-animatronic President Lincoln can say what needs to be said, fulfill his role, and be who he is supposed to be, without the imperfections (irrealities?) of the flesh.

Our world is an imperfect reflection of the mechanized Formal Disney World. Consider, for instance, the residents of the Enchanted Tiki Room. The mechanical birds "interact" with the guests and with each other. They sing and joke and are there for us—there to entertain us, to be consumed by us—as they should be. Birds *really are* machines, and they really are there for us to use and consume. But real-life birds are poor copies, bad machines. They misbehave and do not fulfill their ultimate purpose of perfectly serving Man.

This is, in fact, something the Disney Corporation knows well, as they once found themselves in a fierce court battle in Florida after having violated environmental protection laws which they claimed did not apply to them. When a flock of migratory birds kept returning to Disney World and taking up residence in a themed area in which they did not "fit the look," Disney slaughtered the entire flock (cf. Project 114). Ideal birds would not be so problematic. Ideal cranes would know that they don't belong in the Old West's Frontier. Ideal birds would stay where you put them, go where they are told. And the Tiki Room birds do just that. They joke and laugh and make us smile, and in chorus they sing: "most little birdies will fly away but the Tiki Room birds are here every day."

In Disneyland the animals happily offer themselves up for consumption *as they should*—a point driven home in the Tiki Room, the Jungle Cruise and in particularly gruesome fashion when the mounted heads of slain animals laugh and sing about their having been killed and put on display in the Country Bear Playhouse. Nature is presented in its pure form for the first time. Olive trees have been "chemically trained" to keep from bearing their notoriously messy fruit; the Matterhorn mountain is finally accessible and exists for recreation; flowers never wilt (like Disneyland light bulbs, they are pulled out and replaced while they are still fresh) and they grow in the shape of Mickey Mouse's head—just as is proper and ideal.

Bruce Handy once wrote an extremely entertaining yet misdirected article for the *New York Times Magazine* about Disney taking over Times Square in New York City. The article came out after Disney successfully renovated the Palace and broke attendance records with their "Beauty and the Beast" stage show. In his article Handy imagined what would happen if the Disney Corporation turned Times Square into an amusement park. The result is the "Urban Jungle Cruise," audio-animatronic models of Kate Moss and other billboard supermodels in the Hall of Celebrity Underwear Models, and Mr. Singh's Wild Ride in which a runaway cab only stops its terrifying lurching now and then in order for the guests to experience the "painstakingly re-created . . . sensations of being stuck in traffic while listening to complex discourses on subcontinent politics." Characters from famous movies such as "Taxi Driver" and "Midnight Cowboy" wander the streets ("You talkin' to me, Junior?") and everyone would be in for a good time at the "It's a Nude World" attraction where, Handy tells us, "our merry audio-animatronic cast of multiethnic Girls! Girls! Girls! delight the crowd. . . . ('Caution: May be too nude for some visitors')" (88).

As we have seen, the problem is that Disneyfying something does not mean recreating it as a sanitized shadow of the real. It is to see the thing in its truest and finest form. No one would ever be stuck in traffic in a Disney park because no one ever should be stuck in traffic. This is not to say that we shouldn't have traffic and vehicles in general—on the contrary, Disney is obsessed with transportation. It is to say, rather, that our machines should serve us better. Louis Marin is right to point out that when we leave behind the family car in the Disneyland parking lot it is symbolic of leaving behind the real world (55). Once inside the park, one encounters cars of all shapes and sizes, but they are better than worldly cars. They never (seem to) need fuel; they never get into accidents; they hardly need be attended to at all. Yet they are everywhere. Clearly, transportation is itself the goal—the train runs in circles, the Toontown Trolley meanders a few dozen yards that could be more easily (and quickly) traversed by foot. When the vehicles aren't moving, they are fetishized—but on an Ideal level. That is, we will stand in line to sit behind the wheel of a car that does not move only in Disneyland because here that car is perfectly fulfilling its role—not to get us somewhere, but to strengthen our identity as vehicular people, people whose self-identity is intricately entwined with the automobile, people who are on the go even when they are not moving at all.

It should be clear, I think, that I am not maintaining that the Formal reality of Disneyland really is a Formal reality or that it even is an appropriate or true approximation of these Forms. Platonists can be very wrong about their conception of the Good. That's one reason why we need philosophy. But there is good reason to believe that Disneyland is being presented as Platonic Truth.

Brand-Name Identity

In visiting Disneyland we *become* Disney tourists—we internalize the truth that is presented and become the kind of people who appropriately respond to such truth. Clearly, Disney is responsible for constructing part of our cultural identity. Let us, then, turn to investigate how Disneyland constructs that identity, particularly in terms of the creation of a self and a community within the confines of the park.

It has always seemed to me that there is a bit of ambiguity in the existentialists' claim that existence precedes essence. The idea, of course, is that there is no generic human nature. As Sartre puts it:

First of all, man exists, turns up, appears on the scene, and, only afterwards, defines himself. If man, as the existentialist conceives him, is indefinable, it is because at first he is nothing. Only afterward will he be something, and he himself will have made what he will be. (15)

A lot is riding on this distinction between being and being-something. First we are; then we choose, and by choosing we become something. What do we appear on the scene *as,* then? Before we choose and make ourselves, what is our existence like? And how do we make choices unless there is some set of criteria for choosing—i.e., some unchosen standard that founds our first choice? Sartre says that this condition is the nature of radical choice: you are radically free, so choose. The problem is that there doesn't seem to be much of a "me" to do the choosing until after I choose and construct my essence.

There are various solutions to this problem—all of which would take us in directions we do not have time to explore. The point is that later "Continental" thinkers such as MacIntyre and Carr—who also are in the Heideggerian tradition of thinking about being and "thrown-ness"—suggest that we are less than radically free to construct our own identity. We are engaged in a variety of narratives that were already up and running when we got here. We are often less and never more than the co-authors of these narratives, and thus the project of being is one of providing coherence to a life as one who is engaged in such stories (cf. Carr 80-94).

I have discussed the strengths and weaknesses of these positions elsewhere,[2] and I do not wish to maintain that there is no transcendental ego, for instance, but such authors are useful in getting us started thinking about the construction of personal identity. We live in a necessarily communal world—a world the very foundation of which is socially constituted and experienced as "the same for us all."

In contemporary America, for example, there are varieties of corporate narratives that determine my identity. I am a man who wears boxers or briefs (Hanes or Fruit of the Loom), who uses a Macintosh or an IBM system, who drinks Coke or Pepsi, eats at McDonald's or Burger King, and puts on Nikes or . . . non-Nikes (we are to the point that all other brands are basically just a commitment not to wear Nikes). Surely there is choice here and surely I partially constitute myself by means of these choices, but it seems as if a large part of personal identity has already been determined by the contexts and the choices that are available.

Husserl has said that life is a continual establishing of being, and—like Aristotle—he believes that there is a developmental history to this process. James Hart has interesting things to say as he expands on this theme:

[T]he formative achievements for much of the life of a youth or adult are not the result of unequivocal egological or self-qualifying acts. . . . Rather they are the result of passive position-takings of an imitative and emulative nature founded in the apperception of the position-takings of Others. . . . But this basic trusting spontaneity may not yet be regarded as properly self-qualifying and egological; rather . . . it is the necessary beginning condition for the emergence of the kind of self-reference which proper position-taking acts presuppose and achieve. (61-62)

I would only add that this passive position-taking is perhaps more prevalent in the adult life than is the more proper position-taking. That is, we typically engage everyday life with trusting spontaneity. I trust that one billion burger buyers at McDonald's can't be wrong. I trust that the Coca-Cola company is not poisoning my body—that when they suggest that their product leads to the good life, they are really pursuing the same good that I am pursuing. Drinking Coke, I am apperceiving that good from their perspective, emulating the Coca-Cola company's position-taking on a common good. Furthermore, when "proper position-taking acts" arise, they arise within the context of past achievements and presuppositions. As a Coke drinker I can come to question whether my earlier apperceptions on the common good were correct—was the Coca-Cola company really describing and pursuing the same good I was?—but I come to this self-defining act *as a Coke drinker*.

A theory of "brand-name identity" is even more forceful when one considers the extreme case of having one's standard choices suddenly become unavailable. A friend of mine recently returned to the American Midwest from a year in Taiwan and he brought with him such a story. The grocery store shelves of Taipei held no recognizable brand-names, and sometimes no recognizable food. My friend found that he had to go through a process of trying many foods and many brands in order to see what he liked—a process he likens to a second childhood complete with the gradual emergence of a new, mature self. The new self was constructed by new choices (à la Sartre), but those new choices were mediated by what was on the grocer's shelves (à la Carr). On the level of personal identity this constituted a crisis. It is similar to, though less tragic than, what Hart suggests happens when a dancer loses a leg and there is an "interruption in the flow of life such that both the unity of the world and the unity of him- or herself are an issue" (64).[3]

"We are what we do" is not a historically original philosophic claim. But "We are what we eat" proves no less true. And the point to which we now turn is that in the Magic Kingdom we become a particular kind of person by doing *and* eating.

Licking Mickey

In modern, capitalistic, industrialized states, most people work at jobs that reduce them to interchangeable and dispensable parts in the corporate machinery. Having internalized this sense of self-identity, we "choose" to play out this role on a variety of levels, one of which is in choosing to eat, wear, and display the logos of the corporations we not-so-secretly serve. "In late twentieth-century America," claims Susan Willis,

the cultural capital of corporations has replaced many of the human forms of cultural capital. As we buy, wear, and eat logos, we become the henchmen and admen of the corporations, defining ourselves with respect to the social standing of the various corporations. Some would say that this is a new form of tribalism, that in sporting corporate logos we ritualize and humanize them, we redefine the cultural capital of the corporations in human social terms. I would say that a state where culture is indistinguishable from logo and where the practice of culture risks infringement of private property is a state that values the corporate over the human. (Project 193-94)

Fair enough. But on a certain level there are no humans other than these self-defining corporate citizens. What Willis is after is some concept of authenticity or a real and ideal human way of being—both of which exist, but both of which are also obscured in the Magic Kingdom.

People-watching at Disneyland quickly results in logo-watching. People not only wear the Disney characters and symbols, but they now can purchase parts of "costumes" as well. It is thus possible to see visitors to the park wearing huge gloved hands like Mickey or a variety of hats fashioned after characters (such as Goofy). Updates on the classic pair of Mickey Mouse ears, such corporate costumes allow one to participate in and enter the Disney lifeworld from a "variety" of perspectives. The newly popular "Disney villains" wear, for example, co-opts any rebellion against the Disney ideal of the hero and the happy ending by allowing one to participate *as an outsider, as a rebel*. Disney haters are just another market segment to exploit.

The clothes we wear have long been known to say who and what we are. At Disneyland the mythology is that being in the park and wearing the logo, we can become kids again (read: be happy, innocent, intrigued by our environment, and lust after every neat consumer good we see). The power of the myth is great enough to open up a space in which some people can turn it into a reality. Comments such as the following from a past Disney visitor and later Disney employee are standard:

I saw that the park was the one place I saw my parents be relaxed, be kids again. . . . What was amazing for me to see would be my dad. He's a truck driver, but he would wear this Goofy hat when he was there. He wouldn't wear it after he left the park, but he would wear it there. And I would see them smile and relax, unlike their usual lives. I saw their behavior change. That is what said to me, "There's something special here." (qtd. in Project 139)

Disney provides the space and the equipment to become a (particular kind of) kid again. By consuming Disney we are thus re-defined.

One of the most interesting things about a trip to Disneyland, though, is the sense in which one can literally consume the Disney logo. Mickey Mouse can be eaten in the form of pretzels, pasta, waffles, pancakes, cookies, chips, ice cream, chocolate, Rice Krispie treats, gummie candy, and lollipops—just to name a few.

When we eat, nibble, and lick these images of Mickey we become consumers on multiple levels. We take the cookie together with its meaning, and in this together-taking—this *com sumere*—we become something new. It is a function of choice, of passively apperceived perspectives on what is Good, of the options which stand before us, and of the meaning already built-in to Disney and Mickey Mouse. Choosing to eat an Oreo involves a similar metaphysics, but the experience is different because of the image of Mickey (both in the concrete image stamped on the cookie and in the idealization of Mickey as a set of values—what a Hollywood agent or ad executive might call "Mickey's public image").

To see the point, consider a different kind of narrative. Imagine the experience of eating a Swastika cookie. On the way home from work you stop at a little corner grocery that is not your regular grocery but you've wanted to see what it was like for awhile, so why not now? You grab, among other things, a little package of cookies that look like Pepperidge Farm knock-offs and it's not until you get home that you open the bag, reach for a cookie, and realize that each is topped with distinctly Nazi Swastika-shaped icing. Perhaps you check the bag for any writing, advertisements, or other clues as to the nature of the manufacturer. Little is available apart from the nutritional information on the side panel. You learn that they are low in fat and cholesterol, but apart from that they are a mystery. It might be shocking—or at least a reason to pause and reflect in a new way: Who has made them and why? Who is being supported by your purchasing and consuming them? Is it right to eat them? What kind of person would you be if you did? Could you separate the shape from its cultural meaning and force yourself to eat them *as cookies* and nothing more? Even so, would you hide them away and eat them in private, afraid that you would be unable to explain them to others? Would you return them to the store and demand to know the meaning of all this? Or would you throw them away?

We don't face such a crisis with Mickey Mouse cookies—not because they are not carriers of values and creators of people—but because they are commonplace and generally enjoyed. Their creative powers and values are suppressed in everyday experience. At Disneyland, such powers are multiplied. It is impossible to purchase a non-Mickey pretzel at Disneyland, but who would want to? It is not that we tend to think more about the meaning of the logo when we are inside the park; rather we are freer to not think, freer to be the pure consumer. Just as we should be.

"We": Under Construction at the Park

Indeed, just as we should be. But who, exactly, is this *we*? "We" encompasses so many; it typically apperceives those who are not present. In what sense is there a *we*—a community—at Disneyland?

We are desperate for community, and one of the reasons that Disneyland is so successful is that it offers to fulfill this dream for us. We have already discussed this issue, though not in these terms. When Disneyland offers us a version of Main Street U.S.A., Frontierland, or Tomorrowland, for instance, it is not only offering up an ideal vision of the past, present, and future. It is calling us to be the people who inhabit those times and these institutions. Frontierland creates a narrative to show us who *we* were. By walking down the street, eating at the Golden Horseshoe, and firing the guns at the Shootin' Arcade we participate and become those people. A "we"—albeit a flimsy one—begins to take shape. In Tomorrowland, for instance, we are told that we are high-tech, star-traveling people-on-the-go. And in as much as we participate in the narrative, we become submarine voyagers and rocket jet pilots—we become the people who see this as their future.

All of this is very interesting and important, but it has been discussed quite adequately in other places by other authors (e.g., Smoodin). I would like to focus on how Disneyland draws individual visitors to the park into *we*'s through both a process of shared experience and exclusion.

Most rides at Disneyland seat more than one person. Most, in fact, seat four or more people in a single car or vehicle. Jane Kuenz is right to point out that the seating arrangements, movements of the vehicles, and the added obscurity of the "dark rides" tend to limit the amount of interaction between visitors (Project 62-63). But there are other conditions at work which help to affirm a sense of being together.

In some instances, a community seems to be formed out of a common activity. Paddling the Davey Crockett Explorer Canoes requires common work toward a common goal. Operating a boat, in fact, is an often discussed classic example of communal activity. For Yves Simon, it is close to the prototype of such. He argues:

A team of men pulling a boat . . . supplies a perfect example of a community in act. Of these men, none could cause the boat to move—a thing that the united team does easily. . . . [W]hen men, who know that they exist as a unit for the sake of common purpose, are aware of their common adherence to certain truths, . . . then social life exists more certainly and more deeply than in any transitive action or communication. (125-26)

The problem is that the paid helmsmen and sternsmen on the Explorer Canoes are capable of doing the work all by themselves (Birn- baum's 63), and it is not clear in what sense the visitors are aware of any common adherences to truths—or even really aware of each other. Of course, they must be aware of the mutually appearing world, but this necessary condition of experience—social as it is—hardly constitutes what we mean by an "us" or a "we."

At other attractions, the communicative acts to which Simon alludes are attempts to create community. In the Habermasian spirit, cast members ask groups of visitors to become a unit and participate in some linguistic act. The best example of this comes at the start of the Tiki Room show, where the following exchange is typical:

Cast Member: Are you all ready for a show?
Crowd: Yes!
Cast Member: Our Master of Ceremonies José has been taking a long nap, so I'm going to need your help in waking him up. So at the count of three when I signal you I want you all to say "Wake up, José!" Do you think you can do that?
Crowd: Yes!
Cast Member: Okay, well, here we go. One. Two. Three.
Crowd: Wake up, José!

The result is that *we* woke up José. Acting in unison with a common will toward a common goal that requires common agency, we create a state of affairs through *our* linguistic act. Of course, we were talking to a plastic bird, but at least it was a *we* who was acting, even if the act seems less than communicative in the long run.

Actually, what typically goes on before the show begins is a better candidate for a social-communicative act. Oftentimes the cast member in charge of the show will begin by asking people to identify where they are from. People shout out what country or state or city they call home, or—if they are less than forthcoming with the information—the cast member will ask all of the East Coast residents to applaud, all of the Cal- ifornians to applaud, etc. When it comes to the turn of the latter, she or he will often ask the Californians to welcome the out-of-towners to "sunny Anaheim" with applause. The anonymity of the crowd and the strained nature of the reluctant participation are embarrassing substitutes for community, but there is a sense in which a loose notion of *we* is formed.

Common actions—linguistic and otherwise—can make a move toward community, but common experiences (which form a common past on which to draw, no matter how brief) help solidify the group. We are not only somewhere; we have been someplace—necessarily together. The material conditions of Disneyland can lead to such group constructions through something as simple as the fact that the Indiana Jones jeep holds twelve passengers, all of whom experience the ride as a group—which in this instance means little more than "from the perspective of the same jeep." Recounting the narrative, visitors to the park typically use the first person plural to describe the adventure ("Then we were almost squashed by a huge round rock!") but reserve the first person singular for rides which seat only one or experiences that are essentially non-communal. For example, having gone alone to the park I might say that "I saw the Pocahontas stage show" but "we paddled around the Rivers of America in the Explorer Canoes."

As with most political and social communities, size becomes an important factor. The shuttle to the Moon of Endor holds forty passengers. Little sense of community is formed because there is little time to get to know these Others; there are so many of them that it is an impossible task. Still, and especially in the other rides that do not incorporate the narrative into the queue, even waiting in a long line can create some sense of group identity. As I snake back and forth waiting to board the ships in Peter Pan's Flight or the submarines in the lagoon, I encounter the same faces every few minutes. Not the faces of the people directly behind or in front of me—the narrowness of the aisle prevents me from meeting them unless I am downright outgoing and make a point of it—but rather the faces of people who stand and walk past, people who are side-by-side with me although in terms of the line they are actually several positions ahead or behind. Having to pass them and be in close proximity brings about a "natural" recognition. As the time passes we recognize each other and might even smile. I construct the identity of the Other and myself as "we who are in line."

Stronger experiences shared in a smaller group create a fuller sense of "we." Russel Nye has noticed this phenomenon and remarked that roller-coasters, for example, offer individuals well-known roles to play as individuals, yet create a sense of collectivity as a result of the shared experience of that narrative:

[T]hose who ride the roller coaster . . . are playing roles . . . [such as] the ritual screamer, the front-seat show-off, the marathon rider, the nerveless cynic, and others. People share rides together, eat together, line up together, play games together. . . . Thus the park visitor becomes, in a real sense, a part of a collective unit. . . . Riders . . . often remark on the sudden feeling of camaraderie in the group at the finish at having conquered and survived. (69-72)

The more intense the experience and the smaller the collective unit, the greater the sense of camaraderie. The Indiana Jones Adventure generates this to some degree. Splash Mountain is another good example. In the Splash Mountain log, if one is in a group smaller than four or five, the ride operators will place two groups together in one seven-passenger log. Two families, typically, merge into one "community" as the nine-minute narrative unfolds. Although the design of the boat does not encourage eye contact, one particular addition to the attraction has changed everything. Now a hidden camera snaps a picture of your log-shaped boat just as it tips over the edge of the 52 and a half foot drop. Later, as you float toward the conclusion, video monitors show you the picture. The group is enframed—a unity separated from other groups. Strangers typically turn to laugh and speak with one another. At the exit of the ride one can purchase a copy of the photo to take home, and thus have a concrete manifestation of the unity that existed, even for a fleeting moment. Today in our home we display a photo of my wife cringing in terror, me smiling anxiously behind her, and a family of four who spoke only German behind us and yet were, in some sense, part of that "us." That family purchased a copy of the photo as well. Perhaps my wife and I are part of their photographic, collective memory—with them in a way that forever binds us as a unity. Heidegger has said that being-in-the-world involves being-with the Other. Strangely, in some way that Splash Mountain photo has brought home to me the reality of being-in-the-small-world-after all.

Truth be told, though, this too is a poor stand-in for community. The result is a little taste of togetherness but an even greater sense of separation. While it is true that shared experiences can be an important step in creating unity, the Splash Mountain photo best serves to strengthen my sense of "we" with my wife (i.e., our family) due to the presence of the foreign element that "they" (i.e., the other family) represent. In this way, Disneyland serves to reinforce already established notions of community to a greater extent than it creates them. Disneyland is, in fact, at its best reinforcing community by means of constructing alterity. We are not those pirates who hoard and refuse to spend; we are not those cartoon characters ghettoized in Toontown; and we are not those Germans in the back of the boat.

Other rides make the point in a different way. In the Haunted Mansion, for instance, before the ride comes to an end, the Doom Buggy in which you have been riding spins toward a wall of mirrors in order to show you its contents. In the mirror you see yourself and your companion (the buggies are small enough that only family members or friends need share a vehicle). You see a familiar "us." But there also appears a holographic green ghost hovering on the seat next to you. As the car moves along the wall of mirrors, the ghost stays in the same relative position—a permanent appendage, says the narration, that will "now follow you home." The special effect is a good one. The phenomenological effect is startling. *We* are invaded by the *Other*—and truly no better icon exists for alterity than the non-corporeal, non-living Other who is with us. This image of what we are-not serves to strengthen what we are. Individually, I am not a ghost. Collectively, "we" does not include *that*.

Yet, in some sense it can. In some sense our participation in the common world is changed because the publicity of the world has been enriched. Hart explains that

[t]he opposition of perspectives regarding the common world, the norm, the befitting, etc., enables the appearance of distinctively other points of view or another "we" and the emergence of *"our* world" as contrasted to that of the Others. Before this meeting there was simply "the world" correlated with "us"/"we." Now there is constituted a strange "we"; and now "world" means the way of seeing, the world-view, proper to our country, tribe, etc. World as the correlative of the "we" of one's native land is loosened; now the core is juxtaposed with a dissonant anomalous periphery which demands integration. . . . [N]ow there is the other "we" and "world for us all" has to include them. . . . With the apperception of the strangers' world-view world asserts itself as inclusive of both apperceptions and "we" insinuates itself as inclusive of both us and the strangers—unless imperiously one of the apperceptions, world-views or "we's" is to be dissolved into the other. (223)

Unfortunately, Disneyland tends to construct alterity in just such an imperious fashion. The Other is presented as a modified, malformed, mis-directed version of the self; his otherness is not taken for the alterity that it is. Remembering that Disneyland is a realm of Platonic Formal reality, we learn that this is the finest and purest form of the Other: to be struggling to serve us and to be more like us. A final example will illustrate this point as well as attempt to tie in much of what we have been pondering.

Disney's Heart of Darkness

A phenomenologist charters a boat to go up the river on a Jungle Cruise. We tag along.

Before entering the maze-like queue that leads to the boats, our party typically encounters performers from "another part of the world." Polynesian dancers and musicians put on a show, or a steel drum band plays familiar songs on unfamiliar instruments. There are indications that we are leaving our world and entering another. These Others smile and try to please us—they are there just for us—but we can only pause a moment: the line at the Jungle Cruise is growing.

Working our way toward the boats, we consult our guidebook:

As jungle cruises go, this one is as much like the real thing as Main Street U.S.A. is like life in a real small town—long on loveliness and short on the visual distractions and minor annoyances that constitute the bulk of human experience. There are no mosquitoes, no Montezuma's Revenge. (Birnbaum 68)

It has missed the point. The river which awaits us is not a poor imitation, but rather an ideal realization. It is Asian and African and South American at the same time: unlike our worldly rivers, it is not bounded by the limitations of space. And there are going to be visual experiences which our guide will point out, but no visual distractions. There ought not be such things, but the world, alas, is imperfect. It is filled with distractions. And mosquitoes.

As we enter the boat we take a seat with several strangers. The boats easily hold more than a dozen. We are forced to sit beside these people with whom we did not come to the park. But there is a burgeoning sense of collectivity. We are all going to the same place for the same purpose: to experience the jungle and the river; to get what we paid for. Apart from the close proximity, though, we feel little more attachment to these folks than we do to other drivers who are heading to the mall back home—going the same place for the same purpose. The captain welcomes *us,* though—collectively, as a group—and asks us to turn around and wave goodbye to everyone left waiting on the docks. *We* have acted. A group action—a social-communicative act—has taken place which strengthens the sense of unity by having us engaged in a collective task and by separating *us* from them (they who are back on the docks still waiting).

The captain's spiel begins. Each is slightly different; perhaps ours goes something like this:

As we pass by the entrance to the Indiana Jones Adventure the captain points out the other visitors waiting in line. "Look," he whispers, "the first strange creatures we will encounter: tourists." The joke is on all of us, and we know it, but we laugh at the oblivious visitors above. It is nothing to be ashamed of. In fact, it is good. Disneyland can call attention to what we have become because it is a good thing to be. Throughout the captain's narration, he will make it clear that workers/employees are bad/deprived modes of being, but tourists are on a higher level—honored guests in the realm of the Forms. Couched in such comments as

"Now there's something you don't see everyday . . . but I do; every fifteen minutes" and "I hope you enjoyed the ride; I know I did; so much
so that I'm going to go again, and again, and again, and again . . ." is the
assertion that there is something sad in working for Disneyland, in repetitive labor that is subservient to machines (which, after all, are the main
attraction), in mindlessly serving a function at which one is considered
expendable, interchangeable, replaceable. Indeed, there is great sadness
in all of this—a fact usually obscured by the Disney Magic which inten-
tionally hides the human labor behind the experience. But it is acceptable for our captain to expose us to this here because it only serves to
re-affirm the appropriateness of our own identity and activities. We, too,
are slaves to the system, but in Disneyland we transcend. We are on
vacation.

As we pass the ancient Cambodian shrines, the Captain suggests
that they were built by ancient Cambodian Shriners. The unfamiliar is
co-opted. Audio-animatronic tigers, elephants, and lions appear on cue to
entertain us. The Bengal tiger can jump twenty feet, our captain tells us,
but we know we are safe because in Disneyland the tiger is not unpre-
dictable. He is a fully-understood and controllable machine rather than a
mysterious and malfunctioning machine as in Nature. A group of gorillas
has overtaken an outpost, flipping a jeep and going through the humans'
clothes and equipment. They are pictured trying to wear the clothes and
use the technology—trying to be human. Their true nature is revealed.
Perhaps we think back to the Disney movie "The Jungle Book," with the
monkey leader King Louis singing of how he dreams to be human. Our
identity is more firmly established. We are not those animals; we are
properly human. We are those whom everyone else wishes to be.

Our first encounter with humans strengthens this perception. Dark-
skinned Africans are climbing a pole with funny, ridiculous expressions
on their faces. A rhinoceros has chased them there and is trying to poke
the man on the bottom with his horn. Our captain gives the standard narration: "Look. A native uprising." With one comment African politics
are subsumed under the ridiculous and the comical. We play the role of
the imperial colonialists and take in the scene as such. The eyes see as
such. The Other—note: the darker Other—is politically comical. He also
does not seem able to control the animals and wildlife the way that *we*
can. His alterity is thus reduced to a lesser version of our own subjectivity.

Turning the corner we encounter hippos who, the captain tells us,
are rushing the boat. There seems to be little evidence of this, but the
perception is that *we* are somehow in danger. There is not enough of a
sense of danger to elicit a *thrill,* but we think about the safety of our

boat. The captain pulls out a gun and fires twice at the hippos—some captains say "to scare them," others say "to stop them dead in their tracks." As one of *us,* the captain proves his superiority over the natives. He—and thus we—can control the environment. And shooting the hippo is the right thing to do. Perhaps we'll see his head mounted in the Country Bear Playhouse someday, and we will all have a good laugh when he smiles and thanks us.

The final montages present Disney's attempt to confront us with a more radical Other. To accomplish this they use darker skinned natives who wear masks, shout in an unintelligible language, and practice cannibalism. This is as far from being one of *us* as is possible and still maintain some sense of shared humanity. At first, our boat creeps along and we watch their dancing, trying to "fit in" without incident. The captain yells out a greeting—speaking a gobbledygook that mocks other languages and draws attention to the beauty and logic of our own. But the natives "misunderstand" him and attack us from the river bank. This is no place for *us.* No matter how hard we try, we simply do not belong here and these screaming natives may not become one of us. Back home we will remember: it's a small world after all, but there are some people you don't want to have move into *your* neighborhood—there are some people who simply do not belong with us.

As the ride concludes we pass by Trader Sam who offers to do business with us, selling trinkets and shrunken heads. He is less threatening. He wears a mask, obscuring his racial identity. He is by himself—individualized in the Western tradition. His otherness has been co-opted into our identity and he has become an(other) capitalist. If someone shrinks heads in order to *sell* them, *that* we can understand.

"Prepare yourself for the greatest shock of all," shouts our captain. "The return to civilization!"

As we disembark we are met with a sign welcoming us back: "This Way to Civilization." Passing beneath it we exit into the Adventureland Bazaar and other assorted shops. To be civilized is to consume, we are shown, and we are civilized people. Our boat group breaks up, its members probably never to see each other again. We check our official guidebook to get our bearings and some information on the Bazaar: "Except for the fact that bargaining is impossible, this small market place is well named" (98).

We enter, free to shop. As Joanna promised: "this is gonna be the happiest place you've ever been!"

Notes

1. Earlier Klugman remarks that pictures at Disney are doubly fictional because "when the original is Disney World, then you might say that the resulting image is not a cousin to reality, but a first cousin once removed." Jacques Derrida is concerned about something similar when he wonders about the relationship of counterfeit money to real money and thus to the fulfillment of real Goods. Invoking Plato he claims that counterfeit money is like a copy of something which is itself but a shadow of something else (i.e., currency is not a Good but it is taken falsely as a Good as one may take a shadow to be a thing in Plato's cave; counterfeit money is then a copy of this shadow—a "phantasm") (Derrida 161-62).

2. Cf. Steeves, "Phenomenology and the Possibility of Narrative"; "The Boundaries of the Phenomenological Community"; and "Deep Community: Phenomenology's Disclosure of the Common Good."

3. I cannot begin to do justice to Hart's detailed work. His argument that such occurrences usher in a moment at which "not only is the worldly harmony in question but the I as self or person is an issue because it is not one with itself" (64) is relevant for our current discussions in that the I-pole is to be separated from the self's personal identity. Thus we do not fall into claiming that the self is merely a social construct. I point the reader to these passages in Hart for a full account.

Works Cited and Consulted

Birnbaum, Steve. *Birnbaum's Disneyland: The Official Guide*. New York: Avon and Hearst Professional Magazines, 1996.

Carr, David. *Time, Narrative, and History*. Bloomington: Indiana UP, 1986.

Derrida, Jacques. *Given Time*. Chicago: U Chicago P, 1992.

Francaviglia, Richard. "Main Street U.S.A.: A Comparison/Contrast of Streetscapes in Disneyland and Walt Disney World." *Journal of Popular Culture* 15.1 (1981): 141-56.

Handy, Bruce. "Disney Does Broadway." *New York Times Magazine* 9 Oct. 1994: 88.

Hart, James. *The Person and the Common Life*. Dordrecht: Kluwer, 1992.

Husserl, Edmund. *Ideas: General Introduction to Pure Phenomenology*. Trans. W. R. Boyce Gibson. New York: Macmillian, 1931.

King, Margaret. "Disneyland and Walt Disney World: Traditional Values in Futuristic Form." *Journal of Popular Culture* 15.1 (1981): 116-40.

Koenig, David. *Mouse Tales: A Behind the Ears Look at Disneyland*. Irvine, CA: Bonaventure P, 1995.

MacCannell, Dean. *The Tourist*. New York: Shocken, 1976.

Marin, Louis. "Disneyland: A Degenerate Utopia." *Glyph*. Boston: Johns Hopkins Textual Studies 1. Baltimore: Johns Hopkins UP, 1977. 50-66.

Nye, Russell. "Eight Ways of Looking at an Amusement Park." *Journal of Popular Culture* 15.1 (1981): 63-75.

The Project on Disney [Klugman, Karen; Jane Kuenz; Shelton Waldrep; Susan Willis]. *Inside the Mouse*. Durham, NC: Duke UP, 1995.

Sartre, Jean-Paul. *Existentialism and Human Emotions*. Trans. Bernard Frechtman. Secaucus, NJ: Castle, 1957.

Simon, Yves. *A General Theory of Authority*. Notre Dame, IN: U Notre Dame P, 1962.

Smoodin, Eric, ed. *Disney Discourse*. New York: Routledge, 1994.

Steeves, Peter. "The Boundaries of the Phenomenological Community." *Becoming Persons*. Conference Proceedings. Ed. Robert Fisher. Oxford: Applied Theology P, 1995. 777-97.

——. "Deep Community: Phenomenology's Disclosure of the Common Good." *Between the Species* 10.3-4 (1994): 98-105.

——. "Phenomenology and the Possibility of Narrative." *CLIO* 24.1 (1994): 21-36.

11

FROM EPOCHÉ TO ENTERTAINMENT:
THE CASE OF THE NATIONAL FISHING HERITAGE CENTRE

Karl Simms

From epoché to postmodernism . . .

In the well-known "Vienna Lecture" Husserl argued against a merely geographical notion of Europe, stating that:

In the spiritual sense the English Dominions, the United States, etc., clearly belong to Europe, whereas the Eskimos or Indians presented as curiosities at fairs, or the Gypsies, who constantly wander about Europe, do not. Here the title "Europe" clearly refers to the unity of a spiritual life, activity, creation, with all its ends, interests, cares, and endeavours, with its products of purposeful activity, institutions, organisations. Here individual men act in many societies of different levels: in families, in tribes, in nations, all being internally, spiritually bound together, and, as I said, in the unity of a spiritual shape. In this way a character is given to the persons, association of persons, and all their cultural accomplishments which binds them all together. (273-74)

It is a remarkable passage, one that Jacques Derrida would later describe as "ludicrous . . . comic . . . [and] sinister" all at once (120-22). Particularly remarkable is its double Eurocentrism, for Husserl here advocates a simultaneous inclusion of ethnic Europeans who exceed the geographical bounds, and an exclusion of the non-Europeans within those bounds. This double gesture is based on the premise of *spirituality,* which, as we shall see, for Husserl means inheriting the Greek legacy of theoria and, consequently, of science. The grotesque irony of this passage is, of course, that Heidegger's "Rectoral Address" ("The Self-Assertion of the German University"), which the above passage from Husserl mimics, was one of the principal reasons for this being a *Vienna* lecture. The phrase "wander about," as applied to the Gypsies, immediately brings to mind the image of the wandering Jew, which Husserl himself was, having being excluded from the German University, if not directly by Rector Heidegger himself, then by his successors in their endeavor to enact the principles of the "Rectoral Address." The reference to families, tribes, and nations being internally, spiritually bound together also carries connotations of the twelve tribes of Israel, but whether Husserl considers the Jews to be part of the spiritual Europe, or himself to be either a Jew or part of this (which?) spiritual community or both (is it possible to be both?), he does not say.

What Husserl *does* say is that he's achieved transcendental epoché, something which is "destined in essence to effect, at first, a complete personal transformation, comparable in the beginning to a religious conversion, which then, however, over and above this, bears within itself the significance of the greatest existential transformation which is assigned as a task to mankind as such" ("Clarification" 137). Reading this as Husserl invites us, which is to say, personally, Husserl the wandering double exile (from Israel and from Germany) in effect says "I'm a true, spiritual European because I'm a convert," implying that what he's converted from has now been renounced. Husserl is prompted to this conversion, and to proselytizing for others to be so converted, by a sense of *crisis* in Europe—and through his own crucifixion, or at least martyrdom, Husserl can announce, anticipated by his personal epoché, the dawn of a new epoch. So, what are the spirituality and the crisis on which this argument is premised?

What characterises the *spirit* of Europe, according to Husserl (and again, borrowing from the "Rectoral Address"), is that it lives within the legacy of the Greeks, who were the first to supplant the so-called "natural attitude" by the "theoretical attitude." People living with a natural attitude are concerned merely with their day-to-day lives, and specifically with finite production: what is produced by societies of such people is consumed by them as an end in itself, or at least, in order to enable them to produce more of the same stuff. Hence each such society will have its own truths—ways of being which are valid for that particular society—and the horizons of each of the people living within that society will be finitely bound by those truths. The Greeks, on the other hand, in theorising, produced an ideal, a set of principles which would be true for all peoples at all times (i.e., scientific truths). Therefore, the horizon of the Greeks, and consequently of the spiritual Europeans, is not bounded but is infinite. This is another double gesture: the Greeks are unique in producing *theoria* and hence a properly scientific understanding, but the truths revealed by that scientific understanding are universal or absolute truths, and are thus universally valid for all peoples. It is therefore the duty of the Greeks' spiritual successors, the Europeans, to engage in spiritual conquest by spreading enlightenment, that the truth may be seen (the Greek etymological root *theoréo* means "to see" or "to perceive").

So why is Europe in crisis? Husserl is rather coy about what he really means by European crisis: he writes of "The Crisis in European Humanity," and elsewhere, "The Crisis in European Sciences," and yet, if the European spirit is determined by the theoretical attitude, then a crisis in either of these amounts to one and the same thing. In the final analysis, the crisis is one of just not being scientific enough. The theoretical attitude is seen as merely the second stage of human evolution after the natural attitude. The third stage, heralded by Husserl, is the phenomenological attitude, which is even more theoretical or scientific than the theoretical or scientific attitude. And it is so because it makes theory or science the object, or one of the objects, of its own contemplation. This is where the epoché comes in. Science gains the ideality, and hence the absolute value, of its truths through its objectivity. The localised truths of the natural attitude were merely subjective, or collectively subjective vis-à-vis a given society. The phenomenological attitude, however, in bracketing off the values attached both to day-to-day objects and to scientific facts, is able to make the entire *Lebenswelt* its object of contemplation or, to adopt Husserl's terminology, is able to encompass the entire *Lebenswelt* within its horizon. *This* epoché is transcendental epoché. It transcends subjectivity and objectivity by reflexivity, which is to say, by enabling us to see what is subjective about the subjective, objective about the objective, etc. It will be seen that there are a lot of "ities" in this, and this is precisely the point: in phenomenology, history becomes historicity, science becomes scientificity, etc. This is why Husserl's texts are always "Introductions to Phenomenology": in explaining what phenomenology might consist of, one is already doing it, because (and this is what allegedly makes phenomenology unique and transcendent) it is the only method which self-reflexively accounts for its own methodology.

The anticipated quasi-religious conversion of the whole world to phenomenology does not, of course, come to pass. Rather than the dawn of a new epoch being announced, Husserl's death in 1938 followed by World War II marks the end of an old one. But in the postmodernism which was to come after the war many of the motifs of Husserl's phenomenology are replicated, particularly in the areas of temporality and reflexivity. Phenomenological temporality, as construed by Husserl in *The Phenomenology of the Consciousness of Internal Time,* being grounded in the experience of the subject, depends on a concept of time contrary to the Kantian one of a series of "nows" (cf. Simms). Rather, for the phenomenologist, time is thought of as an already-happened experience of the past mediated by an apprehension of the future, in which "now" disappears in contemplating it (i.e., you can think that you're going to think of a "now," but as soon as you think it, it's already happened). This makes it possible to think through postmodern periodicity: in the postmodern aesthetic, it is the norm to borrow, or make reference to, styles of previous historical periods and combine them in ways which deny their actual historical ordering (e.g., "Tudorbethan" houses which have the brick floor *beneath* the mock wattle-and-daub floor). Indeed, such combinations become the dominant trope of postmodern taste: what used to be "bad" taste is now transcendental taste—"transcendental" because it transcends both historical periodicity and the values attaching to those periods. It follows that postmodernism must be, at least according to postmodern theory, the last historical period, since its aesthetic already anticipates and incorporates any future cultural development.

This leads us to reflexivity, which is also a dominant postmodern trope, and again one which is anticipated by the so-called phenomenological attitude. By anticipating any possible future style and incorporating it within itself, postmodernism also anticipates and incorporates *itself.* Hence we are already seeing phases—early, middle, and late—within postmodernism, so that, for example, the Las Vegas world of pure signs that so impressed Charles Jencks has now been erased in favour of leisure hotel-casinos which incorporate references to that previous postmodern phase within them as part of their "history." In other words, in postmodernism temporality accelerates—everything is always already history before it happens. By 1997, for example, MTV, the most watched form of television programming, important to postmodernism in that it is specifically designed for the short attention span of "channel-surfing," aired a retrospective—of the nineties! The promotion for this imagined itself in some undetermined future, in which various voice-overs made remarks such as "It looks so nineties!"

Postmodernism is the only historical period to hypostatically recognise its own periodicity: the Romantics, for example, weren't so called until the period had come to an end, whereas postmodernism must ever and anew announce its own postmodernity.

From Malraux's museum to the heritage centre . . .

The second edition of André Malraux's *Museum Without Walls* is radically different from the first: in the earlier work (published as *The Psychology of Art I: Museum Without Walls*) the museum as such is "without walls" as a democratic transcultural phenomenon, in that it encapsulates within it the works of any culture and of any time. The museum is therefore to be celebrated as *adding* (cultural) *value*. Take, for example, a display of African masks: a society which has "no culture" can be "transformed" by the transformation of its objects into artifacts, and it is the museum which performs this transformation. The second edition has much less faith in this modernist "making new" (thus leading to the observation that there is a relationship between Malraux and postmodernism [cf. Crimp; Roberts]). Consequently, in the second edition, Malraux finds the double gesture of the first edition—denying other cultures a "culture" combined with European cultural imperialism—something of an embarrassment:

Neither Picasso nor Giacometti consider that they are looking at the masks in the *Musée de l'Homme* with the same eyes as the Africans for whom they were carved and who watched them dance. . . . The more we discover of the meaning of those arts that are united for us by their forms, the more we discover how widely divergent each of these meanings are. . . . How could we admire each of them and all of them together, if it were not for the dazzling common metamorphosis which lights up the dark corners of their individual metamorphoses? We still find it difficult to use the word "admire" without a feeling of uneasiness. (Malraux, *Museum* 210-13)

Malraux's revised view of African masks has the salutary effect of reinvesting them with a cultural value of their own, albeit a *different* cultural value. Again, though, the museum is a mechanism of enlightenment enabling this view. But it does so only partially: while in the first edition the museum as such was without walls, in the second this is only an ideal to which it can merely aspire.

The reason for this change in attitude on the part of Malraux is the development of techniques of photographic reproduction during the years between the two editions, so that in the first edition photography is considered as an art, and a few pages are devoted to it in this capacity, whereas in the second edition photography retains its status as an art, but also becomes the transcendental medium by which cultural value may be globalised, so that it is elevated to being the primary conceptual determiner of the book as a whole.

There is something of Husserlian thinking in the second edition of Malraux's *Museum Without Walls*. The "without walls" here is a theoretical ideal, the realisation of which is made possible by modern photographic reproduction: by its means, the public can have unbounded access to all artworks from any period of any culture whatsoever. As with Husserl's transcendental epoché, this is a matter of broadening one's horizon to encompass the entire *Lebenswelt:* "A museum without walls has been opened to us, and it will carry infinitely farther that limited revelation of the world of art which the real museums offer within their walls" (Malraux, *Museum* 12). If Husserl's world of science has been replaced here by a world of art, nevertheless this theoretical attitude is still a question of sight, of which photography, of course, is a materialisation:

> The museum without walls cannot restore to [recovered] statues the temple, the palace, the church, or the garden they have lost; but it does deliver them from the Necropolis. Because it isolates them; and especially . . . because of the manner in which it lights them. . . . How many works of sculpture move us less than photographs of them, and how many have been revealed to us by photographs? The point has been reached where the real museum is beginning to resemble the museum without walls: its statues are better lit and far less frequently clustered together. Michaelangelo's *Rondanini Pietà* . . . seems admirably posed, awaiting the photographers. It belongs to both the real world of statues and to an unreal world that extends its boundaries. . . . (Malraux, *Museum* 110)

Malraux's position is rather more radical than that of Husserl, however, in that the aim, in replacing the use-value of found objects by a symbolic value as art, is not to spread European culture (or Husserl's "science") globally, but rather to universalise art, which is already global, but isolated. In a charming if somewhat naïvely humanistic gesture, Malraux wants to make all of the cultures of the world equally accessible to all other cultures, and this is to be facilitated by the material light, or transcendental sight, of photography, rather than by the theoretical enlightenment of science.

Since Malraux, however, the museum has not so much reached its ideal; rather, it has been partially replaced by the heritage centre, a kind of consumer-oriented reencoding of the traditional public museum. Heritage centres are now in more or less every town or city of any size in Great Britain. Some of the best known are the Industrial Centre, which is situated in Shropshire, the Maritime Centre in Liverpool, and the Jorvic Viking Centre in York. They're usually "themed" according to the history of their location and they're usually interactive ("bringing the past alive"), and despite their local themes, they are all strangely similar to one another. The growth of this phenomenon questions Malraux's theoretical premises. If the exhibits within a heritage centre invite our admiration, it is not because of their status qua objects, since after all the *objects* within a heritage centre have limited material or "aesthetic" value—their value comes from the purity of their *display*. Hence the picture postcard which one might purchase from the heritage centre shop has, like the picture postcard purchased from the museum shop, a mnemonic function, but the nature of the memory is different: with the museum card, the visitor/customer recalls the artwork, whereas with the heritage centre card, he/she recalls the visit as such. Nor should "display" here be considered purely in visual terms: the heritage centre is an interactive experience, with sound, smell and touch all being brought into play (one of the more popular postcards for sale at the National Fishing Heritage Centre is a scratch 'n' sniff card.) Consequently, one should emphasise that a visit to a heritage centre is an *experience* in a fuller sense than that implied by the passivity of viewing objects in a museum, where visitors are told repeatedly "Do not touch." The upshot of this is that the heritage centre is neither an old-fashioned museum with walls, nor is it a Malraux museum without walls. Rather, it must delimit itself both literally and metaphorically, or else no one would pay to enter (museums, as part of a public service ethos, did not charge for admission), although it also contains a certain ideality within its bounds. This ideality consists in that for which the punter pays, namely knowledge, or, more specifically, that peculiarly postmodern phenomenon, knowledge-as-entertainment.

At this point it is worth pausing over the signification of "heritage." Heritage represents a negotiation between history-as-evolution, or "progress," and the trans-historicality of Malraux's "culture." Heritage re-presents the past, although the past in heritage is not a succession, but is, rather, conceptualised spatially: it is already a collection of artifacts which can be plundered at will with scant regard for continuity. But if culture is a historical product, then properly speaking heritage does not fully represent culture, either. It is significant that heritage is largely an Anglo-American phenomenon. In mainland Europe governments have Ministries of Culture; only in a society which can actively forget history can there be a Ministry of Heritage.

Thus it is the heritage centre, rather than the museum, which offers the better model of the kind of postmodern experience which Jean Baudrillard introduces in his essay "The Ecstasy of Communication" and expands in *Simulations,* by which I mean the *hyperreal* experience:

The "hyperrealism of simulation" [is] the elevation of the domestic universe to a spatial power, to a spatial metaphor. . . . The very quotidian nature of the terrestrial habitat hypostatised in space means the end of metaphysics. The era of hyperreality now begins. What I mean is this: what was projected psychologically and mentally, what used to be lived out on earth as metaphor, as mental or metaphorical scene, is henceforth projected into reality, without any metaphor at all, into an absolute space which is also that of simulation. (Baudrillard, "Ecstasy" 128)

Let us turn now to a specific instance: The National Fishing Heritage Centre, located in Grimsby. A seaport town of 95,000 on the Humber

Estuary about halfway up the east coast of England, Grimsby was once the world's premier fishing port in terms of value of fish landed, although today it derives its wealth principally from general food processing and petrochemicals. The experience begins as the visitor approaches the Centre, since the call of seagulls may be heard even in the parking lot. These are not real seagulls (although Grimsby has plenty of those), but artificially generated seagull noises produced from hidden loudspeakers. Heidegger said that there is no such thing as a pure noise: it is only possible to hear something *as* something, and to do that one must already have language. For Heidegger, one must already have language to hear the call of language, a call which calls us to our being as the animal who speaks (*Being and Time* 203-10; "Language" 187-210). In the artifice of the realistic-sounding heritage seagull the cry is transformed into a call, and it is a call which calls the visitor to be a partaker of an experience. Certainly the call can be described as "welcoming" in a way in which a real seagull's cry cannot (because we know that real seagulls cannot welcome).

Upon entering, the interactive experience begins immediately, when the visitor is invited to choose a "Certificate of Competency" in one of ten areas (e.g., Ship's Cook, Chief Engineer, Deck Hand, and Ship's Cat) as a spur to role-play. Actually, although the exhibition is interactive, no further role-play as such is required beyond this point, so the choosing of a certificate becomes a self-contained *amusette*. I suspect that the real purpose of this is to deflect from the pain of buying a ticket, since the cards are situated *before* the ticket kiosk, so that the visitor has already gone through a symbolic rite of passage in accepting a certificate before having to go through that more typical rite of handing over money.

This is the first instance of the most common of the Centre's motifs, that of a little bit of reality (*petit peu de realité*) or anchoring-point (*point de capiton*), to borrow Lacan's terms. On the front of the certificates it's possible to fill in your own name and the date, which simultaneously projects into the Centre (having the visitor say, in effect, "I am here now and therefore *part of* this experience") and out of it, as a souvenir of the visit (and therefore a spur to the memory of *your own* past). On the reverse are rates of pay, hours of work and duties associated with the role you have decided to play: the Skipper, the Ship's Mate, and the Ship's Cat get the best of it by some way. On the one hand this appeals to the natural inclinations of the visitors, most of whom want to be these people (particularly, it seems, the Ship's Cat). In some sense they already are these people, a popular scenario being to carry the pre-existing domestic situation over into the Centre, so that Dad is the skipper, Mum the first mate, and the kids the crew. This is reassuring for the domestic-minded: whatever the otherness of this exhibition, it's really home away from home. On the other hand, and on the reverse of the card, is the reminder that (and this is another recurring theme) "things were hard in those days." By implication, things are now different and better, so that, just as in Samuel Johnson's theory of tragedy, we partake of the experience in order to pity, which is to say, reassure ourselves that we are *not* those people.

Once you've paid, white bootprints on the ground lead you to the first display, which is on the second floor. It consists of two main features: a 1950s kitchen juxtaposed with a contemporary one, and a 1950s fish-and-chip shop frying range. In the first scenario the theme of carrying one's own domesticity into the leisure experience is continued: the contemporary kitchen could be your very own. Certainly it is a "typical" contemporary fitted kitchen of the "classless" type, that is, neat fitted units as favoured by people who are from working-class backgrounds but who have now accepted bourgeois hegemony. (Most of the visitors to the Centre seem to fall into this category, and this is not surprising, since such centres are designed specifically to fill the leisure vacuum created by this class's emergence from the penury marked by long working hours.) Whilst it might on the face appear bizarre that one should pay to see something that appears for free in your own home, again the comparison is instructional, since the equally "typical" 1950s larder is bare in contrast to the modern one, thus enhancing the already-established Dr. Johnson feel-good factor. Whilst this display establishes comparison, it also establishes unity: by visiting the Centre, particularly if you're from Grimsby yourself (which many of the visitors, like me, are—and in any case, Grimsby is in some respects "any town," being medium-sized and ordinary), you become *part* of the heritage which is being presented.

Which brings us to the fish-and-chip shop—a mock up of the working class street food outlet before the onslaught of corporate fast food franchises. This is metonymic of the whole Fishing Heritage Centre experience, in that it is set in the 1950s, well within the "real" experience of many of the visitors. Back in the days of museums it was considered the norm to exhibit artifacts from other cultures; in other words, things which were beyond the reach of the visitors through temporal, geographic, or cultural distance. Through the Baudrillardian postmodern compression of time and space, there in effect are no "other" cultures anymore. The visitor to the Centre is now in a position of having experienced something in the past which can still be experienced as a memory, but which can now also be re-presented as an actualisation. The comparison between the two kitchens mirrors the comparison between the memory and its actualisation in the now of the Centre as evoked by the frying range. This is reinforced by the accompanying postcard, which, although it purports to represent the frying range, actually represents the model of the fish-and-chip shop assistant. All of the models in the exhibition are modeled on real people, many of whom are still alive and are, of course, free to visit the Centre. Uncanny!

The next scenario is a Grimsby back alley of the 1950s. The representation is as accurate as possible, not only regarding sight, but also sound, smell and touch. The vaguely coal-tar sort of smell which was already present at the first display becomes stronger as one approaches, and when one is completely within the scene it is overlaid by a strong smell of toilet blocks. This is itself a hyperreal smell: as a perfume it has a lost origin in flowers, but one could not imagine a less pastoral scene. The smell has an artificial pungency which is made more disgusting by the thought of that which it is disguising. As one turns the corner, one sees an outside lavatory with a child's swing hanging in the doorway. (*That* was the 1950s leisure experience.) The whole scene is pervaded by the sounds of seagulls, fishwives shouting, and domestic arguments. Moreover, the visitor is not a passive viewer of a tableau, but is *inside* the scene and, again, part of it. Unlike stately homes, where the exhibits are roped off, one can walk around and feel the clamminess of the walls. The scene illuminated by a cold street light, a motorbike propped against a wall, and an exit through a passage adorned with peeling posters of Marlon Brando and Marilyn Monroe combine to make this a *trompe l'oeil* involving at least four senses.

The remaining exhibits succeed in similar vein, the visitor following in the footsteps of a fisherman on a fishing trip (which explains the footsteps on the floor). So, he leaves home, as represented by the back alley, and the next scenario is a trawler radio room. This is a "real" radio room cannibalised from a real trawler, and again made hyperreal by its re-presentation as an exhibit. But again it is not an exhibit in the museum sense, since again the visitor is inside it, looking within it, and free to play with it—there are certainly no signs saying "Do Not Touch" anywhere in the Centre, and at most points tactility is positively encouraged. Once more there is much to smell (the most dominant odor being engine oil), and lots of noise, mainly radio noises and especially the shipping forecast. The next scene is of a deck of a trawler at night, and is heralded by a damp fusty smell. Entry into the scene is also an entry into involuntary movement, a sophisticated mechanism in the floor giving an accurate feeling of the motion of a rolling ship. Sea water is spraying everywhere and is pouring out of a huge net of fish being landed. A stiff cold breeze blows in the visitor's face, and the noise of the sea is almost deafening. Again, one is subjected to what can best be described as a total experience, which leaves one feeling slightly queasy, although in a different sort of way than the back-alley scene. After a museumy interlude of static exhibits (with the added interactive attraction of "Test the weight of a net"), the next scene is of the deck of a trawler in winter. Once more an icy blast hits the visitor in the face, and the smell is of cold air, if that is not too vague a description. The visitor is invited to look into the hold, and the effect of a complete trawler (actually only half) is created by mirrors. The next exhibit is much warmer than the trawler in winter (of course) and the rest of the Centre. There is a burnt-oil enginey smell as one goes down to the boiler room, and the footprints get oily.

This scenario opens out back to the moving deck of the trawler, and from there the visitor proceeds into the galley. Here there is quite a strong smell of spam and baked beans. The galley is the last on-ship exhibit, and the condensation of the fisherman's trip continues back on shore, with a scene of a quayside and lumpers (dockers who handle fish) unloading fish from the hold of a ship. It is accompanied by a tarry smell. From there the visitor proceeds past the settling-up office (where the fishermen were paid), and into the lounge of a typical fisherman's terraced house as it would have been decorated in the 1950s, complete with three flying ducks on the wall. The room smells of coal soot from the tiled fireplace. This scene may be experienced as a pastiche of the country house, although the hyperreal effect also allows for an element of soap opera: a woman is listening to the Home Service on the radio whilst the trawler agent informs her that her husband has been lost at sea. This may be read as a sentimental interlude, although the feeling is rather more uncomfortable than one of sentimentality, since the historical conflation of the experience (it would be possible, if one were a fly on the wall, to witness the same scene for real elsewhere in Grimsby at the same time as your visit to the Centre) reminds the visitor that not only did this really happen (which is true of any museum of social history), but that it really happened and continues to happen to visitors to the Centre themselves back in their "real" lives. There is something uneasy about this, as if the visitor is becoming complicit in pornographisation.

The final scene is altogether more cheerful—it doesn't all end in death, after all!—though the effect is no less uncanny. One enters a pub called the Freeman's Arms, where the fishermen are having a celebratory drink after arriving home safely. This is modeled on a real pub called the Freeman's Arms, in Freeman Street, Grimsby, which hasn't changed much since the 1950s, so that it is possible to compare the Heritage Centre's reality with real reality elsewhere in the town. The only thing not quite perfect is the smell, which in the Heritage Centre is of the cheap perfume worn by the barmaid, whereas the real thing smells of cigarettes and stale beer. The pub opens out onto a quayside which is lined with shops (this is not its location in real life) selling the sort of gifts fishermen would buy for their wives and children. In the water opposite the shops is a trawler, the *Perseverance,* so that when standing on the quay one can see *in toto* as an object what one has just experienced piecemeal.

Finally the exit is, of course, through the gift and coffee shop. Upon entering one is immediately struck (as is the case with each of the scenes of the exhibition) by a smell—but this time it is the smell of fresh coffee. This can be slightly disconcerting, since up to this point the smells have been artificial, and have existed in order to heighten the sense of realism, whereas now the smell is real, and exists as a reminder to consume further. This is odd, since the experience of smelling is identical in either case—the difference lies only in *what* is smelled.

I should like to conclude by discussing my encounter with Peter, one of the guides. There are two reasons for this: first to bring out what Husserl might call the phenomenological essence of the visit to the Centre, and second, to show, through this encounter with the Other (for all his gestures towards ethics in his posthumous writings, and his movement away from Cartesianism in his later works, Husserl remains a self-sufficient being), how postmodernism will no longer sustain the Husserlian epoché.

I met Peter in the galley, although it could have been at any point, since guides are discreetly at hand throughout the Centre. Almost all of the guides are former trawlermen themselves, and they clearly and genuinely enjoy talking about their days as fishermen. From the point of view of the Centre's management, this is presumably why they're employed—again the sense of reality is elevated into hyperreality, so that the visitor is assured of the genuineness of the experience. But it is not quite that simple—one is not quite sure how to respond to this Other. The problem is one of the pornographisation brought about by the breakdown of the distinction between public and private space which the Centre epiphanises. Baudrillard writes that:

This opposition [between public and private space] is effaced in a sort of *obscenity* where the most intimate processes of our life become the virtual feeding ground of the media. . . . Inversely, the entire universe comes to unfold arbitrarily on your domestic screen (all the useless information that comes to you from the entire world, like a microscopic pornography of the universe, useless, excessive, just like the sexual close-up in a porno film): all this explodes the scene formerly preserved by the minimal separation of public and private, the scene that was played out in a restricted space, according to a secret ritual known only by the actors. (Baudrillard, "Ecstasy" 130)

In a hardcore sex film sex is represented, but the representation *is* just sex, so that the "actors" are simultaneously acting and not acting, which is to say, really "doing it." Likewise, Peter was simultaneously a trawlerman and a representation of a trawlerman: by becoming a guide in the National Fishing Heritage Centre, he had become in effect one of the exhibits. In this respect he was like the waxwork woman at the frying range, or one of the characters in the tragic "your husband isn't coming home" tableau, taken one step further: while those characters were static exhibits modeled on real people, Peter was a real person modeled on a real person, namely, his own former self. I found it difficult to imagine what it would be like to be Peter, not because I was alienated from him, but rather for the opposite reason—that in becoming a victim of pornographic obscenity, Peter was a motif of what we all are in the postmodern epoch. This is no longer Johnsonian tragedy—pitying because we are not the Other—but rather human tragedy, pitying because we are the Other.

Fortunately Peter's own humanity shone through, so that initially in his conversation he would explain the exhibits in terms of his own experience of having interacted with them when they were parts of a real trawler, but this would move more generally into anecdotes about his life as a trawlerman in general. According to the information in one of the displays, it appears that it was not unusual for fishermen to marry women at very short notice, and it transpired that Peter had met his own wife three days before marrying her, and that they were still happily married some thirty years later. While giving added authenticity to the exhibition, it also gave added authenticity to Peter, since here was an insight into his "real" life "now." And by this point, in a manner which would doubtless not have endeared him to his employers, Peter began to forget himself (as a guide), and in so doing began to remember his true self. This was inevitably a nostalgic sort of memory: when asked, "Are things better now, do you think?" the answer was that "things are easier now," the implication being that something of more value than mere ease had been lost to Peter. I was left with an uneasiness, however, as I could not help but continually ask myself what it would it be like to follow Peter home after work. What would I see? Presumably, nothing more than I had already seen, since, as Baudrillard writes:

Obscenity begins precisely when there is no more spectacle, no more scene, when all becomes transparence and immediate visibility, when everything is exposed to the harsh and inexorable light of information and communication. . . .

And to drive the point home, Baudrillard repeats:

It is no longer then the traditional obscenity of what is hidden, repressed, forbidden or obscure; on the contrary, it is the obscenity of the visible, of the all-too-visible, of the more-visible-than-the-visible. It is the obscenity of what no longer has any secret, of what dissolves completely in information and communication. ("Ecstasy" 130-31)

I would like to suggest that what is now lacking in Peter's life—the lack which gives a sense of nostalgia—is a sense of vocation. One can imagine having a vocation for fishing—the call of the sea and all that—but not a vocation to be a guide in a heritage centre. The seagulls at the entrance call the visitors, not the workers. Like the Heritage Centre itself, which only opened in Grimsby after the fishing industry had all but died, you only get a job as a guide when the real job you had previously has dried up. Husserl writes that in the epoché:

we establish in ourselves just one particular direction of interest, with a certain vocational attitude, to which there belongs "vocational time." We find the same thing here as elsewhere: when we actualise one of our habitual interests and are thus involved in our vocational activity (in the accomplishment of our work), we assume a posture of epoché toward our other life-interests, even though these exist and are still ours. Everything has "its proper time," and in shifting [activities] we say something like: "Now it is time to go to the meeting, to the election," and the like. ("Clarification" 136)

Husserl does not mention leisure time as having a "propriety," but in the postmodern epoch it seems appropriate to add it to the list. However, in a visit to a heritage centre true epoché seems impossible. We cannot assume a posture of epoché towards our other life interests when visiting the centre if the centre is a representation precisely of those other life interests. Conversely, epoché here is as necessary as it is impossible, since as a "leisure" activity, a visit to the National Fishing Heritage Centre is a departure from vocational activity, and yet the means by which we are entertained by the visit demands exactly this vocational attitude—whether your vocation is to be the Ship's Cat, the Skipper, or any of the other eight choices presented at the threshold. Peter the guide is at the centre of the Centre, since his nostalgia represents the nostalgia we all feel in postmodernism—that true epoché is no longer possible. In 1937 Husserl ("Clarification" 137) claimed a distinction between the *Lebenswelt* epoché of the phenomenologist and the vocational epoché of the cobbler. Once postmodernism has collapsed the *Lebenswelt* into its own representation, this distinction disappears into obscenity, which is disturbing if you phenomenologise it, and entertaining if you don't.

Works Cited and Consulted

Baudrillard, Jean. "The Ecstacy of Communication." Trans. John Jonston. Foster, 126-34.

——. *Simulations*. Trans. Paul Foss, Paul Patton, Philip Bleitchman. New York: Semiotext(e), 1983.

Crimp, Douglas. "On the Museum's Ruins." Foster, 43-56.

Derrida, Jacques. *Of Spirit: Heidegger and the Question*. Trans. Geoffrey Bennington and Rachel Bowlby. Chicago and London: U Chicago P, 1989.

Foster, Hal, ed. *Postmodern Culture*. London and Sydney: Pluto, 1985.

Heidegger, Martin. *Being and Time*. Trans. John Macquarrie and Edward Robinson. Oxford: Blackwell, 1962.

——. "Language." *Poetry, Language, Thought*. Trans. Albert Hofstadter. New York: Harper, 1971. 187-210.

——. "The Self Assertion of the German University" ["Rectoral Address"]. Trans. William S. Lewis. *The Heidegger Controversy: A Critical Reader.* Ed. Richard Wolin. Cambridge and London: MIT P, 1993. 29-39.

Husserl, Edmund. "The Clarification of the Transcendental Problem and the Related Function of Psychology." *Crisis*, 101-89.

——. *The Crisis of European Sciences and Transcendental Phenomenology*. Trans. David Carr. Evanston, IL: Northwestern UP, 1970.

——. "Philosophy and the Crisis of European Humanity." [The Vienna Lecture.] *Crisis*, 269-99.

Malraux, André. *Museum Without Walls*. Trans. Stuart Gilbert and Francis Price. London: Secker and Warburg, 1967.

——. *The Psychology of Art I: Museum Without Walls*. Trans. Stuart Gilbert. London: Zwemmer, 1949.

Roberts, David. "Beyond Progress: The Museum and Montage." *Theory Culture & Society* 5 (1988): 543-57.

Simms, Karl. "The Time of Deconstruction and the Deconstruction of Time." *ImPriMatUr* 1.2-3 (1996): 194-99.

12

VIEWING TELEVISION:
THE METAPSYCHOLOGY OF ENDLESS CONSUMPTION

Beverle Houston

In this essay I will make some distinctions between the positions offered for the spectator by American television—especially network and pay-cable, with some mention of cassette viewing—in comparison with those offered by mainstream cinema, especially with respect to issues of desire. I will comment on the historical context in which these distinctions are being produced.

It seems to me that in practice there is an (albeit ill-defined) interplay between the unconscious dynamics and determinations of subject position and constraint on the one hand, and the activity of the social or historical subject in negotiating readings of a medium and its texts on the other hand. In addition, I also recognize well that the conception of "mainstream cinema" as one single thing is in part a fetish or an imaginary construction. While acknowledging the problems, dangers, and limitations of such analyses as I intend to offer, unless they are articulated with and through specific texts and audiences, and while acknowledging the problematic implications of applying such paradigms to television in the first place, I believe it is of some value to offer a few general distinctions for the purpose of understanding broadly the social work of American television's pleasures at the present time.

Insofar as we may understand spectacle politically and formally/ aesthetically, we may understand that mainstream narrative cinema is far more spectacular than television. This kind of cinema has a fairly rigid enunciative regime in which the source of address is effaced and formal strategies have as their goal to smooth over the medium's play of absence/presence to assist the ego in constructing imaginary unities.

Television structures a very different relationship between the imaginary and symbolic, between a dream of wholeness and the lack that motors it. Institutionally and formally, television insists upon the repetitive reformulation of desire. Rather than suturing the viewer further into a visually re-evoked dream of plenitude, it keeps the ego at a near-panic level of activity, trying, virtually from moment to moment, to control the situation, trying to take some satisfaction, to get some rest from the constant changes, which repeatedly give the lie to television's fervent, body-linked promise. In short, I will try to show that among the pleasures television produces, that of specular mastery is not primary; rather, television offers rhythmic, obsessive, mitigated positions dependent in part on taking something like pleasure in the terror of desire itself.

It may be said that the social work of cinema is to naturalize a certain sense of individual subjectivity by producing cinema-viewing as a timeless and abundant experience. This effect, of course, has a complex role in the circulation of money, power, and sexuality, but its direct goal is to have the spectator say: I want the cinema experience again. At the ideological level, the goal is to reinforce the unified subject as an intermediate step in reproducing a certain social world. This is *not* the definitive work of television. Its function is more directly linked to consumption, which it promotes by shattering the imaginary possibility over and over, repeatedly reopening the gap of desire. Television sets up an obsessive acting-out of desire, which the spectator tries to assuage by consuming the television text itself in its unique promise. Of television we say: I always want it as I have never had it.

Promise and Desire: A Contradiction

This process is motored by American broadcast television's primary contradiction: it offers an extraordinary strong promise of endless flow, which is repeatedly blocked for the spectator by interruption in the delivery of the text. This contradiction keeps the ego active in trying to control and organize the many, numbered items into the "One of a unity whose counting begins with the lost object" (Melman 137). The panicky ego, fearing that desire cannot be endured, but must be silenced, repeatedly seeks a oneness-through-incorporation by watching more television, by consuming it itself and the objects pictured in it, as extensions or displacements of itself. Trained in this disturbingly available partial satisfaction, the obsessional desire for television retains something of the elementary or primal character of the need.

As Williams and others have pointed out, the promise of television lies in its flow, the *uninterrupted* filling of air time modeled on radio. The flow of American television goes on for twenty-four hours a day, which is crucial in producing the idea that the text issues from an endless supply that is sourceless, natural, inexhaustible, and coextensive with psychological reality itself.

Whereas the specularity of cinema's promise evokes the misrecognition of the mirror, and can do so only in the presence of its images, television's promise evokes a much earlier moment and can do so all the time, even when the set is off. In its endless flow of text, it suggests the first flow of nourishment in and from the mother's body, evoking a moment when the emerging sexual drive is still closely linked to— propped on—the life-and-death urgency of the feeding instinct. In its delivery of this flow as visual material, the television also addresses the drive to incorporate in what Laplanche calls its later "fantasmatic scenario" or "analogical . . . line," where the object is no longer directly related to the original object of the instinct by contiguity—as the breast to the nourishing liquid—but has become a metaphorical substitute for the "lost object" (21). Thus the constant interruption or reopening of desire at the analogical level occurs under the pressure of this life-and-death urgency that is re-evoked by the flow. It is no accident that the main textbook in American television studies is called *Tube of Plenty*.

The promise of television is thus not primarily visual, though that has its place, as I will discuss later. Its unique promise is actually more linked with the possibility of liveness, not only in the sense of simultaneity, but more especially in the sense of coextensiveness noted above. Television is as abundant, as plentiful as that which is always already available to the viewer—psychological reality itself. And this flow is available in the home, the privileged location of the everyday and the psychological. Thus television's promise is intensified by a certain relation to materiality. Not only does it lean on the world's body—that is to say, in its liveness—but it is available domestically at all moments—that is to say, in its *livedness*.

The work of the symbolic, of the American television institution, in articulating this technical and imaginary possibility is to break it, interrupt, withdraw it by separating the text into salable parts, breaking up the promise of coherence and wholeness into short sessions, as it were, constantly jerking us out of the dream of coherent signifieds into the world of the endless play of signifiers. The symbolic reproduces this imaginary in discrete, regulated entities—small, discontinuous, easily consumable like the bits of information on a computer screen, like the items in the supermarket, like the small, framed and mirrored segments of the glass-skinned skyscrapers that offer us gleaming reflections of our lives from moment to moment in the high-income, high-tech regions of the American urban environment. TV offers, not access to an imagined coherence of a subject and a signified, but instead an extremely intense miming of the sliding and multiplicity of the signifier.

At the same time that television offers the promise of feeding, it must be remembered that it is also a locus of signification, of symbolic structures, and since it is located in the home, it has family work to do.

As Lacan observed, "Any node in which signs are concentrated, insofar as they represent something, may be taken for someone . . . that which represents a subject for another signifier" (207). In an infant's life, the television, as powerfully as verbal language from other sources, provides a body of signifiers emanating from some unified but mysterious source, an interference from elsewhere drawing the child away from the maternal plenitude. In a scenario of their early months and years together, the mother's eyes are drawn to the shimmering set, and very soon the eyes of the infant as well. The television text intervenes with enough force to prohibit the child's desire to be the exclusive desire of the mother. In their very bedroom, the infant is forced through her to confront this third term, the television and its representational practices. Thus the television substitutes itself partly for other institutions and discourses which constitute the Name-of-the-Father. These discursive positions and cultural imperatives ("meanings") into which the child enters and from which the desire of the Other is learned are thus partly those specific to American television at this moment: aggressive direct address; the single-minded leveling of difference in formal structures, genres, and narrative contents in an attempt to unify all spectators as consumers; the effacement of history as tenses and decades appear simultaneously in programming and are collapsed into nostalgia or myth. At the same time, the apparently contradictory element of television's constant fragmenting and return to difference suggests what Melman calls "a pure play of letters, a pure play of the symbolic, without any voice, without any link to the imaginary" (134). Its disruptions and multiplicities structure it like a kind of barred Other, as Lacan would say, where meaning constantly slips away, eluding the ego and reinstating desire.[1]

Melman suggests that for the obsessive, there is always an interest in signification without meaning or coherence since this allows perpetuation of the basic form of the obsessive idea or activity: "a system of two values based on the exclusion of a third." Thus television's intervention in the family drama helps to found an obsessive movement between seduction by the flow and refusal of its reiteration of lack—turn it off or turn it on—a lifelong dilemma that may be acted out a hundred times a day.

Thus at the level of subject formation, we can see that while the television may to some extent act as another mirror and hold the infant partly in a primary narcissism, and while it may partially block entry into the symbolic by occupying the place of the father, it is perhaps not best examined in these terms. While it may offer its promise as a return to the pleasures of incorporation, it does not finally enable this imagined return. Instead, it regards meaning as somewhat expendable, only a partial compensation, a *distraction* from its endless representation of the sign, of lack, of difference. This is television's excess, its other extremity, if you will, with which it answers the intensity and primal location of its own imaginary promise.

Thus we can understand the phenomenology of television as a "bad object." People often lie about it, claiming always that they watch less than they actually do. Their children, of course, are imperiled by watching too much, etc. In "The Fiction Film and Its Spectator," Metz suggests that a viewer may experience unpleasure, constitute a film as a bad object, when the film offers too little, but also too much, instinctual satisfaction. "In short, every time a fiction film has not been liked, it is because it has been liked too much, or not enough, or both" (111). I suggest that this analysis applies to the television supertext as a whole. It offers too much promise of instinctual satisfaction from the "mother position," so to speak. Yet it also demands too frequent and too brutal a return to desire. And at the same time television gives us very little mirror magic and not much in the way of identification and misrecognition to take away the pain as I shall show later. Thus it is with extreme gratitude that the viewer welcomes the return to the fiction or the sports event. The viewer, in turning on the television, succumbs to the promise of the flow in order to reiterate the pleasure of the return after disruption. Economically and ideologically, American television works! It succeeds in offering itself as the motor, the object, and the field of other objects for the obsessive idea or action that is completed through consumption.

Television's Diffuse Regime

Commercial or network interruption is not, of course, the only way in which television's enunciative structures work against producing the unified experience for the spectator. A key issue in TV's negotiations with its spectators is that it offers a variety of forms of address. While it is correctly argued that ontologically, television is marked by the *possibility* of direct address based on simultaneous presence (impossible in cinema, of course), historically, direct address has been largely divorced from this leaning on the body[2] (as is argued in an unpublished paper by Robert Vianello, "Live Television as an Historical Construction"). There is the simulated or partial direct address and simultaneous presence of the newscast with its re-creations and on-the-scene but after-the-fact reports. Further along the continuum is the oblique direct address of the disembodied network voice-over. Yet another common form of direct address combines the visual pleasure of cinema with the violation of its strongest taboo. This combination is frequently found in expensive commercials such as the recent one in which ex-football star Rosie Greer gazes desiringly into the camera to model for the viewer the pleasure of subscribing to *Sports Illustrated*. However, the seductive power of the gaze is somewhat mitigated by the viewer's awareness of the cinema effect in this commercial. It's a little movie—slickly edited with high production values—so there's no chance that Rosie is present with us, as there was that chance in the news broadcasts. While the television commercial frequently employs the cinematic regime of controlled and controlling enunciation in an effort to reproduce a subject position of mastery, and while network announcements offer a transcendental someone somewhere who's in control, these addresses are only moments among many others in a structure that does not promote identification. The network, or the sponsor, or the program may sometimes enunciate in the cinematic mode, but we are not they.

It might be argued that the deictics of any specific enunciative act in the television text are mitigated by this sliding among and intermingling of various forms of address. It might also be argued that though television is propped on the idea of simultaneity, and though conceptions of its audience are much influenced by ideas of our awareness that we are part of a group, these forms of address or awareness do little to create any felt or functional cohesion among audience members because of a partial but strong absorption of addressee positions and simultaneity into the overriding reiteration of desire and consumption, which are essentially private practices. One is reminded of a new ritual that has grown up on the American streets—or on that edge where the street and the bank come together—the Versateller, the outside, automatic money handler that fronts on the street. No matter how long the line is, no matter how many people are traversing the streets, those in line usually stand well back near the edge of the curb, a good fifteen feet away from the person making the transaction. People who might well push and shove ahead in a movie line or a rock concert, who wouldn't hesitate to position themselves to advantage in any other kind of line—these people, by their atypical discretion, their willful keeping of distance, offer through this new ritual an apparently widely held analysis of money—that its transactions deserve privacy and isolation. I would argue that in the organization of its institutions and format according to salable segments, all transactions between the television and its spectators are inflected to some extent by the secrecy of money as well as by the isolation of desire and obsession. I would argue that matters of address or the awareness that others are watching the same program are insufficient in themselves for interpreting the relation among television's spectators as one of group-in-fusion or community.

Another extremely important aspect of television's diffuse enunciative practice is the role of the cinematic. Cinema functions as a prior discourse for television, one which has demonstrated tried-and-true means of fascinating viewers, of getting them to repeat and reproduce certain kinds of experiences. Thus television calls upon the cinematic in many ways. Its prime-time programming is based on what is offered in cinema, though in altered form, and that is, of course, the fictional narrative, which, between TV's interruptions, structures for television to some extent the same specular relations found in cinema. However, the so-called seamless narrative fiction might be used in a program segment, in a commercial, or in an institutional message of some kind, and each might also involve graphics and direct address. Still, the television depends on the closed fiction of the cinema to make partial delivery on its promise of continued flow.

Those who buy, make, and schedule programming for American broadcast television are well aware of the power of spectacle and its various sutures—the cinema effect—in gaining the consent of the audience to tolerate interruption. We are all familiar with the pattern of beginning programs with long, uninterrupted segments of narrative which, after the first interruptions, grow progressively shorter, until, toward the end, it is often a question as to whether we will tolerate the frequent breaks or simply give up on the program, no longer able to believe in the promise. Visually, such programs as *The Love Boat* (1977-1986) and *Fantasy Island* (1978-1984) call upon the cinema effect—long shots from the moving camera or the helicopter, complex visual fields and detailed surfaces—to hold viewers, not only at the beginning of the program, but at the beginning of individual sections within the interrupted fiction. The evocation of the power of cinema as prior discourse was well in place with the earliest fictions filmed for television such as *Fireside Theater* (1949-1955). Segments opened with brief long shots of exteriors or of character groups before moving into the one-on-one interior intimacy of television's specificity.

The range of television's visual styles may also be understood with respect to the cinema effect. That is, there has been a growing tendency, especially in prime time, to present an image that looks like cinema—that is soft-edged, rich in detail (through camera work, lighting, and the actual environments). The look characteristic of videotape or of much daytime fiction programming, however it is shot, with its harder edge, its minimalist environments, its emphasis on close-ups and facial response—this has fallen out of fashion and a show like *Dallas* (1978-1991) moved steadily toward a more cinematic look. The effective comic-book look of a show like *Star Trek* (1966-1969) would not be produced right now, and this movement toward the cinematic is hailed in many quarters as "progress" for television. However, it can best be understood as another level at which television tries to make a partial delivery on its imaginary promise and at the same time provide a distraction from its work in the symbolic. About twenty minutes spent viewing the movie versions of *Star Trek,* for example, will demonstrate that not every mode of characterization or narrative development can support, or be well supported by, the particular realism of cinematic color and high production values. It's my intention to organize the visual-analysis section of my next television course around this issue, with perhaps *I Love Lucy* (1951-1957) at one pole and *Dallas,* or, better, *Hill Street Blues* (1981-1987) at the other. I think this conceptual structure will provide a way of theorizing visual analysis in television, which has received only limited attention.

However much television may lean on the cinematic, its apparatus in conventional use offers little or no access for primary identification. The image originates, not from a projector behind a viewer, not from a powerful single source postulating a viewer in relation to control-through-aggressive-lines-of-looking. Rather, the television text appears on the front surface of a box in the living room, always waiting in there to be consumed. It is not so much authored as provided.

As David Antin describes typical television camera work, we see that it weakens even further the possibility of formal spectator positioning through identification with the camera since the enunciative position, even in cinema-based fiction, is effaced:

Distinct shots over twenty seconds are practically non-existent. "Distinct" because television's camera conventions include a cameraman who is trained to constantly [make] minute adjustments of the camera—loosening up a bit here, tightening up there, gently panning and trucking in a nearly imperceptible manner to keep the target on some imaginary pair of cross hairs. These endless silken adjustments . . . tend to blur the edges of what the film director would normally consider a shot . . . [and] constantly melt together its various close shots with liquid adjustments and blend scene to scene in recurrent dissolves and fades. (510)

Television's apparatus also includes a channel changer (as well as the off/on switch noted earlier). Our knowledge that we may exercise conscious choice at the slightest sign of dissatisfaction further weakens our chance of immersion; in its suggestion of better possibilities, the channel changer reiterates lack. As a man in the audience of a recent television panel remarked: "I get thirty-one channels and it's *still* not enough."

It's hard to resist talking about the television image itself as never completed, always requiring a scanning process at the unconscious level to assemble lines into a readable image that is always less saturated, smaller, less representative of an imagined signified than is the cinema image—an absence in its very *mode* of effecting presence as well as the absence evoked by its presence. Thus the image itself seems to invite a constant excitation of desire, a work and yearning toward a satisfaction never really available at this level either.

Having noted the variety of forms of address, the range of visual styles, the different modes of textual presentation—commercial network, pay-cable, cassette—we must comment briefly that this variety combines with the location of the set in the home to produce what must be literally an infinite variety of viewing postures or modes of attention. On the one hand, there is the attempt to simulate cinematic fascination by turning the lights down, disconnecting the phone, and putting into the VCR a favorite film which the viewer has been wanting to see, has gone out to rent, and now settles down to enjoy. On the other hand there is the television as "vauditory wallpaper," sight and sound presenting themselves to an empty room, a vanished viewer. Then there is the fragmented viewing of all kinds where you sit before a set and glance at it only occasionally while doing something else, or move in and out of its visual range, perhaps summoned to it from time to time by some aspect of sound. Thus television neither depends on fascination, nor does it require even the glance. Its visual relations with its spectator do not occupy the same privileged role as they must in cinema theory, since television's regime is not primarily specular, as I have shown, but depends on its promise to provide for endless consumption.

Some Implications Regarding Gender

While the model of mental health constructed by Freud is based on the successive vacating of a series of sexual positions, so to speak, the practice and much of the discourse of psychoanalysis is devoted to the fact that these positions tend to be occupied simultaneously by actual subjects. (In fact, it is discourse that constructs this simultaneous occupancy as pathological, or constructs the normatives of psychic "progress" in the first instance.) Lacan's and others' readings of Freud often involve implicit or explicit displacement of models of succession by those of simultaneity, a concern of Freud's as well in his later writings.

But when Freud tried to talk about female subjectivity, he could relax fully in this normative mode and simply affirm that as a subspecies, feminine subjects were *always* regressive, that is, always continued to identify with mothers, with the lawless, pre-oedipal position. The female subject has two objects of desire—the unrelinquished mother and the insufficiently adored father—and two objects of identification as well. The feminine subject *does* learn language, however mysterious her relation to it. Thus she can be said to identify with the Law, which is identified as a masculine position within patriarchy. But as Nancy Chodorow puts it, the feminine subject merely *adds* this male object and position to the continuing female one (7).

Thus feminine subjectivity involves movement among a variety of simultaneously held objects and identifications. For Freud, a regrettable condition; for Julia Kristeva, a contradiction or dialectic common to all subjects, awareness of which allows women to recognize themselves, though we can only *speak* of ourselves through the illusory unity of the dominant paternal language/body. This theoretical work has allowed textual analysts to speak of the capacity for multiple identifications in examining the relation of the feminine spectator to specific genres or texts (cf. Modleski; Williams).

I would like to offer the notion that the strategies of the television institution, enunciation, and apparatus that I have been discussing put all its spectators—both male and female—into a situation that is, in many ways, much like the one that has been theorized for the feminine subject and spectator, but which is, in fact, available for all subjects. As I have argued above, multiple positions are occupied simultaneously by actual subjects; it is a process of differentiation and socialization rather than a sexual essence by which subjects come into existence in culture. The power of the mother position, to which we are never immune; the sliding from the imaginary pleasure of mastery through the passivity of being ourselves the object of direct address and the seductive gaze; the attendant reduced stake in an apparent coherence of the signified; the multiple identifications called for in the movement from fiction to fiction and mode to mode; finally, the forced acceptance of painful delay, deferral, waiting—these characteristics put all of television's spectators into the situation provided for the feminine in theories of subjectivity as well as in her actual development and practice in patriarchy. Television in America requires these forms of behavior, not at the margins of avant-garde alterity or even in special texts produced for and about women, but right at the center of the mainstream of what is arguably—for better or for worse—America's most powerful dispenser of text-for-consumption.

The Politics of Interruption

Having suggested the obsessive reiteration of desire and consumption as television's primary model for negotiating relations between the imaginary and the symbolic through contradiction between flow and interruption, having detailed the formal and technical means by which television's delivery of its text further inflects this position, and having developed certain implications concerning gender, I would like to return to a consideration of interruption itself as a historical and class-linked phenomenon.

Let me clarify what I mean by interruption or fragmentation by examining a break in a theatrical movie being shown on network TV one evening in December. The break to be examined was the hourly one at ten o'clock, containing more discrete items than, say, the next break at approximately eleven or twelve minutes after the hour.

Commercial: Andy Griffith in direct address for the new AT&T. Concludes with graphics.

Commercial: A little parody of a medical soap opera—a commercial for Sheer Energy pantyhose. It's a self-contained little narrative followed by direct address and graphics.

Commercial: A medieval narrative in a kind of historical documentary deconstruction mode—an ad for Riunite wine.

Coming Attractions: For Monday evening. Voice-Over and segments from: *That's Incredible; The Night the Lights Went Out in Georgia.*

Logo: For that night's movie—direct address from voice of the network.

Coming Attractions: For Thursday: *Automan: Masquerade.*

News Brief and Preview: Weather; Salvation Army story; Mid-East report.

Christmas Greeting: Graphics.

Commercial: For Wendy's restaurant. Extreme close-ups of food: baked potato; salads; hot stuff.

Commercial: Toyota—several models.

Public Service Announcement: March of Dimes.

Announcement: Of the 12:25 movie to come. Network Voice-Over. Graphics.

If you count the segments a certain way, there are twelve. But we must bear in mind that each segment is also subdivided not only subtly, as in narrative, but distinctly, as in previews, which present scenes from several different programs, or car ads, which move from model to model. If you count reasonably discernible segments within segments in this particular group, you get about two dozen more or less discrete items.

Television's constant reiteration of desire through fragmentation and interruption is clearly recognized everywhere as a means of enhancing consumption of other products as well. Take, for example, a recent promotion for a new McDonald's breakfast item—Sausage McMuffin. You can get just sausage and muffin, or sausage and muffin with cheese, or you can get everything—sausage, muffin, cheese, and egg. The main emphasis of the commercial is the discrete availability of the items. Apparently the company learned from Egg McMuffin that more money can be made by dismantling the parts than by presenting a unified item. This lesson is reiterated in the history of sponsorship in American television. As Douglas Gomery says:

The television networks have innovated various techniques to garner maximum revenues. During the past two decades, wholly sponsored programs have given way to a "magazine"-type advertising format . . . In recent years by halving the standard advertising slot from 60 to 30 seconds, the networks doubled the amount of "goods" they have to sell . . . Viewers have taken note of this "commercial clutter," complaining to poll takers and making this the number one "problem" with U.S. television. (63)

In 1971, the networks officially converted from the 60-second to the 30-second base for each commercial. By 1980, 87 percent of all network television commercials were 30 seconds long with 10 percent piggy-backed 60-second spots (that is, spots advertising two products from the same sponsor). Only 2 percent of all network commercials were 60 seconds or longer (Poltrack 79).

We note that when Gomery speaks of commercial clutter, he puts the word "problem" in quotes. It's a peculiar fact about American television that no one seems to stop watching it over the long run because of these "problems." But they are a source of worry inside the industry. The following construct of self-regulation taken from the old National Association of Broadcasters code and adhered to by most networks and stations addresses this problem:

Multiple Product Announcement: Advertising more than one product in a commercial of less than 60 seconds is acceptable only if the message for the two or more products is integrated. A message for two products or services is considered integrated if:

—the products or services are related and interwoven within the framework of the announcement (related products or services shall be defined as those having a common character, purpose and use);
[and]
—the voice(s), setting, background and continuity are used consistently throughout so as to appear to the viewer as a single message. (Poltrack 364)

The detail of this regulation, in its effort to arrive at a precise specification of relatedness, reveals the institution at work trying to disguise itemization, trying to transform a "counting" into a "unity" through formal and thematic means. Conversely, even programs such as *Sesame Street,* which don't need to fragment themselves for sponsorship, do so anyway. This is how American television is consumed.

This tendency of American television to increase the strain on its imaginary promise through further interruption and fragmentation is currently heating up with regard to pay-cable networks. In the early years of pay-cable, little else appeared in the text except two things—a brief, unsophisticated channel logo and the movie. At the end of the movie, the logo was repeated and the next movie was presented. At present, movie-channel pay-cable broadcasting has been broken up to include the following: highly spectacular special-effects logos and voice-over network announcements; previews of coming films, sometimes in the form of an organized and narrated program; short subjects of all kinds; direct address "institutional" programs from the cable channel organizations themselves; star interviews; film review programs; "the making of" programs; music videos and frequent mention of corporations and products within or as providing support for this supplementary programming.

Those involved in television marketing—networks and stations that sell time and advertisers who want to buy it—are, of course, eagerly discussing the forms that advertising might take to be acceptable on pay-cable channels. Poltrack's comments in *Television Marketing* are illustrative:

Although I do not believe that the pay cable services will succumb to the allure of Madison Avenue, since to do so would be to give their competition a strong differential advantage, I do believe they might accept a particular form of advertising, the long-form "infomercial" currently seen in movie theaters. These commercials would be short (1-5 minutes), informative, and/or entertaining clips with minimal sponsor identification. Some examples are:

—A series of scenes from a new film promoting that film. [These already exist, of course.]
—A performance or cut from a new album by a group or individual performer. [Also already in place.]
—A great sports moment brought to you by a beer or automobile advertiser.
—A fashion report brought to you by a retailer.

It is felt that this type of advertising preceding and following, but never interrupting, a film would be acceptable to pay TV subscribers. Given the profile of the pay cable audience, advertisers should be willing to switch from the hard-sell 30-second commercial approach to this softer infomercial, or sponsored entertainment approach . . . I expect some such experimentation to begin in the near future. (Poltrack 252-53)

The strategy here is not to disguise differences as in the NAB code, but to create interruptive forms that will be partly misconstrued as belonging to the flow of pleasure rather than to its interruption, or at least be tolerated in the recognition of their gestures in this direction. It should be noted that this form is now common before films on airlines—three minutes on the beauties of a Middle East hotel chain, for example.

Around this issue of interruptibility, we may also engage aspects of the relations of film and television subject positions with certain matters of class. The only thing that prevents the break-up of pay-TV time into commercial segments is a form of economic exchange somewhere between that of the cinema, and that of the apparently "free" broadcast television product. The monthly fee is seen as giving the subscriber some of the same rights as the movie patron—namely, the right to consume a lengthy, uninterrupted fiction. We may understand that right to be to a considerable extent a historical construction.

As is widely known, in the second decade of this century certain changes converged to redefine the activity of the spectator in consuming the American cinema product. The viewing experience no longer consisted of several short pieces, three to ten minutes in length, consumed in the famous storefronts and nickelodeons of the working-class neighborhoods. Instead, a more-or-less standard feature length was established, corresponding roughly to the duration of theater, opera, or dance performances. These long works were viewed in newly constructed movie palaces also modeled more or less after their high-culture counterparts. The new, higher price gave the new middle-class spectator the right to a long, uninterrupted fiction. While early cinema programs often included news and other short subjects, and in the early days were still sometimes packaged with vaudeville variety programs, one by one, the newsreels and short subjects have fallen away. The theater now gives us only the long feature together with some ads disguised as entertainments in the form of coming attractions. There may be the occasional infomercial, but historically there has been great resistance to this direct advertising in American theaters. Robert Sklar is puzzled by this phenomenon:

In the United States, at some point and for no obvious reason, such films were regarded as beneath the dignity of a self-respecting exhibitor and almost entirely disappeared from American screens. (279)

I would suggest that the various elements that came together in cinema consumption after 1915 fetishized non-interruption and the unbroken stretch of entertainment in the American movie theater (unlike, say, India, where uninterrupted length was already a characteristic of pre-cinematic popular or folk forms). But in the U.S., the segmenting of time has not proved viable in the movie theater; the paid ticket for the long feature remains the primary source of revenue. The question for American pay-cable right now can be put a couple of ways: How closely will the spectator insist on maintaining the analogy between the pay-cable film-viewing experience and that in the theater, with respect to the breaking up of time? Another way of putting it is this: Is the power of television's particular imaginary pull—its promise of uninterrupted flow situated in the home—strong enough to support further fragmentation at this interface between film and television viewing?

The subject positions put forward by cinema after the changes around 1915 involved non-interruption above all things and at all levels: that of the narrative, of specular relations, of address, and identification. Those who could afford it were offered a unity, a self, a wholeness which, if the spectator accepted it conventionally, contributed to the continuation of the institutions it represented. All classes would be encouraged to enjoy this experience in an unproblematic way, to shore up their ideological participation. A strong sense of "individual worth" was one of the primary rewards of patriarchal capitalism and cinema was an important means of delivering it.

The dominance of that subject effect as a reward of popular entertainment, and the means of delivering it, are now, it seems to me, in a state of disarray. It has sometimes been said that the movie industry or the early television industry was blind or stupid in not developing the possibilities for pay-TV right away. This argument leaves out the important fact that American broadcast television—network television itself—has been one of the main determinations of the present success of pay-cable. In other words, broadcast television, among a number of other factors (especially the low-cost profitability of satellite networking) has in part produced the desire for pay-cable, in its play of promise and interruption described above.

Again speaking in dangerously global terms and noting as outside the province of this paper the hard questions of the many determinations of broadcast television's success in the first place, we can say there is a kind of circular interplay between pay-television film-viewing and theatrical film-viewing right now, especially in America's urban centers. Various subcultures are effectively altering theatrical viewing conditions. The big cities of both coasts are presently experiencing several waves of immigration, especially from Latin America and Southeast Asian countries where theatrical viewing has not undergone such effective bourgeois restructuring of film consumption and the influence of rural or street-linked viewing conditions may still be strong. Whole families attend the theater, which means the infants must be fed and silenced, older children must be contained. In addition, home-bred Americans whose viewing habits were formed with television bring those habits to the theater. As at home, it's okay to move around, to eat, to talk, to pay a fragmented and punctuated form of attention. .

The technology of viewing conditions has changed also. Under the pressure of reduced attendance, movie palaces have been broken up into small theaters; as new complexes are built with multi-mini theaters, the theater becomes more like the television situation and the class links with theater, opera, and ballet are loosened. In the big theaters with Dolby and 70mm, for which product is specifically created in an effort to re-emphasize difference, the technology is often too much for the personnel. With audience expectations changed, projection is often poor, sound uneven, seats broken; the eating leaves an ankle-deep residue of debris. The "sophisticated" or traditional middle-class viewer may now watch films theatrically only at museums, universities, or archives. Thus the influence of television and the other determinations noted above may reproduce a film viewed under the old theatrical conditions as a nostalgic, aura-intensified, "new" phenomenon. As an ideological apparatus, it could be said that "normal" or "classical" theatrical viewing no longer has it all—an illusion of privileged mastery, the semiotics of the culture palace, together with the frequency and pleasure of popular entertainment.

Under this combination of media-produced and other pressures, movie industry money has flowed into video technology for making and delivering product. Made-for-cable is apparently now the largest source of production funding in the moving picture industry. And middle-class viewing money has followed it. Videocassette or pay-cable movie viewing now offer aspects of the old spectator position. They preserve the personal fastidiousness, sense of higher culture, and illusions of free choice and wholeness which have been the traditional pleasures consumed along with the uninterrupted feature film. The viewer can combine the continuous flow of the television promise while simulating, in altered form, some of the subject conditions of the cinema.

Thus we can see that the traditional position offered to the mainstream cinema spectator as constructed in a regime promoting illusions of mastery in a high-culture analogy is specific to a historical moment that was fully installed with the advent of the feature film screened in a movie palace. Under the pressure of a variety of determinations that have come together since the fifties—the rise of broadcast television; the disruption of Southeast Asia; the political conflicts of Central America; the major decline in the Mexican economy; the presentation of HBO pay-cable television to the public in 1975—under all these pressures, in the context of the continuing crisis of consumerism, that particular historical moment seems to be breaking up with respect to the hegemony of a certain kind of subject effect.

Instead, we are being offered the subject effect I have been describing, which brings us repeatedly face to face with a crisis of desire structured in obsession by the primal promise on which it is propped, diffusing gender relations but providing a far more direct impetus toward consumption. Re-establishment of the older positions now depends in part on further privatization even within the domestic space, where each person needs to have a separate television receiver and VCR so that each person can adopt the viewing posture of his or her choice.

The freedom and anarchy for which television's diffuse regime has been lauded by certain futurist culture critics must be understood in their determinations and functions. It is true that television does not operate to form and reinforce the unified, masculine subject; therefore it can be seen as loosening a particular kind of interpolation. There seems to be a possibility that the spectator of television is not so barred from producing a knowledge of his or her position even while taking television's pleasures. Indeed the link between the level of the economic base and television's role in furthering it seems deceptively clear in comparison with that of cinema. Yet since it is based on a mechanism of desire in which both the dream and its interruption seem to power the viewer toward consumption, it is difficult for a knowledge to be effective.

Notes

1. Martin Scorsese examines television's intervention in subject formation and enunciation in *King of Comedy,* or so I have argued in "*King of Comedy:* A Crisis of Substitution."

2. The unpublished essay of Robert Vianello on the conception of "live" TV as a historical construction has been extremely helpful in thinking about all aspects of this question.

Works Cited

Antin, David. "Video: The Distinctive Features of the Medium." *Television: The Critical View.* Ed. Horace Newcomb, New York: Oxford UP, 1979.

Barnow, Erik. *Tube of Plenty.* 2nd rev. New York: Oxford UP, 1990.

Chodorow, Nancy. *The Reproduction of Mothering: Psychoanalysis and the Sociology of Gender.* Berkeley: U of California P, 1978.

Gomery, Douglas. "Economic Change in the United States Television Industry." *Screen* 25.2 (1984): 62-67.

Houston, Beverle. "King of Comedy: A Crisis of Substitution." *Framework* 24 (1984): 74-92.

Lacan, Jacques. *Four Fundamental Concepts of Psychoanalysis.* New York: Norton, 1978.

Laplanche, Jean. *Life and Death in Psychoanalysis.* Baltimore: Johns Hopkins UP, 1976.

Melman, Charles. "On Obsessional Neurosis." *Returning to Freud: Clinical Psychoanalysis in the School of Lacan.* Ed. S. Schneiderman. New Haven: Yale UP, 1980.

Metz, Christian. "PART III: Fiction, Film, and the Spectator: A Metapsychological Study." *Psychoanalysis and Cinema: The Imaginary Signifier.* Trans. C. Britton, et. al. Bloomington, IN: Indiana UP, 1982. 99-148.

Modleski, Tania. "The Search for Tomorrow in Today's Soap Opera: Notes on a Feminine Narrative Form." *Film Quarterly* 33.1 (1979): 12-21.

Poltrack, David. *Television Marketing: Network, Local, Cable.* New York: McGraw-Hill, 1983.

Sklar, Robert. *Movie-Made America.* New York: Random House, 1975.

Williams, Linda. "Something Else Besides a Mother: Stella Dallas and the Maternal Melodrama." *Cinema Journal* 24.1 (1984): 2-27.

13

THE BLOODY SPECTACLE:
MISHIMA, THE SACRED HEART, HOGARTH, CRONENBERG,
AND THE ENTRAILS OF CULTURE

Michael T. Carroll

Of the many acts of violence in literature, few compare with that which forms the central scene of Yukio Mishima's "Patriotism," in which a young lieutenant performs *seppuku*—the military form of ritual suicide—when he finds that his fellow officers have not included him in a coup attempt. David Lodge, addressing the subject of literature in translation, notes that literary narrative operates a number of codes simultaneously, and in most of them, "(for instance, enigma, sequence, irony, perspective) effects are readily transferable from one natural language to another (and even from one medium to another). A flashback is a flashback in any language; so is a shift in point of view, a peripeteia, or an 'open' ending" (105). Geoffrey Sargent's excellent translation of Mishima proves Lodge's point, for there is one narrative quality that must have been in the original and which is forcefully apparent in the translation. This quality, however, is not one that Lodge catalogues— what Girard Genette calls "focalization," a term which attempts to disentangle "to say" and "to see," the two verbs which are implicated in the Anglo-American term "point-of-view" (Genette 189; cf. Newman 1029). In "Patriotism," Mishima's narration profoundly privileges the gaze:

The lieutenant's eyes fixed his wife with an intense, hawklike stare. Moving the sword around to his front, he raised himself slightly on the hips and let the upper half of his body lean over the sword point. That he was mustering his whole strength was apparent from the angry tension of the uniform at his shoulders. The lieutenant aimed to strike deep into the left of his stomach. His sharp cry pierced the silence of the room. (1187)

Mishima continues to transfix us with this bloody spectacle for several pages; he tells us—or rather, *directs us to see*—the lieutenant's progress as he attempts to complete the ascribed pattern, the blade becoming "entangled with entrails" which push it "outward with their soft resilience," and then the bursting of the intestines through the self-inflicted wound, the "wildly spurting blood," and then the "final flinging back of the lieutenant's head" (1188-89).

It is easy to dismiss this disturbing scene as either an instance of Japanese extremism, or at the very least, Mishima's extremism. After all, the suicide ritual is uniquely Japanese, and it has been noted that Mishima, who took his own life in such ritualistic fashion in 1970, dealt with the theme of violent death in stories like "Patriotism" as well as in the bizarre series of photographs by Kishin Shinoyama called "Death of a Man," one of which has Mishima, hands tied above his head, his torso pierced by airbrushed arrows, in the posture of the Christian martyr St. Sebastian as seen in the Guido Reni painting (cf. Black 203).

But already any culturally specific interpretation has been undermined, for if Mishima and Shinoyama used Reni's painting as a focalizer for their own version of a violent and sacrificial death image, then certainly we are dealing with, if not a cultural universal, then at the very least a transcultural motif. One need not contemplate long before coming to the conclusion that images of a sacrificial victim undergoing what I will call "torsic violation" may be found in a variety of cultures and aesthetic media. The question is, what is the source of their commonality? More importantly, what needs do they satisfy? In short, why do they exist?

The image of violent death, and ritual disembowelment in particular, is something with which Mishima became obsessed, as evidenced not only by "Patriotism" and the Shinoyama photographs, but also by the fact that Mishima himself played the young lieutenant in a 1965 film based on the story; he also played out a similar suicide scene in the 1969 film, *Hitogiri,* about the samurai warrior class. As Henry Scott-Stokes remarks, Mishima "endlessly rehearsed his own death" (26). However, as Joel Black reveals in *The Aesthetics of Murder,* we must bear in mind that Mishima's rather nationalistic interest in this distinctly Japanese ritual is at least partially informed by a study of contemporary philosophy, particularly that of Georges Bataille, who Mishima credits for inspiring the idea behind "Patriotism," that of choosing the moment of one's own death. Bataille refers to violent suicide as a superlatively erotic experience, a moment of "rupture" in which the body overcomes its isolation and reestablishes itself as part of the greater world in a moment that is both orgasmic and transcendent; Mishima himself once referred to ritual suicide as "the ultimate masturbation" (Scott-Stokes 308; cf. Black 205), and in "Patriotism" the ritual is carried out immediately after the lieutenant and his wife make love for the last time and with the understanding that she must play the role of voyeur at this grisly event. And thus we may posit that torsic violation, as a cultural icon and the object of visual focalization, is characterized, in terms of the phenomenology of reception, by its dual, contrary pulls, one towards the body, into the body, and hence sexuality; the other beyond the body, and hence, spiritual and transcendent.

It would be rhetorically and logically appropriate to move from Mishima's highly focalized tale to the realm of iconography, for iconography is a foundational cultural practice, an informing one as regards literary texts which focalize on overdetermined symbolic acts. It might, however, seem less appropriate to move from the profane to the sacred, from the culture of contemporary Japan to that of medieval and early modern France, from, in short, Mishima's "Patriotism" to the Sacred Heart of Jesus.

In its most familiar form, this icon seems to be derived from Christ Pantocrator—the image of Christ with the Bible under one arm and his hand in front, two fingers up, a gesture signifying both wisdom and authority and which is still used in our own time by the Popes. In the Sacred Heart icon, however, Christ's left hand, rather than holding the Bible, is holding open his robe to reveal his disembodied heart. The precise origins of this devotional practice are obscure; there are some passages in the Bible that make reference to the heart of Jesus, but these references, which will be discussed later, seem to have little relation to iconographic practice. Some accounts claim that it dates back to the days of the church fathers, but there is little evidence for this (M. P. Carroll[1] 134; Bainvel 127). However clear the relationship of the Sacred Heart icon to the larger Christian theme of human sacrifice and the attendant image of the Crucifixion, the pagan elements of the worship of the Savior are the more predominant, and thus it is more likely that the icon dates to approximately the 12th century, to the pagan sensuality of medieval Catholicism rather than the post-Alexandrian intellectualism of Augustine and the fathers.

During this era, for instance, several nuns—Beatrice de Nazareth, St. Gertrude the Great, and Mechtilde of Mageburg—had visionary experiences in which they claimed to have seen the physical heart of Jesus. Further, it is from this era that we find what is arguably the earliest form of the icon in crucifixion images of Flemish and German origin. When we compare this image with the Sacred Heart icon as we know it (*see illustrations*), several things become evident: first, there is, to our modern eyes, a peculiar grisliness here in that the most painful and visceral elements of the crucifixion have been amplified. As historian Emile Male says, this "is a strange world. [Here] we breathe an atmosphere of ardent and almost uncivilized piety" (103). Also, during this time we hear the first promotion of this practice on the part of a clerical figure: Dominic of Treves (1384-1461) suggested that devotees kiss a likeness of the sacred heart once a day. In the next century, the Carthusian Lansperg recommended (in 1572) that Christians might assist their devotions by using a figure of the Sacred Heart as a kind of focalizer, a suggestion later echoed by Francis de Sales in 1611. More than a Christian abstraction, then, the Sacred Heart is an image, a focalizer, just as Mishima's fictional, cinematic, and photographic rehearsals for his own sacrificial death served for him as a focalizer.

The ultimate acceptance of this devotion was predicated on its popularity, which in turn was predicated upon the renown of Margaurite Marie Alacoque, a French nun to whom, so it is claimed, Christ made a series of visitations (the Paray-Le-Monial visions, 1675-93) in order to proclaim, among other things, that the worship of his heart was acceptable to him. Alacoque recorded these proclamations in her autobiography, which is, in essence, an imaginary lover's discourse between herself and Christ. Alacoque reports, for instance, that Christ said to her, "I wish thy heart to serve Me as a refuge wherein I may withdraw and take My delight when sinners persecute and drive me from theirs" (8). And later: "Our lord loves you and wishes to see you advance with great speed in the way of His love. . . . Therefore, do not bargain with him, but give him all, and you will find all in His divine Heart. . . . We must love this Sacred Heart, with all our strength and with all our capacity. Yes, we must love Him, and He will establish His empire and will reign in spite of all His enemies and their opposition" (61). Alacoque's visions yield a number of interpretations concerning, for example, the essential imperialism of Christianity and the male/female power matrix expressed within the formulation of male body/female worshiper. Also significant are the psychosexual elements—the veiled language of surrender, of penetration and of exchange. As M. P. Carroll, drawing on Kleinean psychoanalysis, suggests, there is an element of phallic symbolism in the heart image which may explain the enduring power of this icon.

Alacoque's director, a Jesuit priest named D'Columbre, promulgated this practice with particular zeal, and he was soon joined by other Jesuits. While the beatification of Alacoque did not occur until much later, in 1864, the act firmly established the practice, and since that time the feast of the Sacred Heart has been kept at Catholic churches, appropriately enough, on the Friday after the Octave of Corpus Christi. And here it is worth noting that while the Sacred Heart vision in medieval visionary history is seen only by women, men have been primarily responsible for the promotion of the ritual—Dominic of Treves, Francis de Sales, D'Columbre. This suggests a binary code in which the essential creative force is feminine while the bureaucratizing, commercializing force has been male, a code which of course is imbedded in the structure of Catholicism if not all organized religion.

In addition to its manifestation in female visionary experience, the devotion to the Sacred Heart also had an impact on a more ethereal realm of the late medieval superstructure, that of philosophy. This form of devotion was, as one might expect, subject to the controversies which resulted from the conflicts of philosophical and pagan forms of Christianity. The Jansenists, for instance, stood in particular opposition to the practice, and they denounced the "Cardiolartrae" for worshiping a divided Christ and thus giving to the created humanity of Christ worship which belonged to God alone. The conflict here is between the worldly and transcendent elements; between, appropriately enough, the heart and the head of Christianity, an elemental conflict indeed, for as Elaine Scarry remarks, the very fact of Christ's *having a body* is a central preoccupation of the gospel narratives, as in Luke 24:36-40, when Christ asks the apostles to touch and handle him in order to reassure themselves that he is not a spirit. Ultimately, Jansenist objections to the Sacred Heart devotion were censured as injurious to the Apostolic See, which had already approved the devotion and bestowed a large number of papal indulgences in its favor, this under the guidance of Pope Pius VI. In 1794 Pius provided official approval of the devotion in a papal bull which states that the physical Heart of Jesus is not "mere flesh," but is "united to the Divinity." However, the Church did continue to resist the establishment of a feast in honor of the Sacred Heart until the mid-nineteenth century, a fact which makes palpable the official ambivalence towards this practice.

But what has this devotion to do with the *seppuku* ritual, with the self-destructive act imaged by that personification of Japanese machismo, Yukio Mishima? First, there is the sexual dimension that attends the image of torsic violation. In Mishima's rendering of Lieutenant Takeyama's "wildly spurting" blood as well as in Mishima's adaptation of Bataille, the sexuality of death is orgasmic.

Sexuality in a far diminished form may be found in the Sacred Heart images with which most of us are familiar—any one of the thousands of the mass produced portraits, holy cards, statues, and scapulars which may be purchased in any religious goods shop and which are blessed and widely distributed by such Catholic organizations as The Sacred Heart Monastery in Hales Corners, Wisconsin. These images are characterized, in startling contrast to the early and rather gory images, by a dominant tone of sentimentality, which should not surprise us, for such images began to be distributed in an era dominated by sentimentalism—in the 1870s, following Alacoque's beatification.

Sentimentality and sexuality are not, as we know, as far apart as they might appear. In the most common of these images, Jesus gently pulls his cloak to one side with his left hand while his right elbow further parts the cloak, thus suggesting disrobement; further, the soft eyes and the generally inviting demeanor of the portrait suggest something like a "come hither" look. If this reading seems extreme, consider Leo Steinberg's *The Sexuality of Christ in Renaissance Art and Modern Oblivion,* in which various images of Jesus, crucifixions in particular, are discussed in terms of their sexuality, with particular attention to the iconographic tradition of *ostentatio genitalium*—the exposing of Christ's penis. Nor should we ignore the sexuality of the heart itself, at one time believed to be the seat of emotion, that remains to this day an emblem of passionate love in the Saint Valentine's Day celebration. And as the word "passion" has reared its, well, passionate head, we might pause momentarily to consider its dual role, in phrases like "the passion of Christ" and "passionate lovemaking."

If the psychosexuality which informs Mishima's concept of *seppuku* is sublimated in the Catholic icon, so too is the violence. The exposed heart is not violently ripped from the chest, but simply hovers there, mysteriously. Nonetheless, images of violence and violation are evident. The Sacred Heart is surrounded by thorns, a reminder of the humble crown bestowed upon Christ by Pilate's soldiers; and it is pierced on the left, blood dripping from the wound made by the spear of Centurion Gais Cassius. This violent image, perhaps, finds its biblical source in John 19:34, "One of the soldiers struck a spear into his side, and immediately blood and water came forth," while the more idealized element of the icon has its origins in Matthew 11:29, "Learn of me for I am meek and humble of heart." Moreover, the sheer viserality of Christ's heart is contradicted by the transcendent fire of divine love, emanating from the aorta like a sacred gas jet, and by the celestial glow which surrounds this exposed organ.

No treatment of this subject would, I think, be complete without consideration of William Hogarth's series of engravings, *The Four Stages of Cruelty.* This series, a typical didactic narrative, depicts the moral decline of Tom Nero, whose career of gratuitous violence includes acts such as inserting an arrow into a dog's rectum, flogging a horse, and finally, murder. The most shocking picture, however, and the one that warrants our interest here, is the finale, entitled "The Reward of Cruelty," a thoroughly gory depiction of an autopsy being performed on Nero's cadaver following his execution (*see illustration*). The last of the verses accompanying the engraving read: "His heart, expos'd to prying eyes,/To pity has no claim:/But, dreadful!/from his Bones shall rise,/His Monument of Shame."

"The Reward of Cruelty" captures, as does much of Hogarth but rarely as well as here, that odd combination of civility and brutality that was 18th-century England. That dichotomy is pictorially realized in the line of descent which extends from the subordinating gaze of the chief surgeon seated at the center of the picture to the more vigorous engagement of the surgeons who are actually performing the autopsy. As James Twichell notes in *Preposterous Violence,* "we find one freshly killed monster being dissected by other monsters, who are made all the more frightening by virtue of their social and ethical position" (242). The dichotomy is also paradigmatically realized in the contrast between, on the one hand, the symmetry of the surgical theatre—a symmetry informed by the Enlightenment's ideology of reason and order—and, on the other hand, the random disorder of the scholars as they ghoulishly press in to see the dissection and, more significantly, the disorder of the interior of the human body. The victim's intestines and organs are spilling onto the floor, and a dog is warily sniffing at the victim's dislodged heart. One of the surgeons is gouging Nero's eye out with a knife, a gesture that emblemizes the final objectification of the human corpus by denying it the power of the gaze.

More significant still is the way in which the elements established in the discussion of Mishima and Christ—sexuality, transcendence, and focalization of gaze—dominate the picture. In spite of the detachment of the chief surgeon, his gaze suggests an almost prurient interest in the dissection. There is an almost pornographic quality to the 18th-century "medical gaze"—a gaze that lingers somewhere between scientific detachment and sexual or sadistic attraction. In this regard, the chief surgeon's posture is noteworthy: his pointer is held directly in front of his crotch, and it extends in a phallic manner from his hand to the breastbone—where Nero's heart once was. This phallocentric diagonal line follows through in the engraving in both the upheld knife of the surgeon, in the insertion of his left hand into the chest cavity, and, perhaps most explicitly, in the hand of the underling as he removes the intestines.

It is noteworthy that the first and fourth pictures of the series seem to be commonly motived by an interest in "what's inside" the body, an interest we see in both Mishima and the Sacred Heart cult. This interest in internals in "The Reward of Cruelty" is a scientific one, but this does not sever it from other instances of torsic violation, for if Mishima's *seppuku* ritual is an attempt to transcend the duality of self and world, and if through the divine love of Christ, emblemized by his Sacred Heart, we may eventually transcend earthly being and earthly desire, then in this unsparingly satiric depiction of medical autopsy, we glimpse the ideology which, in Hogarth's 18th century, replaced Christianity and its notions of transcendence, or at least usurped a good measure of its authority. And that ideology, of course, is that of science. Institutionalized science is denoted throughout the picture, in the mortarboard caps and in the only object other than Tom Nero's corpse that is the subject of penetrating gaze, a medical book. As this was the era in which medicine became institutionalized, we may then see the frantic activity of the surgeons as an attempt to colonize the body, to force it to yield to scientific explanation and technological mastery. Perhaps their efforts seem so frantic and desperate because, compared to the advances taking place in the natural sciences, the medical establishment was more or less powerless in the face of the mystery of the human body, the mystery of life and death. And of course, by yoking Tom Nero's violation of a dog's body with the violation of Nero's own corpse by medical men, Hogarth suggests that science may not, after all, have gotten very far away from more primitive forms of violence.

Our probing the entrails of culture will conclude with the 1988 film, *Dead Ringers,* the product of the Canadian director, David Cronenberg. Cronenberg's bizarre psychodrama, based on a true story, concerns the lives of identical twins, Elliot and Beverly Mantle, who at an early age evince a peculiar fixation for the internal workings of the female body. They progress from performing mock surgery on a plastic model, to Harvard Medical School, and finally into a lucrative private practice in gynecology, supplemented by research grants bestowed upon them for their innovative techniques. The first of these techniques is the "Mantle Retractor," a device the brothers invented in medical school for holding open the abdominal wall of the patient and which later became, in the words of a speaker at their Harvard commencement, "the standard of the industry." This idyll of prenatal identity, perversely extended into adult life and institutionally legitimated, begins to unravel when the twins are faced with the prospect of "an unexpected turn in the Mantle saga;" that is, a woman, Claire Niveau, comes between them. Niveau's presence causes a "rupture" in the brother's intense psychic bond, a bond which has its roots in the biological bond of identical twins and which lies at the very core of their identities.

And, indeed the problem of identity is the prime motivation for the Mantle brothers' obsession with the internals of the female body, for through visceral knowledge, through the subjugation of the female to their subordinating medical gaze, they hope to solve the mystery of their own origins and to obtain self-knowledge. Their obsession with female internals take a bizarre, aestheticised turn, for as Elliot Mantle proclaims, "There ought to be beauty contests for the inside of the body—you know, most perfect spleen, most perfectly developed kidney." In one alarming dream sequence which has the brothers conjoined at the hip like the Siamese twins, Chang and Eng, Elliot watches as Claire bites through the twins's shared flesh to draw out their shared viscera with her teeth. And in the final sequence of the film, Beverly makes a surgical incision into his brother's abdomen in an attempt to solve their psychic dilemma, a solution which proves fatal to both.

There are of course, many other examples of torsic violation coupled with the transfixed gaze. Examples that readily spring to mind include *Eraserhead,* in which David Lynch's existential nerd/anti-hero, in a moment of what would seem to be irrepressible curiosity, carves open the abdomen of his mutant infant son and watches in fascination as the contents hideously expand. Think also of the disembowelments in the films of Hershel Gordon Lewis, the "godfather of splatter," whose 1963 *Blood Feast* inspired a host of grotesques productions: the comic disembowelments of the Andy Warhol/Paul Morrissey versions of *Dracula* and *Frankenstein,* Tobe Hooper's *Texas Chainsaw Massacre,* George Romero's intestine gobbling zombies in *Night of the Living Dead,* and not coincidentally, the work of David Cronenberg.

But we are left with the question with which we began: why, in terms of cultural motivation, do such artifacts exist? There are a number of possibilities. The most elemental factor is the quality of overdetermination that exists in the bloody spectacle, the presence of the contrary qualities of bodily death, spiritual transcendence, and sexual release, a heady admixture which gives such scenes the power to transfix the human gaze and thus make them spectacular, worthy of intense focalization. In both Mishima's death rehearsals and the Sacred Heart icon we have phenomena which imply transcendent values, for both the *seppuku* ritual and devotion to Christ have at stake the same thing—the possibility of transcending the body/spirit dichotomy—and yet, the scene is inherently corporeal, inherently and perversely sexual. And as we saw in our examination of Hogarth, science too has the goal of transcendence; science too has its transcendent and sexual elements.

The human subject is brought face to face with these dichotomies as well as with the dichotomy which, as Aristotle long ago pointed out, accompanies any true spectacle, that of one's own pity and fear. The pity is inspired by the commonality that we feel for the victim of acts of bodily violation. As Little Alex, the protagonist of Anthony Burgess's *A Clockwork Orange,* proclaims while gazing upon a piece of his violent handiwork, the blood flows the same from all bodies; it flows "like it was all from the same factory." As for the fear—it is perhaps better described as horror. As Milan Kundera says, the horror of death is rooted in two things: the prospect of "non-being" and the "terrifying materiality of the corpse" (171). There is likewise the horrific fear of degradation—perhaps we too will be poked and prodded like Tom Nero.

The bloody spectacle is, seemingly, a moment of truth—a literal seeing into things: into the mystery of Christ's sacrifice, or into the "sincerity," as Mishima describes it, of *seppuku,* or, as in Hogarth, into the empirical truth of scientific examination in 18th-century autopsy, or, as in *Dead Ringers,* into one's identity in the concept of twentieth-century state-of-the-art gynecology.

According to Julia Kristeva, "The corpse seen without God, and outside of science, is the utmost of abjection. It is death infecting life. Abject. It is something rejected from which one does not part, from which one does not protect oneself as an object" (3-4). The bloody spectacle is often seen in the light of God, but never entirely; often in the light of another god, Science, but again, never entirely so. Thus, the spectacle of torsic violation is always somewhere between godliness and defilement, between, on the one hand, the purity of science and transcendent idealism, and, on the other, the degradation of mere brute fascination and sexual drive. It is through this overdetermination that the bloody spectacle is, and will remain, an enduring image in the gallery of culture.

Note

1. Michael P. Carroll, the author of *Catholic Cults and Devotions,* is not to be confused with Michael T. Carroll, the author of this essay and the co-editor of this anthology.—Eds.

Works Cited

Alacoque, Margaret Mary. *Thoughts and Sayings of Saint Margaret Mary for Every Day of the Year.* Compiled by The Sisters of the Visitation of Paray-le-Monial; Trans. The Sisters of the Visitation of Partridge Green, Horsham, West Sussex. Rockford: Illinois Tan, 1935.

Bainvel, Rev. J. V., S. J. *Devotion to the Sacred Heart: The Doctrine and Its History.* Trans. from 5th French. Ed. E. Leahy. London: Burns, Oates and Washbourne, 1924.

Bataille, George. *L'Erotisme.* Paris: Editions de Minuit, 1957.

Black, Joel. *The Aesthetics of Murder.* Baltimore: John Hopkins UP, 1991.

Burgess, Anthony. *A Clockwork Orange.* New York: Abelard-Schuman, 1972.

Callahan, Annice, R. S. C. T. *Karl Rahner's Spirituality of the Pierced Heart: A Reinterpretation of Devotion to the Sacred Heart.* New York: UP of America, 1985.

Carroll, Michael P. *Catholic Cults and Devotions: A Psychological Inquiry.* Kingston, Montreal, London: McGill-Queen's UP, 1989.

Clover, Carol. *Men, Women and Chainsaws: Gender in the Modern Horror Film.* Princeton UP, 1991.

——. Interview with Johnny Ray Huston. [San Francisco] *SF Weekly* 8 July 1992: 23-24.

Cronenberg, David, dir. *Dead Ringers.* Script by David Cronenberg, et. al. Prod. Carol Baum et. al., 1988.

Genette, Girard. *Narrative Discourse: An Essay in Method.* Trans. Jane E. Lewin. Ithaca: Cornell UP, 1980.

Kristeva, Julia. *The Powers of Horror.* New York: Columbia UP, 1982.

Kundera, Milan. *The Book of Laughter and Forgetting.* New York: Penguin, 1981.

Lodge, David. "Milan Kundera, and the Idea of the Author in Modern Criticism." *Critical Quarterly* 26.1-2 (1984): 105-21.

Male, Emile. *Religious Art in France: The Late Middle Ages. Bollingen Series* XC.3. Princeton UP, 1986.

McCarthy, John. *The Official Splatter Movie Guide.* New York: St. Martin's, 1989.

——. *Splatter Movies: Breaking the Last Taboo of the Screen.* New York: St. Martin's, 1984.

Mishima, Yukio. "Patriotism." *The Norton Anthology of Short Fiction.* 4th ed. Trans. Geoffrey Sargent. New York: Norton, 1978. 1171-92.

Moell, C. J. "Devotion to the Sacred Heart." *New Catholic Encyclopedia.* Washington, DC: Catholic UP of America, 1967. 818-20.

Morris, J. U. "Iconography of the Sacred Heart." *New Catholic Encyclopedia.* Washington, DC: Catholic UP of America, 1967. 820-22.

Newman, Beth. "The Situation of the Looker-On: Gender, Narration, and Gaze in Wuthering Heights." *PMLA* 105 (1990): 1029-41.

Scarry, Elaine. *The Body in Pain.* Oxford UP, 85.

Scott-Stokes, Henry. *The Life and Death of Yukio Mishima.* New York: Knopf, 1973.

The Shape of Rage: The Films of David Cronenberg. A publication of the Academy of Canadian Cinema. Ed. Piers-Handling. Toronto and New York: General Pub.; New York Zoetrope, 1983.

Shinoyama, Kishin. "Death of a Man" (photographs of Mishima), 1970.

Steinberg, Leo. *The Sexuality of Christ in Renaissance Art and Modern Oblivion.* New York: Pantheon, 1983.

Twitchell, James. *Preposterous Violence.* New York: Oxford UP, 1989.

14th Century Escutcheon, Flemish or German Origin.

Variations of the Sacred Heart icon.

William Hogarth, "The Reward of Cruelty" (1751).

IV.

THE SOCIAL CONSTRUCTION
OF REALITY

14

PHENOMENOLOGY, AUTHENTICITY,
AND TRUTH IN ADVERTISING

Chris Nagel

As a profession advertising is young; as a force it is as old as the
world. The first four words uttered, "Let there be light," constitute its
character. All nature is vibrant with its impulse.
> —Bruce Barton, founder of the advertising firm
> Batten, Barton, Durstine & Osborn, Inc. (qtd. in Caples 65)

It would be reasonable to assume that the title of this essay is ironic;
after all, our common knowledge is that advertising is at least a bit
untrue; if All detergent really had the laundering omnipotence its name
suggests, this fact would be well-known and the commercials would be
unnecessary. This is an important (yet banal) piece of cultural knowledge:
advertising tells half-truths in order to portray a product or candidate in
the best light. We accept its dissimulating, seductive methods, and
"nobody in his right mind really believes an advertisement or a promotion
piece" (Samstag 97). Furthermore, advertising does not seem to us significant as culture. Ads are the interruptions and fillers in the low-brow
media of TV, radio, and mass-market magazines. This rates their cultural
importance lower than the issue of *People* or the episode of *Friends* into
which they are integrated. Advertising is less significant, and even less
believable, than the main body of misinformation in these media.[1]

On the other hand, according to *Advertising Age,* the annual advertising budget for AT&T is close to $1 billion; each half-minute of com-
mercial time on *Seinfeld* during the 1996-97 TV season cost $550,000;
and President Clinton's call for strict regulation of tobacco advertising
has led ad agencies to lament the potential loss of $1.14 billion in rev-
enue (1-3). These figures point to the tremendous significance of ad
campaigns, but do advertisers really spend these unimaginable sums for
no other reason than to lie to us? Conversely, if advertising's job isn't to
sell products for more than their worth by inflating their images, what is
it?—what else does it do?

My aim here is to clarify advertising as a cultural artifact. In the first part, I will restate four approaches to the interpretation of advertising that make certain assumptions about its nature. Although these interpretations may have their strengths, the assumptions obscure other aspects. Without explicitly rejecting any of these, I will leave them all aside in developing a phenomenology of advertising in part two. On the basis of my phenomenological clarification, I will conclude that the meaning of advertisements is not informational (in the sense of presenting purported facts), though it depends heavily on an accrual of cultural information. In other words, advertising is a cultural artifact which has little to do with making true statements to persuade consumers to buy certain products. Rather, advertising is most essentially an intersubjective practice upheld by a set of tacit agreements, that is, an element of the social construction of reality.

Non-phenomenological Approaches

Criticism of advertising is nothing new; it is, in fact, a minor cottage industry. Many critics complain that advertisements contain truth claims that are false, inflated, or so qualified as to be meaningless. For instance, no rules prohibit subjective or superlative claims about products. The claim that Chrysler makes the "best" cars available does not impose upon Chrysler Corporation any legal responsibility to defend the claim. Roughly speaking, the claim is legally meaningless.

McAllister has devised the categories of "accurate" and "ideological" as a way of sorting through the criticism aimed at the advertising industry. The "accurate" critics complain that such claims imply that the products in question have certain qualities that would warrant the assertion. Legally, no such claim is made, but tacitly, superlative terms lead to the conclusion that the product is actually worthy of praise (Preston 3ff.). This criticism of the accuracy of ads is attacked by "ideological" critics, who consider accurate criticism "naively liberal and missing the larger power and significance of advertising images" (McAllister 152). It is indeed doubtful that consumers faced with an ad claiming Chryslers are the best cars reconstruct the ad's meaning as a syllogism. According to ideological criticism, the more important truth in advertising is more of a question regarding whose interests are served by its power.

These two critical approaches assume that advertising is an attempt to convince consumers to buy a product or a political ideology. How advertising functions as a medium is obscured by this focus on its aims. To follow these criticisms, the capacity of advertising to affect consumers must be presumed unproblematic. In this view, advertising is a direct, unambiguous transmission of information, images and truth claims with the sole end of persuading buyers that a product has good qualities.

On the contrary, according to Samstag, the first purpose of an ad is to be read or seen, and the second purpose "is a secret." Interpreting advertising solely on the basis of the assumption that it is meant to sell something neglects the fact that the differences between the products are usually negligible:

Every now and then, of course, some firm really gets the drop on its competitors and, for a while, information has its day. For a short period there was only one brand of stainless steel razor blades and it was important to know which one it was. For a time (only a short one) Oldsmobile had automatic shifting all to itself. But very soon everyone gets aboard and we are back where we were, seducing with the same body, exaggerating at the same rate and the devil take the hindmost; in this case, the customer.

Perhaps the cause is that our affluent society supports too many choices to make simply informational advertising effective. We have so much money to spend that six or twenty brands can prosper in markets where there are only two or three basic differences possible in the product being offered . . . At any rate, caught without real differentiations to advertise (or blessed with differences they don't dare advertise), a great many advertisers just keep drawing their products longer and sleeker until they outrage every law of perspective or keep faking their TV commercials so obviously that even a feebleminded schoolboy could see through them or persist in describing their oversize art books or perfumes or resorts in phrases that sound like the ravings of those who eat hallucinogenic mushrooms. (26; 90f.)

Samstag remarks that factual information is irrelevant to the success or meaning of an ad. What remains is the appeal of the ad itself, rather than the product it advertises. Marketing research on radio broadcasting in the '30s and '40s shows that consumers do not take advertising seriously as persuasive speech. They complained most often, not about false or misleading claims, but about commercials interrupting the programs with obnoxious music and announcements. What they wanted from advertising was what they wanted from radio in general: entertainment.[2] Advertisers agreed, and so began 60 years of efforts to make commercials more enjoyable and entertaining.

Many commercials are displays of images unrelated to the product being sold. Advertisers spend a great deal of energy and money "branding" themselves—that is, using advertising campaigns not to sell a product, but to associate the brand name with a certain lifestyle or sometimes other abstract images. Print and TV ads for bluejeans, perfumes, automobiles, computers, and nearly anything else one can think of, rely on no qualities of the product, indeed do not even name any. Instead, a great deal of them relate the brand to a certain cultural iconography. There are, for instance, innumerable representations of Marilyn Monroe and James Dean in ads attempting to make a "hip" or "cool" appeal; they incorporate by allusion the entire tragic mythology of these figures. Clearly, accurate and ideological criticism does not penetrate "branding" commercials. One could impose upon these ads a truth-uttering interpretation by once again presuming that the consumer reconstructs the ad as a sort of syllogism (to use a recent example): since Steve McQueen wore khakis, and Steve McQueen was cool, anyone who wears khakis will be as cool as Steve McQueen.

It may be that advertisers rely on an expectation that consumers believe they will look like Steve McQueen in their khaki pants (although no explicit claim is made that Steve is wearing any particular brand of khaki pants); this view presumes that advertising works by tricking consumers into identifying with the cultural icons represented in the ads. Advertisers consider the iconographic branding approach more subtle and sophisticated than this, however: the aim of these campaigns is not directly to sell products but only to give the product an image.

A "subliminal message" interpretation of advertising arises from these more sophisticated techniques and from the work of Marshall McLuhan. In this view, advertising, indeed all media (especially electronic media), operate on a subconscious or pre-logical level; as McLuhan puts it, "any ad consciously attended to is comical. Ads are not meant for conscious consumption. They are intended as subliminal pills for the subconscious in order to exercise an hypnotic spell, especially on sociologists" (*Understanding Media* 218). Instead of appealing to a reconstructed argument guiding the consumer to a conclusion (and purchase), advertising seduces through the id, ego, eyes, and ears of the perceiver (and note that for Samstag, seduction is the primary purpose of advertising). Commercials replay a Freudian drama of desires, traumas, and repressions, as a means to suggest their messages, or, in McLuhan's terms, "[a]dvertising is an environmental striptease for a world of abundance" which has "sprung up as a service for the consumer who hardly knows what to think of his newly bought cars and swimming pools" (Wilson vii; xi).

While most interpreters in this vein consider commercials a kind of hypnosis putting the critical capacity of the consumer to sleep, McLuhan goes further, claiming that advertising forms consciousness and community:

Ideally, advertising aims at the goal of a programmed harmony among all human impulses and aspirations and endeavors. . . . When all production and all consumption are brought into a pre-established harmony with all desire and all effort, then advertising will have liquidated itself by its own success. (*Understanding Media* 227)

McLuhan is optimistic that media will achieve this harmony and produce a human community incapable of conflict, since all of us would always be concerned to produce and consume in an equilibrium matched by the capacities of the global village. War and strife would be virtually advertised out of existence.

Extending beyond McLuhan's subliminal, pre-conscious or consciousness-forming view of media and advertising, Jean Baudrillard dismisses all notions of media having either a beneficial or harmful effect through manipulation. Media cannot have such an enormous influence because there is nothing to counter-pose to media; we lack "in opposition to it an authentic human nature, an authentic essence of the social, with its needs, its own will, its own values, its finalities." Instead, Baudrillard interprets media as a voyeuristic gaze of the masses, at themselves, through an excess of information. Advertising is indeed a seduction, but it is not the seduction of consumers by producers. It is the seduction of the masses themselves, the seduction of the seducers. In seducing ourselves, we the masses delegate "in a sovereign manner the faculty of choice to someone else by a sort of game of irresponsibility, of ironic challenge, of sovereign lack of will, of secret ruse" (*Selected Writings* 209; 216). Thus advertising is the expression of the desire of the masses to have desire imposed. Ads allow us to evade the horrible necessity of choosing from among the indeterminate field of objects, by obliterating meaning and erecting a simulation in its place. Thus, instead of the oppression of deciding between functionally identical toothpastes, we are entertained by the unreality of brands, commit our loyalties to one or another, and stake a claim to a part in the mythological realm of post-consumer society. The masses can only protest by taking on the posture of inertia, by not responding to the seductive advances of advertising; yet this self-objectification cannot counteract advertising's continual progress.

Advertising, Baudrillard contends, is an expanding form of expression, one destined to become ubiquitous. All expressive activity will reach the form of advertising, "a simplified operational mode, vaguely seductive, vaguely consensual . . . in which all particular contents are annulled at the very moment when they can be transcribed into each other . . ." Advertising is the destiny of culture and absolute advertising is a point at which culture implodes, neither communicating nor inform-ing, but only reaffirming itself while effacing the real and its tangible boundaries. The information it presents "devours communication and the social" (*Simulacra and Simulation* 87; 80). Sociality is absorbed within it, and therefore the question of believing in advertising, or in the values of the culture, is impossible to pose: the entire culture is an advertise-ment for itself.

McLuhan and Baudrillard assume that advertising has a powerful influence on viewers. On the basis of this assumption, they seek the effects of this power. Interpreting media and advertising as general social phenomena, they hypothesize a set of aims or a trajectory of advertising. In their ominous views, advertising is a social force inde-pendent of human interests and not the result of human practices. Adver-tising does not merely inform, it does more: it forms its audience.

Phenomenology of Advertising

Phenomenology requires interpretation to follow description; that is, all theoretical assumptions must be laid aside. This does not necessar-ily mean that theoretical approaches lead to incorrect interpretations. It could be the case that ads lie, that ads serve capital, that ads seduce sub-liminally or alter our perceptions; it may be true that commercials create desires or express desires the masses desire not to take responsibility for. Phenomenology asks instead what advertising is, what the experience of advertising means, beginning with a description of the phenomenon.

How can one delimit the field of phenomena proper to advertising? I will assume only that something which is presented with the meaning "an advertisement," is an advertisement. This does not mean that only *such things* are advertisements, nor that such things are *only* advertise-ments. Furthermore, advertising is a cultural artifact, an objective expression of social relationships. By taking actual advertisements as my examples, I hope to gain some essential insight into advertising. Imagi-native variation (as well as the actual variety of ads themselves) will clarify the essential core of advertising, as a promotion of things. The meaning of "promotion" will be examined in the end.

It will be helpful, in identifying what is entailed in the social rela-tionships involved in advertising, to sketch out the relevant elements of the phenomenology of the social world. Alfred Schutz orders forms of communication along a continuum from those which are most immedi-ate to those which are most mediate, corresponding to forms of intersub-jective relationship that are more and less authentic (*Phenomenology* 80). The basic structural unit of sociality, according to Schutz (and echoed in different ways by Maurice Merleau-Ponty, Peter Berger and

Thomas Luckmann, and Emmanuel Levinas), is the face-to-face or We-relationship. The face-to-face situation is one in which I and the Other share "a community of space and a community of time," in which I and the Other are co-present and maintain "an actual simultaneity with each other of two separate streams of consciousness" (*Phenomenology* 163). The Other is given to my experience (and I am given to the Other's experience) distinctly and directly as a person, as a "Thou" with "life and consciousness" (164). In the We-relationship founded upon the face-to-face situation, I and the Other direct our consciousness toward each other, we intend an understanding of one another as living persons, and communicate with one another in a shared or common environment. Merleau-Ponty gives concreteness to this authentic experience of co-presence through the example of dialogue:

Our perspectives merge into each other, and we co-exist through a common world. In the present dialogue, I am freed from myself, for the other person's thoughts are certainly his; they are not of my making, though I do grasp them the moment they come into being, or even anticipate them. And indeed, the objection which my interlocutor raises to what I say draws from me thoughts which I had no idea I possessed, making me think too. (354)

On the other end of the spectrum, Schutz places inauthentic, indirect, mediated They-relationships, the relationships we have with "contemporaries." The difference between authentic and inauthentic relationships with others, according to Schutz, is simply a matter of direct vs. indirect, immediate vs. mediate, one in which the other is a co-present Thou, and one in which the other's existence is not directly apprehended at all (*Phenomenology* 181). Furthermore, inauthentic relationships are "derivative" upon the authentic. All of the intimacy and understanding of the authentic We-relationship is missing in the They-relationship, and others are attended to only through abstract descriptions. Berger and Luckmann describe the They-relationship as the employment of "typificatory schemes" to classify others as, for example, "consumers," "television watchers," etc. (31). The utter lack of empathy for the Other which characterizes the They-relationship suggests antipathy to some. Merleau-Ponty considers the Other outside of the co-presence of dialogue "a threat" (355), and Levinas claims that only within the They-relationship is murder possible (86f.). Yet, according to Schutz, even close relationships with friends are sometimes drained of their immediacy, and it is only by way of the derivative, taken-for-granted typifications of a They-relationship that we continue to understand or attend to a friend who is distant (*Phenomenology* 179-80).

Understanding other selves, whether authentically or inauthentically, entails interpreting behavior in terms of the motivation of acts. Schutz claims that there are two forms of act-motivation: the "in-order-to" motivation and the "because" motivation. The expectations an actor has, or the result the actor means to bring about through a set of particular actions, are "in-order-to" motivations; they are "projected in the future perfect tense" (*Phenomenology* 88). Having such a motivation requires the presumption of certain relationships within the world and between objects within it, relies on a fantasy of the projected aim, and hence is a non-genuine understanding of behavior. In contrast, the "because" motivation is the genuine explanation of the meaning of a deed. A "because" motivation is a comment on a lived experience, hence a past-tense experience; it is a way of explaining, in the pluperfect, why one did what one did. A "because-motive" can only be established after the act has taken place, and on the basis of the actual, lived experience of the act. Note that the "in-order-to" motive is quite independent of the "because-motive," and it is only the contemplation of the "because-motive," in the pluperfect tense, that can establish the genuine meaning-context of the action. That is to say, a "because-motive" explains the act, while the "in-order-to" motive merely establishes the project.

These two forms of motivation are important in the interpretation of social behavior. Of key importance in a phenomenology of advertising is the motivation of persuading an audience. Schutz describes a similar situation:

I may so project my action that I picture you as being moved to a certain kind of behavior as soon as you have grasped what I am doing. I am then picturing your interpretation of my action as the because-motive of your behavior. Suppose, for instance, that I ask you a question. My in-order-to motive is not merely that you understand the question but that I get an answer from you. Your answer is the reason why (the "for-the-sake-of-which") of my question. (*Phenomenology* 159-60)

The questioner presumes that the question will be answered, and the precise nature of this presumption is that the question will be sufficient reason, a because-motive, for being answered. If the person responding takes up the gambit of the question, the question is accepted as a because-motive, or, to put it in Schutz's terms, "his answer must be such that the questioner will accept it as a real reply to his question. The orientation of the answerer, therefore, reflects that of the questioner" (*Phenomenology* 161). The importance of this analysis of social behavior is that responding to others requires, according to Schutz, the adoption of the other's project as a genuine because-motivation. The response is due to, produced by, drawn from the respondent, by the project of the sender of a message.

Finally, the meaning-context of an act is established by the projection of the act. This means that the in-order-to motive of the projection sets forth the entire meaning-context, "for it gives unity to all the intentional acts and all the actions involved in its performance" (*Phenomenology* 75-76). Sending a message, or asking a question as in the above example, is an act whose projection establishes the unity of meaning of all acts related to that project. An answer is an answer specific to the question asked, because the act of asking the question sets out the meaning-context in which the answer takes place. In other words, the in-order-to motive which founds the project of sending a message also establishes a unity of acts, a meaning-context, to which the response to that message inevitably must pertain. If you respond to the message I send you, your actions enter into the meaning-context, the unity of my project of communicating, and your response is due to (has its because-motive in the act of) my message.

Preliminarily, using these theoretical terms, we can say (1) that advertising has a promotional in-order-to motive, (2) that it is a form of communication that is based in an anonymous They-relationship (the advertisers are not co-present), and (3) that advertising sets up a meaning-context in which a response to advertising is meaningful on the basis of taking up the project of advertising.

(1) As a cultural product, ads are one of those "objective configurations of meaning which have been instituted . . . and which have a kind of anonymous life of their own" (181). The anonymity of ads does not imply that advertisers seek in every case the most general audience. In fact, this is most often not the case: advertisements are directed toward demographic groups. Of course, the identity of a certain demographic group is determined through the anonymous means of statistics. An advertiser fixes on a number of people who are likely, according to the data collected, to have a certain income, education, etc., and who will be affected by certain appeals.

(2) From the Schutzian viewpoint, all of these analyses of the advertiser's market are inauthentic They-relationships. So advertisers appeal to audiences as typifications rather than as actual people, regardless of the narrowness of the targeted group.

(3) More obscure, perhaps, is that the experience of advertising depends on a certain intersubjective understanding of the media. The media bear sets of assumptions or "taken-for-granted" characters. Television has a certain meaning in general for the viewers. At a very basic

level, the images and the sounds are closely associated, so that an aspect of the meaning-context of television is the typical relation of visual and aural experience. In our typical, taken-for-granted interpretation, what appears is what makes the noise we hear. In quite another vein, television is constituted socially as not a "serious" or intellectually challenging medium; according to this wisdom, "TV is not an art form or a cultural channel; it is an advertising medium . . . it seems a bit churlish and unAmerican of people who watch television to complain that their shows are lousy. They are not supposed to be any good. They are supposed to make money."[3] We watch, not because we are stimulated, excited or even well-entertained by TV, but because it is something that does not seem to require effort. The terms associated with watching TV—"idiot box," "boob tube," "couch potatoes," "vegging out," etc.— suggest, in accordance with McLuhan, that TV is a form of hypnosis, a super-cool medium to which we are not prompted to react. The meaning-context of TV is a highly typified interpretation that is taken for granted by viewers. Armed with this set of assumptions, we watch the set and make sense of what appears.

Since the 1960s, most national ad campaign money has been spent on television. In addition, TV ad campaigns have set the tone for national print and radio ads. The style, sensibilities and meaning-context of television have carried over to other media, and trickled down from national advertisers to local, small-budget campaigns. For these reasons, I will use TV commercials as my leading examples of advertising, but the results apply to all advertising.

In 1996 Levi's advertised *Jeans for Women* with a series of animated TV commercials. Because viewers rely on the typical presentation of elements on television, the highly stylized and sketchy figure has the sense of a depiction of a woman. This "woman" is composed of a roughly outlined triangle for a "torso," a roughly outlined oval as a featureless "head," and two long blue daubs extending as the "legs," or more specifically, her "jeans." The blue daubs are the only solid-colored elements of the "woman," who would appear to have the overlong, emaciated figure of a Barbie doll. The "head" and personality are totally effaced or given simply as blanks. She has no race, no age, no eyes. Along with the visual elements is a soundtrack of an assured-sounding female humming. The commercial's artsy style is striking; if one accepts the suggestion that it represents a female form, the movements of the figure are alarming. As the animation sequence unfolds, the "woman" stretches, leaps, runs, zips around the screen, and shoves aside apparent obstacles of considerable weight and size. "She" moves well beyond human limits of flexibility, speed and strength. At the end of the 15 or 30 seconds, the Levi's logo and the name *Jeans for Women* appear on the screen for the first time.

Once again relying on the socially constructed meaning of TV ads, the presentation of the logo indicates an association of the brand with the rest of the content of the ad. In other words, the appearance of the logo and slogan refers the figure's movements to the Levi's brand. Two facts are implied: that the figure is a woman, and that "she" is wearing Levi's. Yet the ad does not assert that these facts are true—on the contrary, they are patently not the case. All that is presented are "her" extraordinary movements and the logo at the end; the meaning-context of the medium allows the constitution of the intelligibility of the ad. Female humming and a set of shapes vaguely acceptable as a human form=a woman; blue daubs as "legs"=jeans. Since we can establish a more or less coherent meaning for the animation, the movements of the figure take on their senses as "flying," "jumping," "pushing something heavy," etc., in a way that is reminiscent of a human being and yet at the same time beyond human capacity.

The connection of these superhuman images with Levi's is rather obscure, not just because it is only indicated by the inclusion of the logo at the very end of the ad, but also because nothing about the ad makes a claim that Levi's has anything to do with the transcendence of the "woman." Nor does the ad present a persuasion to *buy* anything. The advertiser does not make explicit an in-order-to persuading motive which would help the viewer constitute the ad's meaning. The viewer of the Levi's ad does not rely on the explicit expression of its posited aim to make sense of the ad, because this pre-posited meaning is taken for granted already, in the meaning-context of watching TV. Thus the ads themselves need not present the meaning of persuading the audience. Since viewers interpret the ad according to the typical meaning-context, the persuading-sense of the ad is constituted by the viewer. It does not express its attempt to sell, and to that extent, the ad does not attempt to sell. The case of the Levi's ad is somewhat extreme in the tenuousness of the connection of the ad's content to the persuading motive of the company. All that appears is the company logo, at the very end of the ad. The logo indicates the company, the slogan states the name of the product; we do the rest of the work of constituting the meaning of the commercial. In this way we understand what advertisers want, and do not require to be told. No one needs to see a particular ad to tell what it is for; the particular ad simply indicates the object about which we already understand that we are supposed to be persuaded. In short, as we constitute the ad's persuasive sense, it is we who assume the burden of persuading, not the advertisement or the advertiser. Nothing actually presented or expressed in the Levi's *Jeans for Women* ad makes a persuasive case for the product. This meaning is left implicit, and it is the viewer who does the actual persuading.

(This aspect of the experience of advertising may explain the early complaints of radio listeners. Since the commercials are obviously broadcast in order to influence the audience, "hard sells" are always overkill. Listeners grudgingly accepted the presence of ads and the motives driving them, conceded to the broadcast of advertising as a way of funding radio programs, but wished advertisers would entertain more and interrupt less.)

The second example is for a Polaroid instant camera. This ad, cited by *Advertising Age* as one of the best of 1996, consists of an overwhelming number of quick shots, probably more than 60 in a half-minute ad. It is unclear to a casual viewer what exactly is present, and what is filled in. There is a shot of an overturned trash can and garbage strewn on a kitchen floor. A woman scolds her dog, while a cat struts in the background. She leaves, and the cat jumps up onto a counter top adjacent to the trash can. The dog looks on, with apparent anxiety, as the cat leaps onto the can and upsets it to begin rummaging through the garbage. The scene cuts to a shot from the dog's perspective, a shot which jumps from the cat to a cleaver, to a rolling pin, and finally to a camera. At the end of the ad, the woman re-enters, and a quick cut to the trash can shows the garbage across the floor again. Cut to the dog with photos in its mouth, offering them to the woman's hand. Photos of the cat on top of the pile of garbage appear, and the woman's voice is heard, saying "Oh dear."

Advertising Age published a review of this commercial, along with the results of a survey of sample viewers, which revealed that 100 percent of the viewers called the ad "excellent"; 31 percent found it humorous; 27 percent creative; 86 percent retained the dog or the cat. Strangely, only 6 percent retained that the product was an instant camera, and a matching 6 percent retained that the camera was "easy to use" (Vadehra 16). The "excellence" of the ad evidently does not consist in its presenting an unequivocal claim that Polaroid makes easy-to-use Instamatic cameras. To conclude that the advertisement sells the product seems premature at best. Yet as an advertisement, it has the social meaning of a promotion which attempts to influence the behavior or attitudes of the audience.

What the survey reveals is that the heart of the ad is the dog and the cat. The dog's behavior is especially fascinating. The ad depicts the dog reacting to a scolding for a crime it did not commit and feeling the desire to avenge this injustice. The dog understands the abstract ideas of right and wrong. Furthermore, it understands the use of human tools in the creative way depicted. Not only does the dog know that a cleaver can cut, but is also aware of the cultural cliché of the rolling pin as a domestic weapon. Even more amazing, the dog decides upon vengeance, not the mere infliction of harm to the cat. The dog presumes that presenting evidence of its innocence will help its case, so the farfetched implication that the dog could use the camera is the least of its accomplishments!

The common knowledge or social assumption that advertisements are selling devices hides the more important significance of ads—that aside from selling, they get themselves seen, heard, and read. If ads sell products, it is not necessarily on the basis of any qualities of the products. When those qualities are named, the claims made for the products are usually inflated, distorted, or composed of meaningless distinctions. But the Levi's and Polaroid ads I've described contain practically no information about the products. Nevertheless, Levi's and Polaroid are no less motivated by the urge to sell products, and that is the ultimate aim of their efforts as corporations. In these cases, advertising's content is not about the products, but about the advertisers themselves. In a recent column in *Advertising Age,* Bob Garfield writes:

In so many categories these days, advertising is called upon not merely to highlight the brand's value but to be the brand's value. In the imagery of the Marlboro man, in the attitude of Pepsi commercials, in the ethic of "Just Do It" resides not just brand information and brand personality but also brand meaning. The advertising is, in fact, part and parcel of the brand. It is itself a brand benefit. (55)

Advertising connects a brand to a certain corporate image. This image is a "brand benefit," that is, a reason to prefer one brand over another. In Schutzian terms, brand benefit is a because motive for the consumer's purchase. I buy Marlboro cigarettes because I take up the image of the Marlboro man; I buy Pepsi because I am postured in a certain attitude. The in-order-to motive of advertising is to present the consumer with a because motive to behave or believe in a certain way. In other words, advertising relies on the viewer's act of constituting the meaning of the ad (and assuming the in-order-to motive of advertising in general, i.e., to promote things) to associate the thing promoted with a set of images or ideals which provide a reason to prefer the thing promoted (a post-hoc because motive).

All of this takes place through the anonymous They-relationship of mass media. Advertisements present information about the consumer as a typification, and associate the product or brand with this stereotype. Ads present the consumer with an image of himself or herself or, in other words, tell consumers who the advertisers think we think we are. Furthermore, the stereotypes are necessary to constituting the meaning of the ads in the first place. Levi's advertises *Jeans for Women* with a schematic, cartoon superhero, surpassing human bounds, as well as the already-surpassed bounds of sexism (in the limited sense of restricting the activities of women to what we used to call "traditional roles"). The ads do not claim that the jeans enable this transcendence, but only associate the jeans with it. Unless one already takes for granted the typification of a certain "young, strong, and assured woman," the Levi's ad is totally unintelligible. The "liberated woman" typification is required both to make sense of the images and sounds actually presented in the ad, and to make sense of the appeal of the ad (its motivation structure). The demographic target is a typified group who identify themselves with the ideal of womanhood portrayed, and it is this typified ideal which makes possible the meaningful constitution of the commercial's images. The womanhood ideal must be recognized to render the ad intelligible; if the ideal is accepted as an ideal, the ad's persuasive message emerges. The ad both depends upon and promotes a stereotyped notion, at a constitutional level of experience. The viewer does not deliberately assent to the stereotyped ideal promoted by the ad. Instead, in seeking to constitute the intelligibility of the ad, the viewer must adopt the typified ideal. Actually to have seen the commercial means that the viewer has already taken up the motivation of the advertisement. Merely by viewing, one is persuaded of at least the interpretive validity of the images which promote the product or brand.

Likewise, the Polaroid ad is absurd without the background typification of anthropomorphized cats and dogs. Pet owners imbue their animals with human traits and motivations. These cultural meanings of pets are played upon in the ad, to render it intelligible. The story told in the commercial requires the assumption of this way of typifying pets to a fantastic degree. The viewer also takes up, in the act of making sense of the images presented in the ad, the value of pets as entertaining companions. Moreover, the viewer *must* adopt a set of beliefs about justice and fair play, without which it would appear meaningless for the dog to take a photo of the cat instead of attacking it with a weapon.

Advertising plays upon cultural information that has been established as a general social structure of reality. The intersubjectively constructed meaning of the medium of an ad—that is, the socially pervading meaning of media—is fundamental to the constitution of the ad. A whole set of expectations establishes where one is likely to encounter ads and what one does when faced with an ad. Persuasion is an essential element of the meaning-context of advertising, a meaning that viewers bring to the experience of advertising in order to constitute the sense of particular ads. Particular ads connect individual products and brands to the general sense of advertising as a means of promotion.

This sense of advertising clarifies both assertorial and vague ads, those that purport that a certain product is good, and those that give an image to the brand. Advertising is in every way bound up with a certain truth-claim; but unlike verifiable truth-claims in reference to the factual performance of a product, the true utterances advertisements make are references to goodness. All advertising asserts that the thing being promoted is good. But this goodness has nothing to do with the product's or brand's qualities. A good product is a means to some desirable end; a good brand is one that refers abstractly to desirable ends or images. The goodness is presumed in the meaning-context, so all the advertiser needs to do to promote the product is to name it. The Levi's ad promotes (or gives a good name to) the ideal of liberated, strong womanhood which viewers use to meaningfully interpret the ad. Its images of female transcendence are given a promotional pitch, as it were, in the eyes and ears of the viewer. The Polaroid ad refers to the goodness of pets, of a cultural anthropomorphization of pets, and of an ideal of justice. Less abstract ads have the same structure. As Samstag points out, the differences in products are few; the purpose of advertising is to connect one brand more intimately with good ends. All detergent does not advertise an objectively demonstrable superiority over other brands, but celebrates the goodness of clean clothes and refers All to this good end.

If one responds by rejecting the ad's message, one is nevertheless rejecting it in terms it establishes. The deliberate, critical rejection of the ad's message is founded upon an act which has already promoted that message. Reacting in any way would appear on this basis to achieve the aim of advertising. Accurate critics attack measurable truth-claims. This is inept since truth-claims are not the locus of the promotional sense. Whether all the claims made were true or false, the ad would already have promoted the product or brand. Ideological criticism fails for the same reason—neglecting to consider how the meaning of advertising as an expression of social conditions of labor (or as a cause of consumerism) is founded upon the general, constituted, promotional sense of advertising.

McLuhan's optimistic view of advertising's power to form a harmonious global community has no phenomenological warrant. Advertising is anonymous, and has no way to approach individuals as individuals or to form the We-relationships at the heart of communities. The content of advertising is the set of promotional ideals developed in accordance with inauthentic, typified conceptions of people and the good. This set of typifications may be endlessly recalculated, demographic research and marketing surveys infinitely conducted, yet there is simply no way for this naive approach to establish intimacy, empathy, and authentic intersubjectivity. The equilibrium of production and consumption McLuhan foresees could only be struck on the basis of understanding persons as sets of statistics. Advertising may indeed tend toward the leveling of desires and available goods, and it decidedly appears that advertising can do nothing other than promote typified goods to typified viewers. But such a social form is not a community.

Baudrillard's interpretation more closely fits the phenomenology developed here, except that Baudrillard too extends beyond the warrant of phenomenological clarification, by speculating that media destroys meaning and sets up a relation to the audience that would not rely on the audience's act of constituting meaning. Baudrillard ambiguously claims that the masses are responsible for the state of media, and that media has already set up conditions which make this responsibility impossible. But his diagnosis of mass media as absolute advertising fits the present interpretation insofar as anyone who is part of the audience of advertising cannot avoid complicity with its promotional motivation (and even someone who avoids mass media as entirely as possible still has contact with members of a society who bring the social meaning-context of advertising to bear in all relationships). As our culture deepens its commitment to media technology, it broadens the range of operations of mass media. This commitment also lends legitimation to the techniques of media. In a sense, to be an American is to take part in American mass media, to adopt the meaning-context of media, to engage in the promotion-motive of advertising, and seduce ourselves.

Baudrillard does not explain what makes this mediated self-seduction possible. As a result, his analysis is a dead-end: there is evidently nothing that can be done to change the situation. According to the phenomenology of Schutz, Berger and Luckmann (and also of Merleau-Ponty and Levinas), advertising, as a form of communication, is inauthentic. But inauthentic social relationships, they all agree, are derivative of authentic We-relationships. Media relations—which are the central form of intersubjectivity in mass society—do appear to correspond to the inauthentic mode or the They-relationship. If inauthentic intersubjectivity is presumed to be derivative of authentic intersubjectivity, then it would have to be the case that in our face-to-face relations we agree to submit ourselves and one another to the seductions of advertising (and the alienation of media). Furthermore, media and advertising would be intelligible through interpretive schemata we negotiate with one another. Does this mean that inauthentic communication, and the interpretation and understanding of inauthentic communication, depends upon a set of authentic arrangements which establish its legitimacy? What direct, immediate face-to-face relationship sets out the terms for the typified interpretive schemata viewers use to understand advertisements?

There is no way for social phenomenology to answer these questions or to comprehend the phenomena of media and advertising adequately on the basis of the presumed binary opposition of authentic and inauthentic intersubjectivity. Advertising shows the need for a phenomenology of media and intersubjectivity without the presumption that there are authentic and inauthentic relationships. When advertising overtakes understanding—that is, when understanding advertising requires submission to the typifications and motivations of advertising—we witness a social relation in which media(ted) intersubjectivity informs face-to-face relationships. When media(ted) intersubjectivity legitimates typifications, it sets the terms of all social relations.

Notes

1. The mistrust of news media, for instance, is well-documented. In *News and the Culture of Lying,* Paul H. Weaver cites a Nielsen study showing that the public lost confidence in the press and TV in general at rates of 22 percent and 36 percent, respectively, from the period 1973-1983 (19ff). Where the deceitfulness of media is not backed up with statistically verifiable facts, it is argued that "[t]he news media and the government are entwined in a vicious circle of mutual manipulation, myth-making, and self-interest" (Vandewicken 144.) In order to sell papers or increase ratings, the news media must find or invent crises, the focus on which prevents the media from seeing "what's really going on."

2. There is a considerable and fascinating literature on radio broadcasting from this period, taking up the "problems" of improving the entertainment and advertising on radio. In *Time for Reason—About Radio,* Lyman Bryson presents the results of a survey of radio listeners which showed that 64 percent either liked or didn't mind the commercials. In the transcript of a radio interview with Atherton W. Huber, who was Chairman of the Benton & Bowles, Inc. advertising firm, Bryson and Huber read and address the complaints of radio listeners about ads. Especially irritating, it seems, were "singing commercials." But Huber asserts his belief that "[u]nless consumers like products and repeat their purchases, no amount of advertising will keep them alive" (107). A study published in 1946 shows that the most frequent and severe complaint about commercials was that they were noisy and distracting (0.70 on a scale of 0 to 1), followed by boring and repetitious (0.52) and in poor taste (0.52); far

down the list was the strong claims made by advertisers (0.35) (Lazarsfeld and Kendall 72).

3. The quote is from a 1966 New York Times Magazine article by David Karp that was referenced in *Advertising Age* website in 1996 under "History of TV Advertising."

Works Cited and Consulted

Advertising Age. Website. http://www.adage.com

Baudrillard, Jean. *Selected Writings*. Ed. Mark Poster. Stanford UP, 1988.

——. *Simulacra and Simulation*. Trans. Sheila Faria Glaser. Ann Arbor: U Michigan P, 1994.

Berger, Peter L., and Thomas Luckmann. *The Social Construction of Reality*. New York: Doubleday, 1966.

Bryson, Lyman. *Time for Reason—About Radio*. New York: Stewart, 1948.

Caples, John. *Tested Advertising Methods*. Englewood Cliffs: Prentice-Hall, 1974.

Garfield, Bob. "Steel Wool Dino Roars a Powerful Message." *Advertising Age* 16 Sept. 1996: 55.

Hettinger, Herman S. ed. *Radio: The Fifth Estate*. Philadelphia: American Academy of Political and Social Sciences, 1935.

Karp, David. "TV Shows Are Not Supposed to be Good (They're Supposed to Make Money)." *New York Times Magazine* 23 Jan. 1966: 6-7, 40.

Key, Bryan Wilson. *Subliminal Seduction: Ad Media's Manipulation of a Not-So Innocent America*. New York: New American Library, 1974.

Lazarsfeld, Paul F., and Patricia L. Kendall. *Radio Listening in America*. New York: Prentice-Hall, 1948.

Levinas, Emmanuel. *Ethics and Infinity*. Trans. Richard A. Cohen. Pittsburgh: Duquesne UP, 1985.

McAllister, Matthew P. "Re-Decoding Advertisements." *Journal of Communication* 46. 2 (1996): 150-57.

McLuhan, Marshall. *Understanding Media*. Cambridge: MIT P, 1995.

Merleau-Ponty, Maurice. *Phenomenology of Perception*. Trans. Colin Smith. London: Routledge & Kegan Paul, 1962.

Preston, Ivan L. *The Great American Blow-Up*. Madison: U of Wisconsin P, 1977.

Samstag, Nicholas. *How Business Is Bamboozled by the Ad-Boys*. New York: Heineman, 1966.

Schutz, Alfred. Collected Papers, Vol. 1: The Problem of Social Reality. Collected Papers. Vol. 1. Ed. Maurice Nathanson. The Hague: M. Nijhoff, 1962-66.

——. *Phenomenology of the Social World.* Trans. George Walsh and Frederick Lehner. Evanston, IL: Northwestern UP, 1967.

Vadehra, Dave. "Campaign Clout." *Advertising Age* 26 Aug. 1996: 16.

Vandewicken, Peter. "Why the News Is Not The Truth." *Harvard Business Review* Mar./Apr. 1996: 144-51.

Weaver, Paul H. *News and the Culture of Lying.* New York: Free P, 1994.

15

ON AMERICAN TIME:
MYTHOPOESIS AND THE MARKETPLACE

Steven Carter

I.

Literary characterizations of time as a thief or a cheat are common to most if not all Western literatures. Poetical and fictional treatments of time in Continental and British fiction and poetry are generally expressed in four fashions: as elegies or laments for the lost years; as attempts to relive the past; as expressions of *carpe diem;* as desires to escape from time altogether—i.e., the Romantic longing for the infinite. In American literature and culture we most often find an obsession with the fourth, or characteristically Romantic, attitude toward time. As we will see, however, a particular longing for the infinite also exists which appears to be characteristic of American consumer culture, wherein the notion of a "perpetual now" takes palpable form in the "perpetually new" products of mass advertising.

In my view the enduring and familiar American passion for the new is really a symptom of a deeper collective urge: the desire to escape time altogether. In early American fiction, Washington Irving's "Rip van Winkle" represents the best-known characterization of this transcendent desire for states of timelessness, but there are many others. Kay S. House has noticed, for instance, how the men on Huckleberry Finn's raft are "typically American," because they are "chillingly alone:" "[t]hey are strangers," she adds, "having no histories, no futures, no loyalties, no names . . ." (194). In short, Twain's riverbound lowlifes exist outside of time; consequently they are, for Twain, literally nobodies.

In twentieth-century American fiction, Jay Gatsby is the best known exemplar of the deracinated American who, in Harry Levin's memorable phrase, is perpetually caught in "a state of suspense between wanderlust and nostalgia" (4):

His heart beat faster and faster as Daisy's white face came up to his own. He knew that when he kissed this girl, and forever wed his unutterable visions to her perishable breath, his mind would never romp again like the mind of God. So he waited, listening for a moment longer to the tuning-fork that had been struck upon a star. Then he kissed her. At his lips' touch she blossomed for him like a flower and the incarnation was complete. (Fitzgerald 112)

Gatsby hesitates because the instant Daisy blossoms for him "like a flower," they both tumble into post-lapsarian time.

Gatsby thinks he wants to repeat the pre-lapsarian past, to recapture the "now" that existed while he listened to "the tuning-fork that had been struck upon a star"; what he really desires, however, as the metaphysical language of this passage makes clear, is to banish time from experience, or, as Ihab Hassan puts it, to achieve "the [American] timeless vision" (325).

There is, of course, a certain grandeur about Gatsby's dream. But for Fitzgerald and for other American novelists like William Faulkner, the timeless vision also constitutes the nearest American equivalent to original sin. For different reasons, Quentin Compson of *The Sound and the Fury* struggles with an impulse which is similar to Gatsby's. On the day of his suicide in Cambridge, Quentin pulls the hands off his watch, as if he could stop time altogether. In Bernard Malamud's *The Natural,* published 23 years after *The Sound and the Fury,* Roy Hobbs carries no timepiece at all. His denial of time even extends to the home runs he hits into stadium clocks: "the clock spattered minutes all over the place, and after that the Dodgers never knew what time it was" (162). When Hobbs' lover tells him she is a grandmother, he turns away from her, as from a corrupting odor of mortality. Faulkner's and Malamud's fictional characters are both dehumanized by their desire to escape time.

Symptoms of chronophobia in the American past may also be found in the very processes of mythopoesis. As David Brion Davis has written,

In our mythology, the cowboy era is timeless. The ranch may own a modern station wagon, but the distinguishing attributes of cowboy and environment remain. There is, it is true, a nostalgic sense that this is the last great drama, a sad knowledge that the cowboy is passing and that civilization is approaching. But it never comes. This strange, wistful sense of the coming end of an epoch is not something outside our experience. It is a faithful reflection of the sense of approaching adulthood. The appeal of the cowboy in this sense is similar to the appeal of Boone, Leatherstocking, and the later Mountain Man. We know that adulthood, civilization, is inevitable, but we are living toward the end of childhood, and at that point "childness" seems eternal; it is a whole lifetime. But suddenly we find that it is not eternal, the forests disappear, the mountains are settled, and we have new responsibilities. When we shut our eyes and try to remember, the last image of a carefree life appears. For the nation this last image is the cowboy. (246-47)

In both fictional and mythopoetic projections of the early American psyche, the desire to annihilate time is narcissistic because it represents an inability to accept the otherness of nature on its own terms. And although the roots of this desire can be traced back to the beginnings of American civilization, it is only in contemporary American culture that we see the denial of time in conflict with the narcissistic quest for a "homemade" or manufactured word of self-extensions: commercial environments which simultaneously inspire and deny the possibility of transcendence.

II.

Today the perverse imp of technology is time: age, obsolescence, stressful boredom which slows the clock and stressful work which speeds the clock. In the culture of technology, the war against time turns workplaces into battle stations where, according to an IBM ad of the early eighties, we must use computers to gain "power over time"[1] in order to survive. These battles are not merely fought on the job, however; ironically, the "power over time" syndrome also embraces the recreational quest for a perpetual future as an escape from the stress of battling time in the workplace. In the view of Arthur Kroker and David Cook, this quest is epitomized by the slogan, "Are we having fun yet," which they interpret as oracular, as "the truthsayer of a culture of altered minds" (16).

Kroker and Cook fail to add that the cultural impulse to internalize the power of time really points in two directions. Recent Hollywood films, like *Grease, American Graffiti, Back to the Future* and *Peggy Sue Got Married,* reverse the arrow of time; films like *Star Wars, Blade Runner, Outland and Alien*(s), point the arrow toward the future. As in the pages of American fiction, or the senescent dream of the eternal cowboy, these and other films are also symptomatic of a deeply-rooted chronophobia.

In American mass media, when disc jockeys regularly introduce new recordings by announcing, "Here's a future memory;" when they promise that "It's always the weekend all week long on the Oldies Station;" when an NBC sports promo claims, "We're building tomorrow's memories today;" when a CBS ad assures the viewer that the first annual Tour de Trump bicycle race will be "the dawning of an American classic;" when a syndicated program for ABC affiliates is touted as "Future Legends of Baseball"—these promos and spots reflect and reinforce the twin values of transcendent desire to snap the arrow of time altogether, and the demand for instant gratification which TV ads for programs described as classics before they exist are designed to meet.

The line from the Tour de Trump ad, "The dawning of an American classic," suggests the mass appeal of marketable duration, a degree zero of time in which everything happens at once. It concretizes the mass desire to gain "power over time" by internalizing, then reconstituting time into an artifice created in our images and likenesses to suit our tastes and specifications. If the endemic restlessness of a culture which is notorious for its pursuits of instant gratification won't permit us to wait for an event to become a classic, that's fine: we will simply make it one right now. Never mind that the integrity of age and endurance, which only the natural passage of time heretofore bestowed on "classics," must be sacrificed in the process.

As he clicks through the channels, the American TV watcher is constantly persuaded that he needn't be a slave to time if he chooses not to. In the fall of 1989 an ad for the TV series *Baywatch* told viewers, "Your summer doesn't have to end!" During the same season, an ad for *Main Event Wrestling* promised, and perpetually delivers, a "never-ending struggle for ring supremacy." The appeal of all these ads, promos and radio spots is fundamentally metaphysical; Peter Conrad also sees this metaphysics of time at work in TV soap operas:

The defining characteristic of the soap opera is after all its mournful, unassuageable continuity—its touring protraction of time (since everything on the soaps takes so tantalizingly long to happen), its recurrence from day to day. The soaps aren't a relief from the domestic routine which oppresses their viewers but a confirmation of it: watching them becomes another unshirkable daily chore. The soaps are occupiers of vacant time, and as their titles suggest they have made their own remorseless tedium into a cosmic principle. One of them is called *As the World Turns;* introducing another, the lugubrious voice of Macdonald Carey declares that "as sands through an hour-glass, so are the days of our lives." The title of *One Life to Live* makes existence itself sound like a dreary domestic grind—an indentured expanse of time which must somehow be passed, or killed. (71)

The appeal of soap operas, in Conrad's view, is almost masochistic; because they offer the viewer "an indentured expanse of time," they ultimately become part of the problem rather than the solution. Why then do people watch them? It may be that turning on a soap opera reflects the crudest of existential gestures, wherein the act of watching *The Days of Our Lives* becomes a sort of Sisyphean stone rolled up the hill of every afternoon in a TV watcher's life, only to roll down when the TV is turned off and be dutifully rolled up the hill all over again the next day.

But what is the solution to the sense of "unassuageable continuity" which Americans who cannot stand to watch soap operas suffer from? The answer is simple: find a way to destroy the sequential nature of time. N. Katherine Hayles believes that this "solution" is what chiefly characterizes the postmodern experience of American adolescents, who live in "a world of disconnected present moments which jostle one another but never form a continuous (much less logical) progression." Hayles elaborates:

The prior experience of older people act as anchors that keep them from fully entering the postmodern stream of spliced contexts and discontinuous time. Young people, lacking these anchors and immersed in TV [but not, one assumes, soap operas] are in a better position to know from direct experience what it is to have no sense of history, to live in a world of simulacra, to see the human form as provisional. (282)

The Tour de Trump TV ad, of course, represents one example of what Hayles means by "spliced contexts." The duration of time needed for an event to become a "classic" has been surgically excised in the present so that the dignity of the past, which one traditionally associates with classics of literature and music, may be grafted onto a future which is then packaged and sold as a product along with the television show itself. Other commentators have noted ways in which "spliced contexts" assume ominous political configurations. According to John Leo,

In politics, as elsewhere, the loss of sequence leads to an ever-shortening attention span. After the appalling reports about Dan Quayle [during the presidential campaign of 1988] Jim Baker told Republicans not to worry: It would blow over in a few days because there was nothing left to say on the subject (i.e., no story line to keep it alive, no smoking gun to look for). This sort of discontinuity means that amnesia afflicts our collective memory and there is no longer any such thing as a permanently impaired reputation. (68)

If it is true, as Ralph Waldo Emerson argued, that civilizations interpret themselves in the act of interpreting nature, then there is much to be learned about mass American culture through these internalizations of the existential meaning(s) of time.

III.

One way of describing a hermeneutics of time for the American marketplace is to say that consumers are encouraged to think of themselves not "in" time, but "with" time.

The inness of time, as I choose to call it, is the most commonly experienced form of psychological, impressionistic or noetic time, a phenomenon which thinkers from Henri Bergson to James T. Fraser have investigated with the sort of rigor once associated only with the hard sciences. Fraser calls noetic time "a part of our mental apparatus" (43). Nootemporality "is the temporal reality of the mature human mind. It is characterized by a clear distinction among future, past, and present; by unlimited horizons of futurity and pastness; and by the mental present, with its changing temporal horizons, depending on attention" (367). Noetic time and human sense-of-self are intimately related. According to Fraser,

Noetic time is the human brain's way of minding the affairs of the body. It does so with the help of the symbol we know as the self. The self is the only mental image that may be attributed to both an external and an internal reality. The changing speed of experienced time, the feeling of free will, the use of human creativity and destructiveness in the name of distant goals: all these manifestations of being human may be interpreted as the efforts of the self to maintain and expand its control over behavior. (357)

When a human being or an entire culture refuses to accept what C. W. E. Bigsby aptly calls "the pressure of time" (146), and desires to escape from it, then they fall into a state of noetic time which might be termed "withness." Withness denotes an ontological separation: one is not felt to exist in time, or to be contained by time, as a glass contains water or as water contains fish; nor is one's experience felt to be constituted of time, as water is constituted of hydrogen and oxygen atoms. On the contrary, the desire to escape from time automatically makes time a separate entity detachable from the self, a "thing" which always exists somewhere or "somewhen" else.

Fifteen-, thirty- and sixty-second television spots which are sold to advertisers, for example, demonstrate in familiar fashion pragmatics of the withness of time: time's function as a commodity, a product to be packaged, consumed, disposed of and forgotten. If the restless desire to disassociate oneself from time-present is strong, a person can escape by purchasing a new appliance in order to feel, thanks to its seductive "space-age technology," that the future has crowded the present aside, that it is "here." Martin Heidegger has argued that it is precisely this ontological stance toward time on the part of individuals which imperils a healthy sense-of-self: "Time must be brought to light and genuinely grasped as the horizon of every understanding and interpretation of Being" (61). When time is not "brought to light"—i.e., existentially lived in—then, according to Heidegger, there is "no selfhood and no freedom" (106).

If Heidegger is right, and if, furthermore, "the deadening of the sense of the time sequence in society inevitably kills it in private life as well" (26), as Vaclav Havel has argued, what then are the implications of Heidegger's ontology for the individual writ large—for mass culture? Specifically, what are the consequences when a society such as our own fails to "genuinely grasp" the existential inness of time? From a social perspective, Havel argues, a collective willingness to live in as opposed to with time

makes the more prominent the element of uniqueness and repeatability within the time flow. This in turn, of course, makes it easier to reflect its sequential character, to represent it, that is, as an irreversible stream of non-interchangeable situations, and so, in retrospect, to understand better whatever is governed by regular laws in society.

"The richer the life the society lives," Havel adds, "the better it perceives the dimension of social time" (25). But when a culture ceases to privilege the "sequential character" of social time, Havel concludes, "everything merges into the single grey image of one and the same cycle" (26). I would argue that this is in fact happening in contemporary American society, as the persistent cultural ideal of the "eternal now" is gradually transformed from a mythopoetic ideal into a commodity. Acting as a sort of surtax on these transactions is, of course, the erasure of the perceived value of history itself, a familiar process to any university teacher in the last generation who asks his or her students to talk intelligently about events and personalities before 1960. For many of them, as Ernest van den Haag has observed, "[t]he culture of nearly everybody today" has become *ipso facto* "the culture of nearly nobody yesterday" (316). Note also the similarity between Havel's description, of the withness of entropic social time and John Leo's comments on the "loss of [a sense of] sequence" in American political life, which leads to the easy forgetting of government abuses.

IV.

How then does mythopoesis become incarnated in the marketplace? To properly answer this question, we must recall that since the advent of

Taylorism in the 1920s, chronology has been reconfigured in American workplaces and marketplaces into the concept of "man-hours" where "time is money" or some other form of accountable capital. More recently, the arrival of high-tech products in the workplace has made of computer cyberspace a killing field where workers must engage in a power struggle—a war—against time. But there is another aspect to the conversion of time into finite capital on the one hand, and the gaining of power over time via cybernetics on the other, that has gone largely unnoticed: the tendency for free market capital to destabilize the irreversibility of social time.

According to Jean-François Lyotard, "the daily practice of [capital] exchange" depends on the cultivation of a habit of mind wherein "the future conditions the present." Lyotard elaborates on the connection between exchange and temporality:

Exchange requires that what is future be as if it were present. Guarantees, insurance policies, security are means of [forestalling] eventualities . . . money here appears as what it really is, time stocked in view of forestalling what comes about. (9-10)

In essence, Lyotard suggests, money invested in "a better" future—i.e., a more prosperous one—concretizes the witness of time by indefinitely deferring states of unpleasantness.

This is true, however, from two distinctly different perspectives. For an insurance company, for instance, present time (t) represents a moment to invest in by laying actuarial odds against any undesirable comings-to-pass in the consumer's future time (t'). The insurance company's hope, needless to say, is that time t' never occurs: for them to do business successfully, ideally the future must come under erasure, while the present becomes an ideal eternal now. It is in this way that "the future conditions the present" for the company. For consumers, on the other hand, it is time t' which becomes a moment to invest in and time t which comes under erasure; for them, the future is converted into an ideal eternal now—something to be bought and paid for. In both cases, however, the meaning of money transcends its quantifiable value as accountable capital, because clock or calendar time is reconstituted into a Platonic—i.e., a metaphysical—commodity.

Lyotard does not apply his temporal formula to the actual exchange of capital for consumer goods, but I would argue that the pattern of such exchanges in the American marketplace constitutes nothing less than a hidden law of economics, what might be called the law of "disappearing nows" (Tyler 18). For generations this strict law has governed the advertising of an infinite array of "new and improved" American products from insect repellant to breath mints to laundry detergent—Tide, for instance, which has gone through 55 "new and improved" incarnations since it appeared on the American market in 1947.

What is most striking about the economic law of disappearing nows is its relative anonymity; over the years it has gradually eased into the mainstream of American consumer culture to be taken for granted as part of the natural order of things. The reason for this, as I have suggested, is that the law represents nothing radically new: it is simply the most recent symptom of what Ihab Hassan has diagnosed as a collective "refus[al] to acknowledge time" (325) in American life from the beginning, or what I call chronophobia. Centuries ago, it was perhaps the supreme mythopoetic progenitor of the American law of disappearing nows which governed the voyages of Ponce de Leon, the Spanish captain who sailed the coasts of Florida in search of a fountain which sang a siren song to men eager to invest their energies in the promise of an orgiastic future.[2] In *In the American Grain,* William Carlos Williams reprises that deathless song:

In the wind, what? Beauty the eternal. White sands and fragrant woods, fruits, riches, truth! The sea, the home of permanence, drew [de Leon and his crew] on into its endless distances. Again the new! (43)

Notes

1. The IBM ad is reproduced and discussed by Andrew Wernick (198ff).

2. The famous phrase, "orgiastic future," is taken from the ending of *The Great Gatsby:*

Gatsby believed in the green light, the orgiastic future that year by year recedes before us. It eluded us then, but that's no matter—tomorrow we will run faster, stretch out our arms farther. . . . And one fine morning—. . . (182)

Works Cited

Bigsby, C. W. E. "Who's Afraid of Virginia Woolf?" *Edward Albee.* Ed. Harold Bloom. New York: Chelsea House, 1987.

Conrad, Peter. *Television: The Medium and Its Manners.* Boston: Routledge and Kegan Paul, 1982.

Davis, David Brion. "Ten-Gallon Hero." *The American Experience.* Ed. Hennig Cohen. New York: Houghton, 1968.

Fitzgerald, F. Scott. *The Great Gatsby*. New York: Scribners, 1925.

Fraser, James T. *Time, the Familiar Stranger*. Amherst: U of Massachusetts P, 1987.

Haag, Ernest van den. "A Dissent from the Consensus Society." *Daedalus* 89 (1960): 315-24.

Hassan, Ihab. *Radical Innocence: Studies in the Contemporary American Novel*. New York: Harper, 1961.

Havel, Vaclav. "Letter to Dr. Gustav Husak." *Living in Truth: Twenty Two Essays Published on the Occasion of the Award of the Erasmus Prize to Vaclav Havel*. Ed. Jan Vladislav. London: Faber and Faber, 1986. 3-35.

Hayles, N. Katherine. *Chaos Bound: Orderly Disorder in Contemporary Literature and Science*. Ithaca: Cornell UP, 1990.

Heidegger, Martin. *Basic Writings*. Ed. David Farrell Kroll. New York: Harper, 1977.

House, Kay S. *Reality and Myth in American Literature*. Greenwich, CT: Fawcett, 1966.

Kroker, Arthur, and David Cook. *The Postmodern Scene: Excremental Culture and Hyper-Aesthetics*. New York: St. Martin's, 1986.

Leo, John. "Wait! Don't Turn That Page!" *U.S. News and World Report* 14 Nov. 1988: 68.

Levin, Harry. *The Power of Blackness: Hawthorne, Poe, Melville*. New York: Vintage, 1958.

Lyotard, Jean-François. "Time Today." *Oxford Literary Review* 11.1-2 (1989): 3-20.

Malamud, Bernard. *The Natural*. New York: Avon, 1952.

Tyler, Stephen A. *The Unspeakable: Discourse, Dialogue, and Rhetoric in the Postmodern World*. Madison: U Wisconsin P, 1987.

Wernick, Andrew. "Vehicles for Myth: The Shifting Image of the Modern Car." *Cultural Politics in Contemporary America*. Ed. Ian Angus and Sut Jhally. New York: Routledge, 1989. 198-216.

Williams, William Carlos. *In the American Grain*. New York: New Directions, 1956.

CONTRIBUTORS

Editors: **Michael T. Carroll** is Associate Professor of English at New Mexico Highlands University. He has published a number of articles on popular culture, and he is editor of *No Small World: Visions and Revisions of World Literature* (NCTE, 1996) and the author of *Popular Modernity in America: Experience, Technology, Mythohistory* (SUNY, 2000). **Eddie Tafoya** is Assistant Professor of English and Creative Writing at New Mexico Highlands University. He has published in a number of fiction journals as well as the *Journal of Popular Culture,* and he is currently at work on a critical anthology entited *The American Fool.*

Ralph Acampora has published essays on environmental phenomenology and environmental ethics. He is Assistant Professor of Philosophy at Hofstra University, and has been an urban park ranger (N.Y.C.).

Harris M. Berger is Assistant Professor in the music program at Texas A&M University. At Indiana University, he completed a Ph.D. in ethnomusicology and folklore. Based on interviews and participant/observation fieldwork, his work explores the political dimensions of heavy metal and the interplay between culture and agency in music perception. Articles by Berger have appeared in *Ethnomusicology, Popular Music,* and *The Journal of Folklore Research.* He is the author of *Metal, Rock, and Jazz: Perception and the Phenomenology of Musical Experience* (Wesleyan UP, 1999). Berger is currently the lead guitarist for The Bee Dreams, a Texas-based rock group.

James Brusseau teaches Philosophy and Comparative Literature in the graduate division of the Faculty of Philosophy and Letters at the Universidad Nacional Autónoma de México in Mexico City. He is the author of *Isolated Experiences* (SUNY P, 1998).

Felicia Florine Campbell is Professor of English at the University of Nevada, Las Vegas. She is editor of *Popular Culture Review,* and has published a variety of essays on popular culture in *Studies in Popular Culture, The Mid-Atlantic Almanac,* and *The Futurist.*

Steven Carter is Professor of Literature and Communications at California State University at Bakersfield. He is the author of *Bearing Across: Studies in Literature and Science* and *Leopards in the Temple: Studies in American Popular Culture,* both from International Scholars Publications, 1998.

Beverle Houston (1935-1988) was Director of the Division of Critical Studies in the School of Cinema-Television at the University of Southern California from 1982 until her death in 1988. Though she was originally trained as a scholar of 18th-century English literature and from the 1960s to the 1980s published many influential articles on cinema in leading film journals (such as *Film Quarterly, Wide Angle, Framework, Sight and Sound, Women and Film,* and *Cinema*), she was best known for her essays on television spectatorship and for her groundbreaking 1978 issue of *Quarterly Review of Film Studies* on "Feminist Theory." She collaborated on two books with Marsha Kinder: *Close Up: A Critical Perspective on Film* (Harcourt Brace Jovanovich, 1972) and *Self and Cinema: A Transformationalist Perspective* (Redgrave, 1980). In 1984, as one of the first American film scholars invited to China, she was the first to use melodrama to strengthen the bond between the two cultures.

Don Ihde is Professor of Philosophy at SUNY-Stonybrook and a major proponent of contemporary phenomenology. His work is particularly important in terms of a relationship between phenomenology and technology, a question first probed by Heidegger. He has also taken the lead in establishing the place of phenomenology in the era of post-structuralist criticism. His many publications include *Instrumental Realism* (Bloomington: Indiana UP, 1991), *Technology and the Lifeworld: From Garden to Earth* (Bloomington: Indiana UP, 1990), and *Postphenomenology* (Northwestern UP, 1993).

Daniel Mackay completed his M.A. at New York University's Performance Studies Program. His book on the aesthetics of the role-playing game is forthcoming from McFarland Press. His heart lies secluded within the confines of a Russian Orthodox Monastery in the mountains of Northern California.

Sam McBride received his Ph.D. from the University of California, Riverside in 1997 with a dissertation on Laurie Anderson. He currently teaches at DeVry University, Pomona, California.

Chris Nagel earned his Ph.D. (thesis: "Merleau-Ponty's Hegelianism") at Duquesne University in 1996. He has published and presented papers on Merleau-Ponty, Hegel, and intersubjectivity. He is a Lecturer in Philosophy at California State University at Stanislaus.

Janice A. Radway is Professor of Literature at Duke University and a leading authority in the study of popular literature. Her publications include *A Feeling for Books: The Book-of-the-Month Club, Literary Taste,* and *Middle-Class Desire* (U of North Carolina P, 1997), and *Reading the Romance: Women, Patriarchy, and Popular Literature* (U of North Carolina P, 1991).

Karl Simms is Lecturer in English Language and Literature at the University of Liverpool, and is former editor of the journal *Language and Discourse.* His publications include *Ethics and the Subject, Language and the Subject,* and *Translating Sensitive Texts: Linguistic Aspects,* all published by Editions Rodopi.

H. Peter Steeves is Assistant Professor of Philosophy at DePaul University where he specializes in ethics, social/political philosophy, and phenomenology. He is the author of *Founding Community: A Phenomenological-Ethical Inquiry* (Kluwer, 1998) and the editor of *Animal Others* (SUNY P, 1999). He has visited Disneyland three times—all in the name of philosophical research.